Praise for Liberating Structures

This book is so needed and so useful. The authors understand that the world is changed through small, elegant shifts in the protocols of how we meet, plan, conference, and relate to each other. The genius of this book is how it puts in the hands of every leader and every citizen the facilitative power that was once reserved for the trained expert. This will be a required text for all programs on leadership and change.
Peter Block Bestselling author of *Flawless Consulting, Stewardship,* and *Community: The Structure of Belonging*

A treasure trove of simple, practical methods to stimulate critical conversations and liberate the full potential of any group, from the frontline to the C-suite.
Cheryl M Scott Global Programs Senior Advisor, Bill and Melinda Gates Foundation

Liberating Structures will forever change the way we look at collaboration, learning and leadership by showing us how structures are critical in the world of work. Simply put, this book is for every leader who wants innovative but proven methods to transform his or her organization and engage its members in that journey of discovery.
Pat Witherspoon Dean, College of Liberal Arts, The University of Texas at El Paso

As a Wall Street Journal columnist covering executive leadership, I discovered Lipmanowicz and McCandless in the early days of their work with Liberating Structures. Today, as an entrepreneur in a complex industry, I use those practices routinely. Any group, anywhere is inherently poised for rapid transformation. Liberating Structures make it simple to turn this potential into reality.
Thomas Petzinger Jr. Founder of five life science companies and former Wall Street Journal "Front Lines" columnist

The authors have drawn on pioneers in complexity science research, making insights immediately useful for people in the field. Liberating Structures invite frontline ownership of challenges by engaging everyone in a way that encourages them to become part of the solution and take action.
Brenda Zimmerman Associate Professor of Strategy/Policy, Schulich School of Business, Toronto

Liberating Structures have given me not only many powerful new ways for engaging employees and customers; they have also succeeded beyond my imagination in providing endless new approaches to improve productivity and creativity, all in a fun and enjoyable way!
Guy Eiferman President, Healthcare Services & Solutions, Merck & Co

Billings Clinic has been using many Liberating Structures for a decade. The engagement and emergence of new and stronger teams that include staff, leaders, physicians and nurses has helped us to improve patient experience and safety while reducing costs in an extremely complex healthcare environment. Highly recommended.
Nicholas Wolter, MD CEO, Billings Clinic

Bringing Liberating Structures into my work is restoring my soul. Thank you.
Deb Witzel Executive Director, Longmont Community Justice Partnership

Being able to manage interactions with Liberating Structures helps me be more self-confident and a better leader in the eyes of my team and my customers. Being an early adopter increased my influence in the organization and is one of the reasons I'm now a member of the senior management team. Liberating Structures helped me grow in my career.
Vanessa Vertiz Business Unit Director, Lima, Peru

For the past eight years in Latin America and Italy Liberating Structures has helped me and my teams work through a wide range of issues. They became a way of doing business and to move organizations and people to new heights.
David Raimondo General Manager Latin America, Coopervision

There are those rare but delicious moments when you stumble across a resource that transforms everything. Liberating Structures have provided a delightfully rich repertoire of methods that live up to their bold name—liberating participants to engage, collaborate and reach into their collective wisdom to address their concerns and goals. And not just for my practice, but increasingly as fruitful tools for managers and staff across the Yukon Government organization.
Barrett W. Horne OD Consultant with the Yukon Government, Canada

A must-read guide to transform how you engage others. Liberating Structures offer elegant approaches to get the most out of every discussion, meeting or workshop. Our NGO uses them internally and with our partners around the world. From Tanzania to NYC, from St. Lucia to Liberia, I have been amazed watching Liberating Structures unleash the potential of each gathering.
Sean Southey Executive Director, PCI Media Impact

Holy smoke: www.liberatingstructures.com might be one of the most useful websites I've been introduced to since Google. The only words that come to mind are swear words, and I'm on county email.
Ryan Murrey Acting Executive, Washington State CASA

The Surprising Power of Liberating Structures

Simple Rules to Unleash a Culture of Innovation

Henri Lipmanowicz   **Keith McCandless**

Published by Liberating Structures Press

ISBN 13: 9780615975306 (Liberating Structures Press)

ISBN: 0615975305

CONTENTS

Part Three: Stories from the Field   **115**

Part Four: The Field Guide to Liberating Structures   **163**

Prologue

As Easy As ABC

Do you remember learning the alphabet? And learning to spell your first words? Cat, dog, bat. Alphabets are not only easy to learn, they are endlessly adaptable and universally useful. They are the building blocks of words, ideas, and actions. With the twenty-six letters of the Roman alphabet, millions of different combinations can be strung together, enough to write all the words of many languages.

Now imagine having access to only a five-letter alphabet. How many different words and ideas could you structure with five letters? How diminished would writing, reading, and talking be? How frustrating would it be to communicate with just a few words? How boring and repetitive would your dealings with others be?

This is precisely the situation in which most people find themselves when working with other people. They are boxed in by the equivalent of a five-letter alphabet, which consists of the five methods everybody everywhere uses to organize how groups of people work together. These five conventional methods are the presentation, the managed discussion, the status report, the open discussion, and the brainstorm. This tiny alphabet is in good part the reason why so many meetings or classrooms are boring, unproductive, or frustrating. Also these conventional methods fail to create a fertile ground where innovation can emerge easily and flourish.

The purpose of this book is to greatly expand your alphabet of possible ways to interact and work with others to achieve exceptional results. It describes and explains thirty-three new "letters," simple methods that you can learn without difficulty, with only a small amount of practice.

Figure 1
The Liberating Structures "Alphabet" of Simple Methods

These so-called Liberating Structures make it easy to transform how people interact and work together in order to achieve much better results than what is possible with presentations, reports, and other conventional methods. We call them Liberating Structures because they are designed to include and engage everybody. They "liberate," so to speak, everybody's contribution to the group's success.

How well you interact and work with other people often determines not only your success at work but also in other areas of your life. You will find that each Liberating Structure has its own specific benefits. By learning to use some or all of them, you will create your own alphabet and build a different vocabulary for getting things done with others. Your new language will be endlessly adaptable and applicable as you create more combinations to fit every situation that you face in your life, whether challenge or opportunity, large or small, simple or complex.

You will also find that the power of Liberating Structures is not only surprising but also infectious. When you use Liberating Structures, people around you will enjoy the experience and see the unexpected benefits; this will likely help and encourage them to expand their own alphabets. They will become your practicing partners and be grateful that you helped them acquire skills that will serve them forever.

You will find as well that Liberating Structures scale up and down easily for use by a small or large team, a department or function, an organization, a class, a school, a community, or a social movement. That makes them useful for anything from a single meeting to a large project to a system-wide transformation initiative. You will also discover that they can help you bring more structure to one-on-one conversations and make them more productive. And, of course, they can also help you converse with yourself more effectively and transform how you think, plan, and make decisions.

When asked who are perfect candidates for using Liberating Structures, our modest response is simple: everybody. Liberating Structures are for CEOs, senior executives, middle managers, and frontline workers; professors and teachers, administrators, support staff, and students; hospital leaders, doctors, and nurses; military officers and soldiers; government employees and politicians; consultants and coaches; community leaders and philanthropists—and many more. By everybody we mean everybody!

If the notion that Liberating Structures can be universally useful sounds to you too good to be true, join the crowd; this is a common initial reaction and is understandable. You will not believe it until you discover what Liberating Structures can do for you by using them yourself and then using your imagination to extrapolate adaptations and new applications. In other words, this book contains many important ideas, but it is not a theoretical or conceptual book. Instead, it is a practical field guide written to make it easy for you to get started and make significant progress quickly so that you can find out what place to give Liberating Structures in your work and in your life.

Liberating Structures are methods for a purpose: to improve performance. If this were a book about tennis, golf, or skiing, you would read it knowing that its value would come only when you have practiced the methods and learned from them. This is the secret of how to learn and benefit from Liberating Structures: just do it, plunge in, explore, and practice as often as possible, taking advantage of the opportunities that abound daily. Be assured that no matter which Liberating Structure you try, in whatever situation, you will generate surprisingly better results than expected.

When asked who are perfect candidates for using Liberating Structures, our modest response is simple: everybody.

If this were a book about tennis, golf, or skiing, you would read it knowing that its value would come only when you have practiced the methods and learned from them.

Chapter 1
Small Changes, Big Differences

For months, a father had been unable to go beyond monosyllabic responses from his teenage daughter. Then, one day, he made a small change in the way he started their conversation, and she talked to him for over an hour.

For months, fifteen managers had been getting nowhere arguing about transforming their biweekly meeting, which they all agreed was frustrating and unproductive. Then, one day, they made a small change in the way they usually worked as a group. The payoff? Within thirty minutes, they figured out what their major problem was and decided how they would address it together.

For years, each new batch of students in a required course attended it with little enthusiasm, doing the bare minimum to get a decent grade. Then, one semester, after small changes in the professor's teaching methods, the students were animated and eager, feeling engaged and having fun learning concepts they found relevant to their personal lives.

For years, the briefings for replacement officers going to Afghanistan were more numbing and overwhelming than illuminating. Then one day, thanks to small changes in the briefing process, returning officers were able to convey to their replacements the nuances of how to hit the ground running. Their replacements listened avidly, asked and got answers for

"Not hammer strokes, but the dance of water sings the pebbles to perfection."
R. Tagore

all their remaining questions, and felt more confident to start their challenging deployment.

For decades, infections had been increasing in a hospital unit despite regular campaigns to train the staff and introduce best practices. Then one year, the unit implemented a small change in its approach to infection reduction and was able to bring down transmissions to near zero in just twelve months' time.

As far back as anybody could remember, strategic plan reviews had always been stressful and unpleasant; you presented your plan to the management team and they did their best to find faults in it. Then one year, a small change turned the review into an energizing, productive, and pleasant event.

All these vignettes encapsulate true stories with a common story line: small changes in people's routine practices produced big differences in the results they were getting.[1] All that each individual or group did was to replace what we call a "conventional microstructure" with something called a "Liberating Structure."

What the teenager's father did differently was to take his inspiration from a Liberating Structure called **Appreciative Interviews**. His small change was to ask his daughter, "What was the best moment of your day today?" This prompted her to tell a story, and then another, and another ...

The small change made by the managers stuck on how to transform their biweekly meeting was to use two rounds of a Liberating Structure called **1-2-4-All** to address their issues and settle differences of opinion without conflict.

What the professor did differently was to introduce seemingly minor variations in her classroom approach: she replaced her lectures with a few Liberating Structures such as **Impromptu Networking, Troika Consulting,** and **Conversation Café** and created an interactive environment that provided many spaces for self-discovery and peer-to-peer learning.

The Afghanistan briefing used to consist mostly of white-paper and PowerPoint presentations. The simple change the briefing officers made in the process was to use a Liberating Structure called **Users Experience Fishbowl** in which a small group of returning officers shared their on-the-ground stories with each other while their replacements listened and later asked questions.

The hospital unit reducing its infection rate simply stopped promoting top-down campaigns and gradually engaged everybody on the unit in small and diverse group conversations. How did they do that? They used Liberating Structures such as **Discovery & Action Dialogues** and **Improv Prototyping** to have participants discover for themselves how they could contribute to reducing infections. Without buy-in imposed from the top, people volunteered to take actions on their own.

In the case of the confrontational strategic plan reviews, the small change was to eliminate the presentation routine and substitute the Liberating Structure called **Ecocycle** to engage the whole management team in assessing strategic options and cocreating the plan together.

The Invitation

Check all that apply when you think about a group or organization you work with:

- Deadly boring or frustrating meetings
- Someone else's best practices imposed
- Deciders separated from the doers
- Brain-numbing PowerPoint presentations
- Difficult conversations routinely avoided
- Fear and politics getting in the way
- Teamwork that feels like drudgery
- Group process that is chaotic
- More training but no changes
- Great ideas that never leave the drawing board
- People excluded because they would "complicate" decisions
- Structural changes that don't deliver the Promised Land
- Being expected to know and anticipate everything
- Change driven by resorting to fear or "bribery"
- More and more bureaucracy and requests for data
- Accountability without adequate autonomy and support
- Things that everybody knows don't work but are never changed

If you are like most of the people we have worked with around the world, you experience some of these situations and events day in, day out. It doesn't matter whether we look at business, government, NGOs, education, health care, or community service—or neighborhood or civic groups, advisory committees, or similar organizations—these realities block most groups' ability to work together to achieve remarkable results.

This book is an invitation to use the methods called Liberating Structures to organize and engage people in a new way. Too often, we rely on experts to design our world while overlooking the people directly in front of us. With the constellation of methods and principles explained here, it becomes practical for people at any skill or hierarchical level to quickly become expert contributors in taking next steps and innovating.

Too often, we rely on experts to design our world while overlooking the people directly in front of us.

You can use this book to generate innovative results for yourself, with your family, with your team at work; these methods will work to improve your interactions with leaders in your organization and with neighbors in your community. Everyday use in a conversation or meeting can be as powerful as application to the big transformation initiative.

At the core of the book is the practical idea that simple shifts in our routine patterns of interaction make it possible for everyone to be included, engaged, and unleashed in solving problems, driving innovation, and achieving extraordinary outcomes. Small changes generate big results without imported best practices, more training, or expensive buy-in strategies. This alternative approach is both practical and feasible because, as you will see, Liberating Structures are quite simple and easy to learn; they can be used by everyone at every level, from the C-suite to the front line of any organization, from the neighborhood block club to the global issue-advocacy association. Rather than complicated frameworks or elaborate processes to guide work together, Liberating Structures employ simple rules that are extremely spare and very specific. Liberating Structures have been used by managers and salespeople, by doctors and nurses, by professors and students, by military officers and administrators, in business, government, and the nonprofit sector—all together in more than thirty countries. No lengthy training courses or special expertise is required. No dependence on expert facilitators is necessary.

What's Ahead

We assembled this collection of Liberating Structures by tapping great ideas in the public domain, simplifying them, and adding a few of our own. Our purpose is to make all of the structures accessible for use by anyone from the bottom to the top of any organization. Whether you are a leader, facilitator, or part of any group of people who want to be more innovative, adaptive, and quick off the mark to achieve better results, this book shows you how to put the power of Liberating Structures to work immediately.

Part One: The Hidden Structure of Engagement will ground you with the conceptual framework and vocabulary of Liberating Structures. Chapter 2 introduces key concepts and contrasts Liberating Structures with the conventional ways of how people work together. In Chapter 3, we explain in more depth the features of Liberating Structures and show the benefits of using them to transform the way people collaborate, how they learn, and how they discover solutions together; also included in this chapter are two key performance indicators to assess what we are calling Engagement Expertise. The intent of Chapter 4, Liberating Leadership, is summed up in its subtitle: "How leaders can avoid perpetuating the problems they complain about." Here we offer insights and alternatives to leaders at all levels.

Part Two: Getting Started and Beyond offers guidelines for experimenting with Liberating Structures and learning from your experience in a range of possible applications, from one-off, small-group interactions to system-wide change initiatives.

Part Three: Stories from the Field is a collection of real-life case examples provided by people who have used Liberating Structures around the world. Their stories unfold in all types of organizations, from health-care to academic to military to global business enterprises, from local judicial and legislative systems to national and international R&D efforts. They are snapshots of the depth and breadth of what Liberating Structures can make possible in a broad variety of situations.

In **Part Four: The Field Guide to Liberating Structures,** we give you a repertoire of thirty-three Liberating Structures. Each Liberating Structure is carefully designed to include only what is absolutely necessary to generate innovative results. The Field Guide provides the minimum specifications for each Liberating Structure (shortened to Min Specs) in a standard format so that they are easy to follow and easy to use. In describing how to use each Liberating Structure, we provide a step-by-step explanation of what to do and what to expect, including:

- What is made possible
- Five microstructural design elements

Our purpose is to make all of the structures accessible for use by anyone from the bottom to the top of any organization.

- Purposes for use
- Tips and traps
- Riffs and variations
- Examples

Throughout the Field Guide, we point you to a host of supporting materials on our website www.liberatingstructures.com to make it easy for you to start experimenting immediately.

In the **Afterword**, we share our thoughts about what it means for people individually and as a group to become regular users of Liberating Structures.

We believe Liberating Structures are transformational because they are purposely designed to make it easy to accomplish what is missing in most organizations, namely to include and engage people effectively and to unleash their collective intelligence and creativity. They provide a wide variety of ways to:

- Accommodate groups of any size
- Let go of control safely
- Give everyone equal opportunity to contribute
- Facilitate progress through rapid sifting and sequencing
- Maximize active participation
- Routinely generate better-than-expected results

One Liberating Structure can transform a meeting, a classroom, or a conversation. Using many of them together, on a regular basis, can transform an organization, a community, or a life.

Most important, Liberating Structures are simple enough to fit within normal work routines and schedules. They can save enormous amounts time by making it possible to include all the right people from the start.

The thirty-three Liberating Structures included in this book can be combined in an infinite variety of designs that can be tailored to whatever needs to be accomplished. This makes them adaptable for shaping next steps in everything from personal relationships, to tomorrow's meeting, to big projects, to strategic work, to organizational transformations, to social movements.

PART ONE
The Hidden Structures of Engagement

Part One contains the necessary background for working with Liberating Structures. We introduce the concept of Liberating Structures, contrast them with the conventional ways people work together, and describe how using them can transform the way people collaborate and discover solutions together. The last chapter speaks to leaders at all levels about why the strategies they use to address perpetual problems in organizations usually do not improve the situation and often make it worse. We propose the use of Liberating Structures as a proven way to get things done while overcoming perennial leadership challenges.

"The aspects of things that are most important to us are hidden because of their simplicity and familiarity."
Ludwig Wittgenstein

Chapter 2

Why Microstructures Matter

How invisible structures shape everything that gets done

One day, a CEO preparing for a merger spoke to a large group from the acquired company. He found himself totally unable to establish contact with the hostile crowd in spite of his repeated attempts to reach out. The next time he addressed the same group, he didn't have any positive news to deliver, yet he was able to connect easily with them and even exchanged pleasantries that sparked laughter.

The only thing the CEO did differently the second time was to change the physical structure where he interacted with the group. He moved the venue of his meeting from a long rectangular room to a square one. Then, instead of standing on a podium at one end, he stood in the middle of the group and moved around. This made it possible for him to engage people with stories and questions. Small structural change, big difference in content!

"How difficult it is to be simple."
Vincent Van Gogh

Whatever we *do*, there is always a structure to support or guide what is being done. Without structures, there is just chaos. We see this even in our most routine activities. When we have dinner with our family, the structure is provided by the room, the table and chairs, the dinnerware and eating utensils, and more subtly by who sits where. Most of the time, we pay no attention to this structure because its elements rarely change. What we notice is what matters to us: the food, our dining companions, the conversation. We take the structure for granted and don't even think of changing it to transform our dinner.

The same happens at work or at school. We know that big structures such as buildings, strategies, policies, and processes support and constrain our activities, but we are not constantly aware of their influence. We tend to be even less conscious of the way smaller or intangible structures—such as the room we select for a meeting or who sits where—influence our interactions with other people. All sorts of structures shape all our undertakings and accomplishments, and we will explain how and why.

First, a Few Definitions

Buildings, strategies, policies, organization structures, and core operating processes are examples of what we call **macrostructures**. They are built or designed for the long term and can't be changed easily or cheaply.

In contrast, meeting rooms, offices, presentations, agendas, questions, and discussions are examples of **microstructures.** They are the small structures that we select routinely to help us interact or work with other people. They can be changed easily from one event to another or even in the moment.

Tangible microstructures are the physical spaces where interactions or work takes place. They are like the room where the family eats dinner. They also include how we choose to arrange the tangible **structural elements** within that space, such as tables, chairs, flip charts, and the like. **Intangible microstructures** are how we micro-organize our interactions with elements such as agendas, presentations, processes, discussions, questions, seating arrangements, and so forth. Table 2.1 shows some examples for each type of structure.

For most organizations, the familiar microstructures become fixed in routine—the usual meeting room, who sits where, the use of PowerPoint presentations, the format of discussions. Since they are so often the same, they fade into the background and go unnoticed. In fact, when we started our work together, these small structures didn't even have a name. We coined the term "microstructures" to make talking about them easier.

When we started our work together, these small structures didn't even have a name. We coined the term "microstructures" to make talking about them easier.

Microstructures may sound like small things, but they have a big impact. Consider three different configurations for a group meeting: long rows of rectangular tables, clusters of small round tables, chairs with wheels but no tables. Each one will enable and constrain in a different way what is possible for the group to accomplish. More subtly, questions will do the same thing. Asking, "Why is our customer strategy failing?" will launch a search for solutions in a different direction from asking, "When and how have you been successful in satisfying a customer?" Both questions enable searches, but each question constrains the range of appropriate answers.

Microstructures may sound like small things, but they have a big impact.

	Tangible Structures	Intangible Structures
Macrostructures	Office building School Hospital Shop Ship Factory	Strategies Organization structure Policies and procedures Compensation/Incentives Core operating processes Grants of authority
Microstructures	Boardroom Classroom Meeting room Restaurant Office Water cooler	Presentation/Lecture Managed discussion Status report Open discussion Brainstorm Liberating Structures
Structural Elements	Large round table Large rectangular table Small table Chair Flip chart Post-its Projector Screen	Purpose/Agenda Question Theme Seating arrangement Group configuration Time allocation Standing instead of sitting Formal or informal

Table 2.1
Hierarchy and Examples of Structures

The Neglected Power of Microstructures

People, resources, and structures are conventionally seen as the three ingredients that drive the performance of all organizations. Simply stated, *people, supported by resources and macrostructures, make decisions and take actions that generate results.* Every organization is looking for the ideal formula, the precise combination of people, resources, and strategies that will produce top performance (see figure 2.1).

In Figure 2.1, "People" includes leaders and managers, the organization's workforce, suppliers, and customers. For a school, the people would be board members, principals, teachers, administrators, students, and parents. As Table 2.1 shows, "Macrostructures" would include factories, offices, or other buildings, as well as things like strategies, organization structures, policies, and procedures. "Resources" include products, services, patents, property, equipment, capital, and cash flow.

What is missing from Figure 2.1 is the role microstructures play in shaping decisions, and affecting results since nothing ever happens without some form of interaction, some exchange of information, and some discussion, formal or not (see Figure 2.2).

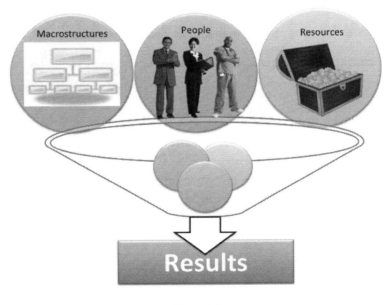

Figure 2.1
An Incomplete Picture: Structure, People,
Resources Drive Performance

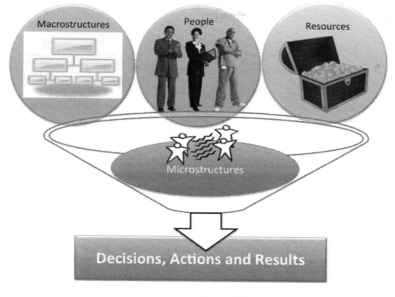

Figure 2.2
The Role of Microstructures in Producing Results

Microstructures Enable and Constrain

Microstructures are the way you organize all your routine interactions, consciously or not. They guide and control how groups work together. They shape your conversations and meetings. They enable *and* constrain what is possible. For our purposes, we can say they come in two flavors: conventional microstructures and Liberating Structures. Liberating Structures are adaptable microstructures that make it possible for groups of people of any size to radically improve how they interact and work together.

Conventional microstructures, in one form or another, have been around for centuries. They are designed for convincing, teaching, debating, brainstorming, controlling, or some combination of these purposes. Their usefulness, however, is limited by side effects that are difficult or impossible to avoid, such as unengaged participants or audiences, excessive power dynamics, and competition for attention, bodies present but minds absent. The resulting frustrations spark much talk about the need for engaging employees (in academia, the talk is about engaging students), but, in actual practice, there is too little expertise on how to engage people effectively and broadly. Routinely uninspiring meetings, classes, or conversations

In organizations large and small, the standard decision-making formula is: meet with a small circle of coworkers, decide, and then tell the others.

reinforce the dominant belief that engaging people is very difficult and reserved for the charismatic few. Because of the perceived difficulty, the myth is compounded by excluding the vast majority in shaping next steps. In organizations large and small, the standard decision-making formula is: meet with a small circle of coworkers, decide, and then tell the others. The presentation, the managed discussion, the status report, the open discussion, and the brainstorm are the most frequently used conventional microstructures in group interactions—we call them the Big Five. They also shape one-on-one meetings and conversations. In fact, they dominate all activities in pretty much all organizations, small or large, no matter their mission.

Whether employed in a sales meeting, a managers' meeting, an executive meeting, a customer contact, or a classroom discussion, the impact of the conventional microstructures is greatly dependent on the skills and personalities of their users. The reason is that, as structures go, they are either too tight or too loose in terms of how much control is exerted on the participant group. For example, presentations, status reports, and managed discussions are at one end of the spectrum: too tight. Open discussions and brainstorms are at the other end of the continuum: too loose. Each of these qualities—too tight or too loose—has its limitations. What's more, all conventional microstructures make it impossible to engage more than a small number of participants. Liberating Structures make it possible to include and engage everybody, no matter whether the group is small or large.

The Elements of Control

All microstructures—Liberating Structures and conventional structures—are made up of the same five structural elements (Figure 2.3). These elements determine how control is exercised over a group of people who are working together:

1. The invitation
2. How space is arranged and what materials are used
3. How participation is distributed among participants
4. How groups are configured
5. The sequence of steps and the time allocated to each step

The invitation provides direction in the form of a question or a request. In other words, participation in the group's work together will depend on someone's invitation, explicit or implicit, to listen or speak up, to contribute to an objective, and so on.

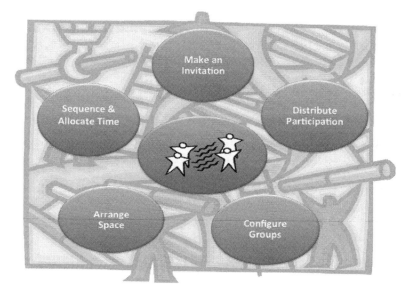

Figure 2.3
Microstructure Elements of Control

How space is arranged and what materials are used refers to all the choices that can be made about the tangible and intangible elements such as tables, chairs, podiums, projectors, flip charts, where people are located, whether they are standing up or sitting down. These arrangements can contribute to the invitation but often conflict with it as, for example, when a large group is sitting classroom-style and people are invited to ask questions.

How participation is distributed refers to how much time every participant will be given to contribute.

How groups are configured refers to the freedom that exists to change the composition of a group—for instance, by breaking up into small groups then reconfiguring into another formation.

Every microstructure contains **one or more steps,** each with a specific purpose and **time allocation.**

Conventional Microstructures: Too Much Control and/or Too Little Structure

Liberating Structures are fundamentally different from conventional microstructures in the way they control and structure people's interactions. Conventional microstructures tend to provide too much control of content or too little structure to include everyone in shaping next steps. To illustrate, let's look at the three most frequently used conventional microstructures.

Presentation (or Speech or Lecture)

Participation in shaping next steps is very limited, if present at all, in the Presentation structure.

The Presentation is designed to make it possible for one person to tell and show the same information to many people simultaneously. Its purpose is to give one person full control about the content while restricting everybody else to listening ... or not. Participation in shaping next steps is very limited, if present at all, in the Presentation structure.

The structural design of the Presentation is:

1. **The invitation**: Audience members are invited to listen to the presenter from beginning to end (except for questions).
2. **How space is arranged and what materials are used:** Audiences large or small are usually sitting and facing the same direction, toward the presenter. PowerPoint slides dominate, whether in face-to-face presentations or virtual broadcasts. A podium or a stage is used for large audiences.
3. **How participation is distributed:** One person, the presenter, gets nearly 100 percent of the time with the discretion to invite questions from others either during the presentation or at the end. Everyone else is given little or no time.
4. **How groups are configured:** The configuration is static, with the presenter in front and everyone else in one group.
5. **Sequence of steps and time allocation:** The first step, the presentation, gets 90 to 99 percent of the allotted time; the second step, questions, gets the balance.

The Presentation is neither an inclusive nor an engaging process since a single person controls the content. Furthermore, that person is the "expert," the one who has prepared and is intimately familiar with all details. Participants are "forced" into a silent role that, instead of engagement, may invite passive acceptance, defensive reactions, or withdrawal. When the Presentation is used to convince or persuade others of a predetermined idea or decision, it tends to discourage engagement and spark resistance. In a time-constrained agenda, time allocated to the Presentation means time stolen from group interactions. When the Presentation takes up most of the time available, it becomes the dominant structure and sets the tone for the whole meeting (same thing for a class dominated by lectures).

Open Discussion

An Open Discussion is one that is not managed or facilitated. It can have many different purposes: to collect feedback, share viewpoints, attempt to reach a consensus, allow people to ventilate, create the illusion of inclusion, search for new insights.

The structural design of the Open Discussion is:

1. **The invitation**: Participants are invited to respond to a topic, a question, or a presentation in any way each sees fit.
2. **How space is arranged and what materials are used:** One large group or several smaller groups sitting in a fixed configuration within a room (or connected virtually). Microphones are used if needed.
3. **How participation is distributed:** Participation is not distributed. Individuals assert their idea or opinion to the whole group at any time for any amount of time.
4. **How groups are configured:** The initial configuration remains unchanging.
5. **Sequence of steps and time allocation:** A few minutes may be used to restate the topic. Participants use the rest of the time for expressing their views and for discussing. Total duration is variable and may or may not be specified in advance.

In contrast to the Presentation, the Open Discussion operates with very little control of content, if any. If used to engage people in shaping direction, it easily turns chaotic, becoming too unconnected to be productive or too random to shape decisions or next steps. As groups get larger, Open Discussion becomes less and less open for all as a few people will inevitably dominate the discussion. In short, the Open Discussion has too few or too weak microstructural elements to provide everyone a chance to shape next steps. In simpler

Open Discussions easily turn into a mess

terms, Open Discussions easily turn into a mess. This usually incites someone with authority to take control and manage the discussion.

Managed Discussion

The standard way of avoiding a mess is to put somebody in charge. In a Managed Discussion, someone is in charge (leader, chair, professor) and responsible for guiding the discussion. Managed Discussions frequently come after a presentation or a status report. Their purpose can be to come to a conclusion or reach a decision or make some progress.

The structural design of the Managed Discussion is:

1. **The invitation:** Participants are asked to respond to specific questions by a person with authority/power.
2. **How space is arranged and what materials are used:** Participants sit around a long or U-shaped conference table, or are seated classroom-style, with the leader in the "power seat." A presenter may or may not remain standing during the entire discussion. For large groups beyond a dozen participants, seating is multitiered.
3. **How participation is distributed:** Distribution is determined by the leader, by power relations, by expertise, or by whoever imposes himself or herself.
4. **How groups are configured:** The initial configuration remains unchanging. For regular meetings (or gatherings or classrooms), the configuration is usually the same, time after time.
5. **Sequence of steps and time allocation:** Total time is determined beforehand by an agenda or decided in the moment by the leader. If addressing the issue requires several steps or tasks, the leader decides, usually in the moment, how time is allocated between each.

The Managed Discussion puts control entirely into a single hand, with all the difficulties and complications that this entails.

The Managed Discussion puts control entirely into a single hand, with all the difficulties and complications that this entails. The most common challenge for the leader (or chair, or professor, or expert) is giving to all participants the time they need for comfortably expressing their views. Making it safe for everybody to speak up is another common challenge since acquiescing is the easiest option. Achieving true depth and quality of content within a predetermined amount of time is often impossible.

Chairing Managed Discussions at senior levels is a special challenge. Even though senior leaders are likely to be more skilled in expressing themselves in group discussions, the issues they address are much more complex and power dynamics tend to be significantly stronger. The boss may want more participation in shaping next steps, but if everyone doesn't step up, this reinforces the pattern of making decisions at the top. Including participants from lower levels as equal partners in a Managed Discussion with a group of senior people is an art form too often neglected.

From Too Much Or Too Little Control To Well-Structured and Distributed Control

By definition, full engagement means that everybody plays an active and unrestrained role in contributing ideas, discussing options, and shaping next steps. The descriptions of the Presentation, the Open Discussion, and the Managed Discussion make it clear how and why conventional structures fail to make this possible. They provide too much control of content or too little structure to effectively engage more than a few people in shaping next steps. In the next chapter, we will describe a Liberating Structure called **1-2-4-All** to exemplify how Liberating Structures make it possible to easily achieve full engagement regardless of group size.

Figure 2.4 provides a visual summary of these differences between Liberating Structures and conventional microstructures. It illustrates that:

- The Presentation puts maximum control of content in the hands of one person and has no structure to include/engage others.
- The Status Report is essentially like a series of presentations, putting the control of content into the hands of one person at a time and with no structure to include/engage others.
- The Managed Discussion puts into the hands of one person the control for including/engaging a small number of participants.
- The Brainstorm provides a structure to include/engage a few people in expressing their ideas without constraints.
- The Open Discussion has no control of content and no structure to include everybody.
- Liberating Structures make it possible to include everybody regardless of group size and distribute the control of content among all participants.

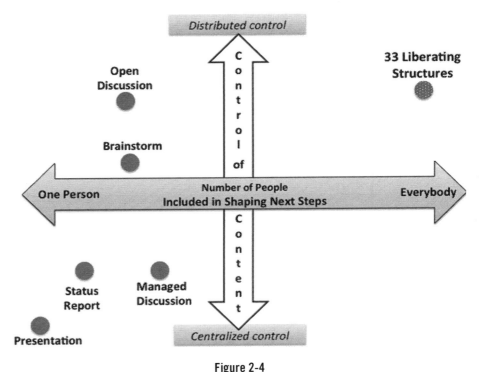

Figure 2-4

Liberating Structures and Conventional Microstructures Differences in Control and Structure

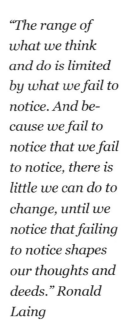

"The range of what we think and do is limited by what we fail to notice. And because we fail to notice that we fail to notice, there is little we can do to change, until we notice that failing to notice shapes our thoughts and deeds." Ronald Laing

Conventional microstructures perpetuate long-running traditions. They are huge time wasters. In many organizations, people, and leaders in particular, spend an enormous amount of time passively listening to PowerPoint presentations. This was unavoidable decades ago but not anymore. Current communication technologies make it possible to share information very effectively without people having to be in the same physical space. This frees up face-to-face time to be used for truly interactive activities designed to generate new ideas or solve problems. To take advantage of this opportunity, a different kind of microstructure is needed that can fully engage participants. Liberating Structures are designed precisely for that purpose.

Chapter 3
Liberating Structures For Everyone
How easy it is for anyone to radically improve the way people work together

Liberating Structures are adaptable microstructures that make it quick and simple for groups of people of any size to radically improve how they interact and work together.[1] In contrast to the Big Five, Liberating Structures are specifically designed to include, engage, and unleash everyone in contributing ideas and shaping their future. They can be used to complement the Big Five approaches that people use all the time—or simply replace them.

Instead of oscillating between too much control (Presentation), too little control (Open Discussion), and too centralized control (Managed Discussion), Liberating Structures distribute the control of content among all the participants so that they can shape direction together as the action unfolds. This liberates energy, unleashes participants' contributions, stimulates creativity, and reveals the group's latent intelligence. Liberating Structures are designed to transform the way people collaborate, how they learn, and how they discover solutions together. They support and spark creative adaptability. A description of a basic Liberating Structure called **1-2-4-All** shows how these features work in practice.

"To be free is not merely to cast off one's chains, but to live in a way that respects and enhances the freedom of others." Nelson Mandela

A Liberating Structure in Action

We know that the group is smarter than any single individual. The challenges are: How to tap into a group's collective intelligence and creativity when discussing an issue? How to prevent a conversation dominated by a couple of people? How to avoid a discussion that goes on, and on, and on?

1-2-4-All is one of the most effective methods for overcoming those challenges. It is so simple that it can be used anytime, anywhere, by anyone. Learning to use **1-2-4-All** makes it easy to work your way into some of the other Liberating Structures detailed in Part Four: The Field Guide to Liberating Structures.

1-2-4-All is so simple that it can be used anytime, anywhere, by anyone.

1.   **The invitation**: Reflect and share what questions, comments, or suggestions you have in response to a presentation or question.
2.   **How space is arranged and what materials are used:** Participants must be able to be face-to-face in groups of two and then in groups of four. Small tables with four chairs are easiest but not indispensable—people may sit or stand. Microphones may be needed for groups of four to share with the whole group if it is large.
3.   **How participation is distributed:** Everybody is given equal time.
4.   **How groups are configured:** First alone, then pairs, then groups of four, then the whole group
5.   **Sequence of steps and time allocation:**

     -   Reflect alone and write down your thoughts (1 minute)
     -   Share/compare/improve/expand in pairs (2 minutes)
     -   Share/compare/improve/expand in groups of four (2 minutes)
     -   One group at a time shares one important answer with the whole group moving quickly from group to group and avoiding repetitions (3 minutes)

The whole cycle can be as short as three minutes and shouldn't be longer than fifteen minutes. If an issue warrants more time, it is more productive to do a second cycle. Two cycles of ten minutes are better than one cycle of twenty minutes.

Why the Structure Works

Why does the insertion of a four-step structure elevate discussions consistently to a higher level no matter who the participants are or how senior or sophisticated they are? First, effective use of **1-2-4-All** does not hinge on expertise or talent. All you have to be able to do, we often say, is count to four.

Second, unlike Open or Managed Discussion, **1-2-4-All** gives everyone both more time and equal time to contribute. The structure does this automatically without a "boss" having to give permission to anyone.

Third, it makes space for silent thoughts that otherwise would stay in people's heads to surface and be written down. Reflection in silence is an extremely valuable but consistently underutilized structural element in meetings

Harvesting action ideas with 1-2-4-All in Peru

Then, working in pairs provides the safest possible space for everyone to articulate and test thoughts for the first time. It guarantees that everyone will express himself or herself at least a little. Since every voice is heard, the amount and, most importantly, the diversity of ideas are multiplied compared to a Managed or Open Discussion, resulting in much richer initial content.

In the groups of four, ideas—especially controversial ones—get a chance to be discussed and sifted to get them ready to be shared with the whole group. The stepwise progression provides support and time for ideas to be formed, modified, and strengthened before being exposed to a large group.

Finally, in the last step, going quickly from group to group and collecting one main idea at a time levels the playing field to make space for all ideas to be aired.

Overall, the progressive nature of the conversation, as it moves from one to two to four people, provides everyone with the repetition and time for greater depth and meaning to develop.

1-2-4-All levels the personality playing field, giving safe spaces for the more timid and preventing the more vocal ones from monopolizing the entire

Working in pairs provides the safest possible space for everyone to articulate and test thoughts for the first time.

discussion. Many more good ideas are given the chance to get picked up. Without having to jostle for space to be heard, participants are freed to focus on listening. Cocreation rather than advocating for one's position becomes more possible. As all participants hear the same information at the same time, they can discover patterns together. Better ideas, and more of them, are generated. Open, generative conversations unfold. Ideas are sifted in rapid fashion and "painlessly." Solutions, conclusions, or decisions are reached more quickly.

What else is made possible?

1-2-4-All transforms discussions from a linear sequence of single contributions into a series of simultaneous conversations. This makes it possible to engage within the same amount of time groups much larger than what is feasible with a Managed Discussion; getting contributions as wide and diverse as an issue requires is to be expected. More broadly, shared ownership of codeveloped initiatives means simplified and faster implementation; there is less of a need to explain actions, convince others, or push for buy-in.

1-2-4-All is so simple that it may easily be seen as a trivial change, something childish even, that is unlikely to make any difference, particularly with a group of more senior people. Nothing could be further from the truth. Replacing any of the Big Five microstructures with **1-2-4-All** is one of those tiny changes that can totally transform the outcome of any group's discussion.

Seeing **1-2-4-All** in action, or even reading about it, illustrates how, with distributed control, Liberating Structures make maximum use of the time available by replacing sequential interventions/contributions with simultaneous interactions. In other words, Liberating Structures like **1-2-4-All** allow parallel versus linear processing. This gives everybody not only a lot more total time to contribute but also a lot more equal time than conventional microstructures. Well-structured parallel processing makes it possible for groups of any size to work effectively and productively together. This dramatically increases the possible number of stakeholders who can contribute to shaping decisions.

1-2-4-All also exemplifies how Liberating Structures prevent the common side effects of conventional microstructures. Liberating Structures give everyone equal opportunity and time to participate. They provide clear boundaries within which energy and creativity can be unleashed but channeled. They create lots of

Liberating Structures make maximum use of the time available by replacing sequential interventions/ contributions with simultaneous interactions.

safe spaces that minimize power dynamics and encourage candid exchanges. They invite and facilitate the cocreation of both agendas and solutions.

These features transform how people collaborate, and how they discover and cocreate new solutions.

Harnessing the Power of Small Changes

Logic suggests that big progress can only come from big changes and that small changes will have little or no impact. Hence, the focus of leadership is nearly always on the larger and more visible ingredients of organizational performance, for example:

- Change "people": replace, train, increase, or decrease the workforce or its leaders.
- Change "resources": introduce new product, new equipment; increase or decrease funding.
- Change "macrostructures": reorganize, change strategy, revamp some core operating processes.

Changing people often includes training managers, leaders, and others to develop their skills. Using training to change people is unfortunately a very slow process and a complex challenge. In contrast, replacing a conventional microstructure with a Liberating Structure in group work is very quick and quite easy. It mostly takes the willingness to take a small risk and suffer through a bit of anxiety the first couple of times around. It takes getting used to trusting that the structures will—so to speak—"do the work of engaging people" and the people will do the rest. Multiple experiences reveal that it takes learning that the structures provide enough control to avoid chaos. A little *believing before seeing* is required.

Liberating Structures also provide many practical ways to make one-on-one discussions more productive and thereby transform the overall engagement capability of an organization. The process often starts with learning how to use Liberating Structures in groups. From this experience, it becomes possible to select from among the variety of liberating invitations or questions those that fit the purpose of each one-on-one meeting—for instance, "What is your **15% Solution**?" Similarly, the steps included in many Liberating

Liberating Structures challenge the myth that engaging people in an organization is difficult.

Structures are easily adaptable to what needs to be accomplished in a group of two—for instance, the debrief structure of **What, So What, and Now What?**

Liberating Structures challenge the myth that engaging people in an organization is difficult. First, they are easy to learn. Second, they don't require charisma or any special skills to use. Third, they spread person-to-person, without formal training, making it possible for everybody to join in shaping next steps. Liberating Structures quickly boost creative adaptability across an organization.

Without changing people, resources, or macrostructures, each instance of using a Liberating Structure will have an impact by affecting how ideas emerge and are filtered, how choices and decisions are made. The vignettes at the beginning of Chapter 1 are examples of the power of small structural changes and their impact. Many changes will have a small impact, but some will be significant. Cumulatively, their effect will be large because there is an endless number of opportunities every day for using Liberating Structures in every corner of any organization.

With Liberating Structures, it is possible to change patterns of interactions, decisions, and actions between individuals, then within a team, then across teams, and then across other boundaries. This "liberates" changes that can radiate in all directions: down, sideways, and up (figure 3.1).

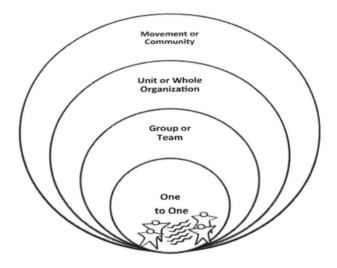

Figure 3.1
Radiating Change in All Directions

Principles and Practices

With Liberating Structures, it is possible, and not that difficult, to tap an organization's collective intelligence and address opportunities and challenges together. This approach to including and unleashing everyone ensures that every individual not only has influence but also the structure to contribute something unique. Our experience with groups using Liberating Structures around the globe confirms that much more can be achieved by inviting those contributions. In fact, key contributions often come from unexpected sources when Liberating Structures are used to create the right conditions.

From our own experience, and the stories our clients have shared, we have identified ten principles that emerge in organizations when Liberating Structures become part of everyday interactions:

1. Include and unleash everyone
2. Practice deep respect for people and local solutions
3. Never start without a clear purpose
4. Build trust as you go
5. Learn by failing forward
6. Practice self-discovery within a group
7. Amplify freedom and responsibility
8. Emphasize possibilities: believe before you see
9. Invite creative destruction to make space for innovation
10. Engage in seriously playful curiosity

Table 3.1 summarizes the full range of what gradually becomes possible in an organization when Liberating Structures replace or complement conventional microstructures.

In other words, the principles listed in Table 3.1 become ongoing practices for how to stimulate positive changes and innovation. For example, in every situation where we have been involved, without exception, Liberating Structures made it quickly obvious when a group's purpose was not clear or shared by all participants. This happened because, as everyone became engaged, confusion and differences that might otherwise have been suppressed came to the surface immediately. A clear, commonly held purpose is rarely seen for the simple reason that all the participants are almost never invited to generate jointly the answer to the question, "What is our purpose for working together now?"

"Everyone thinks of changing the world, but no one thinks of changing themselves."
Tolstoy

Principle **When Liberating Structures are part of everyday interactions, it is possible to:**	**Liberating Structures make it possible to:** **START or AMPLIFY these practices that address opportunities and challenges with much more input and support:**	**Liberating Structures make it possible to:** **STOP or REDUCE these "autopilot" practices that are encouraged by conventional microstructures:**
1. **Include and Unleash Everyone**	Invite everyone touched by a challenge to share possible solutions or invent new approaches together. Actively reach across silos and levels, beyond the usual suspects.	Separate deciders from doers. Appoint a few to design an "elegant solution" and then tell all others to implement it after the fact. Force buy-in. Confront resistance with hours of PowerPoint presentations.
2. **Practice Deep Respect for People and Local Solutions**	Engage the people *doing the work* and familiar with the local context. Trust and unleash their collective expertise and inventiveness to solve complex challenges. Let go of the compulsion to control.	Import *best practices*, drive *buy-in*, or assume people need more training. Value experts and computer systems over local people and know-how.
3. **Never Start Without a Clear Purpose**	Dig deep for what is important and meaningful to you and to others. Use *Nine Whys* routinely. Take time to include everyone in crafting an unambiguous statement of the deepest need for your work.	Maintain ambiguity by using jargon. Substitute a safe short-term goal or cautious means-to-an-end statement for a deep need or a bold reason to exist. Impose your purpose on others.
4. **Build Trust As You Go**	Cultivate a trusting group climate where speaking the truth is valued and shared ownership is the goal. Sift ideas and make decisions using input from everyone. Practice "nothing about me without me." Be a leader and a follower.	Over-help or overcontrol the work of others. Respond to ideas from others with cynicism, ridicule, criticism, or punishment. Praise and then just pretend to follow the ideas of others.
5. **Learn by Failing Forward**	Debrief every step. Make it safe to speak up. Discover positive variation. Include and unleash everyone as you innovate, including clients, customers, and suppliers. Take risks safely.	Focus on doing and deciding. Avoid difficult conversations and gloss over failures. Punish risk-takers when unknowable surprises pop up.

Principle When Liberating Structures are part of everyday interactions, it is possible to:	Liberating Structures make it possible to: START or AMPLIFY these practices that address opportunities and challenges with much more input and support:	Liberating Structures make it possible to: STOP or REDUCE these "autopilot" practices that are encouraged by conventional microstructures:
6. **Practice Self-Discovery Within a Group**	Engage groups to the maximum degree in discovering solutions on their own. Increase diversity to spur creativity, broaden potential solutions, and enrich peer-to-peer learning. Encourage experiments on multiple tracks.	Impose solutions from the top. Let experts "educate" and tell people what to do. Assume that people resist change no matter what. Substitute laminated signs for conversation. Exclude frontline people from innovating and problem solving.
7. **Amplify Freedom AND Responsibility**	Specify minimum constraints and let go of overcontrol. Use the power of invitation. Value fast experiments over playing it safe. Track progress rigorously and feed back results to all. Expose and celebrate mistakes as sources of progress.	Allow people to work without structure, such as a clear purpose or minimum specifications. Let rules and procedures stifle initiative. Ignore the value of people's understanding how their work affects one another. Keep frontline staff in the dark about performance data.
8. **Emphasize Possibilities: Believe Before You See**	Expose what is working well. Focus on what can be accomplished now with the imagination and materials at hand. Take the next steps that lead to creativity and renewal.	Focus on what's wrong. Wait for all the barriers to come down or for ideal conditions to emerge. Work on changing *the whole system* all at once.
9. **Invite Creative Destruction to Enable Innovation**	Convene conversations about what is keeping people from working on the essence of their work. Remove the barriers even when it feels like heresy. Make it easy for people to deal with their fears.	Avoid or delay stopping the behaviors, practices, and policies that are revealed as barriers. Assume obstacles don't matter or can't be removed.
10. **Engage in Seriously Playful Curiosity**	Stir things up—with levity, paradoxical questions, and Improv—to spark a deep exploration of current practices and latent innovations. Make working together both demanding and inviting.	Keep it simple by deciding in advance what the solutions should be. Control all conversations. Ask only closed *yes* or *no* questions. Make working together feel like drudgery.

Table 3.1

Liberating Structures: Principles and Practices

What is standard in most organizations is importing best practices or imposing practices from above.

Working with Liberating Structures has taught us that self-discovery and cocreation are the only reliable way to clarify purpose and ensure that it is both common and meaningful. The idea is to marry Principle #3, "Never start without a clear purpose," with #1, "Include and unleash everyone, and #6, "Practice self-discovery," and use appropriate Liberating Structures to make all three come alive. Otherwise, many group members likely will not endorse a purpose generated without them. They will not put their energy to advance it or, worse, will resist or block it.

The importance of self-discovery and cocreation doesn't stop with purpose. They are just as essential for making sense of challenges and for developing solutions that are likely to be adopted, adaptable, and successful. What is standard in most organizations is importing best practices or imposing practices from above. The assumption that a best practice will work everywhere is just too convenient to resist. So is the assumption that local context and people, though important, will not matter enough to make the difference. Plus, best practices fit nicely with the deep-seated notion that reinventing the wheel is a waste of time and money. Unfortunately, importing or imposing best practices usually involves trying to fit a square peg in a round hole. Context, culture, and people do matter more than we like to admit, and resistance inevitably emerges when we discount them.

Customer Service the Best-Practice Way

Consider this example of a conventional expert-driven approach to a customer-service issue (Figure 3.2). The leader of an organization perceives there is a problem with customer service and competition is increasing for the attention of customers. An external consultant is brought in to analyze the dimensions of the problem and report to top management. An external expert is then hired to generate a solution in the form of a series of best practices for exceptional service. A plan to launch the new service concept is hatched by a leader-sponsor who is inspired by a best-selling management book with success stories from other companies. A training program is designed that addresses the dimensions of the problem identified in the initial analysis. Training for frontline employees follows, cascading down the organization. A series of communications strategies are implemented to generate buy-in and overcome resistance to change. The project is reported as "Mission Accomplished." A few months later, momentum has evaporated and nothing much has changed about the quality of customer service. Now the program is rarely mentioned.

The unspoken principles here in the minds of the leaders were: *"We don't know how to solve this problem, so the people in the middle of it (those who created the problem and who are less smart than we are) are even less capable of figuring out what to do. Solutions and innovations can only come from external experts."*

We would suggest that the so-called nonexperts, the frontline people close to the challenge, are the ones who are most likely to come up with and sustain workable solutions to the customer-service issues. **BUT**, getting there requires tapping the hidden or unexpressed know-how of the frontline workers. This is where Liberating Structures come in.

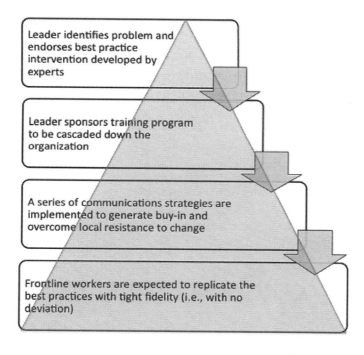

Figure 3.2
A Top-Down, Expert-Driven Change Progression

Customer Service the Self-Discovery Way

With Liberating Structures, the difference is that from the start, frontline people, leaders, and users agree there is a problem with customer service (Figure 3.3). Several project leaders from the internal organization are invited to step up. The team's approach to exploring the challenge of providing great service is primarily focused on learning from frontline staff and the organization's customers. They use **DAD, Simple Ethnography, Appreciative Interview**, and **TRIZ** to gradually engage all frontline groups and a variety of customers. These structures engage the people with the best knowledge of the situation in identifying successful behaviors and practices in current use. **Improv Prototyping** sessions are organized to spread learning and improve existing practices. New informal leaders step up as local ownership inspires more people to take action and networks are reinforced with **Social Network Webbing**. Barriers are identified and local managers take the initiative to remove them, calling on more senior leaders only if needed. As progress on addressing the customer-service situation builds, confidence grows to look for bolder ideas through **25/10 Crowd Sourcing**. More innovative approaches emerge and spread within and across units through the strengthened networks. More people are invited to gather information and ideas with **Simple Ethnography** and to spread these with **Users Experience Fishbowls**. Frontline people create metrics to measure their own progress, maintain gains, and continue innovating. Good ideas from the outside seep in without any pressure from above.

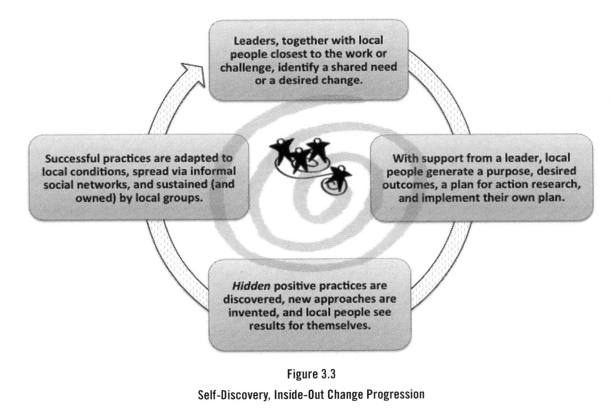

Figure 3.3

Self-Discovery, Inside-Out Change Progression

The principles openly expressed by the leaders in this case are: *"We don't know how to solve this problem, but the people closest to the work (including our customers) collectively can do it. They are the ones who know what is happening; they are the ones who need to decide to change; they are the ones that will need to sustain momentum and continue to innovate over time. Our job as leaders is to remove obstacles and create the conditions for self-discovery and cocreation."*

Tapping the Collective Capacity

The strategy of developing homegrown solutions internally, with or without inspiration or support from outside, requires being confident that they will be more successful than conventional approaches. If such confidence were widespread in organizations, internal development would undoubtedly be the more common approach. Clearly that isn't the case; otherwise, best practices would not be so popular. Why is that so?

Two reasons: one, many leaders, no matter their level, don't realize how smart their organization as a whole is and can be and, two, they and those below them haven't learned how to liberate and tap their organization's collective intelligence and creativity. Why is that so?

An organization's collective capacity comes in three layers: what the organization knows it knows, what it doesn't know it knows, and what it has the potential to invent. Only the first layer is visible to leaders and the view is often incomplete. The other two layers are invisible; the knowledge in layer two is there but must be uncovered before its potential contribution can be developed, and layer three doesn't even exist until successful experiments generate valuable innovations.

Leaders who are confident about practicing self-discovery believe that layers two and three can be exposed to deliver homegrown solutions that will be successful. They also believe that they and others will know how to unlock those layers reliably time after time. They build widespread faith and confidence in the process through repeated successful experiences at many levels. Creating a growing wave of successes is the only way to build a more self-sustaining and resilient organization that doesn't continuously depend on external experts.

Our job as leaders is to remove obstacles and create the conditions for self-discovery and cocreation.

Groups that discover their innate productive capacity and creativity through the power of self-discovery don't want to return to having external solutions imposed on them. This is their incentive for developing their own ability to facilitate self-discovery and invite experts only as needed. They own the changes they have to make, which is the best preparation for implementation and adaptation. A look at any of the field stories in Part Three will show that self-discovery is a common thread in all of them.

Users of Liberating Structures quickly start seeing the drawbacks of conventional microstructures. It becomes difficult to go back once "liberated." Frontline people are no longer left out of the innovation action. The top no longer decrees solutions to problems. Experts no longer tell people what to do. Resistance to change fades as conversations flourish and trust blossoms.

Measuring Inclusion and Engagement: IE Quotient

According to recent research by Gallup Inc., 70 percent of American workers are not engaged in their work.[2] Of that number, 18 percent are actively resisting what the organization is trying to get done!

These distressing statistics show how big the need is for organizations of all sorts to transform how they engage people across all levels and functions. Gallup's research shows that engagement drives greater business productivity, lower turnover, and better work quality; other findings from its study show that organizations in the top 10 percent of engagement outperform their peers by 147 percent in earnings per share and have a 90 percent better growth trend than their competition.

Statistics like these explain why achieving high levels of engagement often is a leadership priority. Unfortunately, the vast majority of people at all organizational levels have not developed the expertise to include and engage others effectively. To assess what we are calling Engagement Expertise, we have created two new key performance indicators (KPI):

- One measures the Engagement Expertise of individuals
- The second measures and illustrates the Engagement Expertise of entire groups—teams, departments, functions, or entire organizations

- Both serve as diagnostic tools that identify what needs to be changed or improved

We call these indicators Inclusion and Engagement Quotients, or IEQs—not IQ or EQ, but IEQ because engagement must be preceded by inclusion. While broad engagement metrics such as Gallup's are useful in grasping the scope and significance of the problem of disengagement, they are measurements of the outcomes or consequences of the inability to engage people. In contrast, IEQs measure the ability to engage directly and therefore are useful and to the point of what needs to change in order to build the expertise for achieving higher levels of engagement across the board.

Individual IEQ

An individual's IEQ is the score achieved from answering a simple questionnaire (Table 3.2) which can be found on pages 36 and 37.

The questionnaire can be self-administered, filled in through observations, or done through a 360-degree process. The range of possible scores is from zero to ten. The answers also provide an immediate diagnosis of which practices need to be changed to improve engagement expertise.

Table 3.2
Individual IEQ Questionnaire

This questionnaire can be used by or for anyone who regularly or periodically leads meetings or manages projects. Use the following scale to score points for all questions except for #3 and #4. When the questionnaire is used to assess what someone else does, replace "you" and "your" in all the questions by "he/she" and "his/her."

Never...	Rarely...	Periodically...	Routinely...	Always
1　2	3　4	5　6　7	8　9	10

Score

1. At the end of your meetings or projects how often do you assess specifically the level of engagement among participants?　　　　　　　　　_____

2. At the start of your meetings how often do you take time for all attendees to generate together a common purpose for their participation?　　　　　　　　　_____

3. On average, in your meetings or work sessions, what percentage of the time is spent listening to presentations? Give yourself 10 points for 10% or less, 7 points for 10 to 20%, 4 points for 20 to 30% and zero for above 30%.　　_____

4. How many different methods of interaction do you use in your meetings to engage every attendee and improve the effectiveness of the working group? Give yourself one point per method with a maximum of 10 points.　　_____

5. In the agendas of your meetings or work sessions how often do you specify the method of interaction that will be used for each topic and its purpose?　　　　　　　_____

6. In your meetings or work sessions how often is someone acting as the facilitator?　　　　　　　　　　_____

7. In your meetings or work sessions how often do you change the configuration of the group––for instance, from working together as a whole group to working in small groups or pairs or working individually?　　　　　　　　_____

8. In your meetings or work sessions how often does the role of facilitator shift among members of the group?

   _____

9. How often do you make an intentional decision to include new people with different perspectives or functional roles in your meetings or work sessions?

   _____

10. How often do you make the decision to include in your meeting or work sessions all or most of the people that will be affected by the decisions that will be made?

   _____

11. With your working group, how frequently do you engage as a group without presentations and with the freedom to co-create the agenda together?

   _____

12. How frequently do you create opportunities for everyone to share their own ideas for moving forward together without regard to formal position or rank?

   _____

13. How often do you deviate from your agenda to engage group members in unscripted sessions formed to respond adaptively to themes that emerged in the moment?

   _____

14. How frequently do you create opportunities to innovate (create something new) with diverse people from other functions or with the clients you serve?

   _____

15. How frequently do you work together in a space that makes it possible and easy to creatively mix and re-configure participant groups?

   _____

Total points   _____

IEQ score (total points/15)   _____

Add up the points to all the questions.

Divide by 15; this is the IEQ score.

Group IEQ

A group IEQ is derived from plotting the cumulative distribution of the individual IEQs of all group members, as illustrated in Figures 3.4 through 3.6 below. The Group IEQ is obtained by measuring the area under the curve; it can range from zero to ten. Figure 3.4 illustrates a "perfect" group IEQ: 100 percent of its members have individual scores of ten.

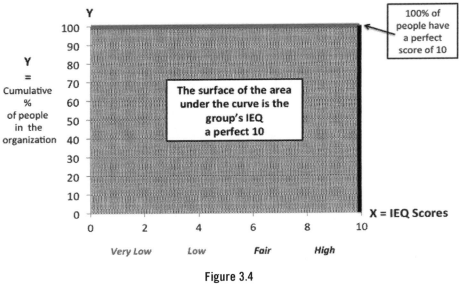

Figure 3.4

IEQ Distribution for a Perfect Group

IEQ of a Group Using Conventional Microstructures

In the example illustrated in Figure 3.5, the Group IEQ is approximately 2. The curve illustrates the distribution for an organization where only a select group of people have developed a high level of Engagement Expertise, either from natural talent or specialized training. Everybody else is using the Big Five conventional microstructures.

In such an organization, only a small percentage of people have IEQ scores of five or more (in this example, about 10 percent). The vast majority have IEQ scores of less than five (in this example, about 90 percent) and a large proportion have scores between zero and one (in this example, 50 to 60 percent). The resulting IEQ curve is deeply concave, which is typical of an organization where the majority of people use traditional structures for meetings and for working together.

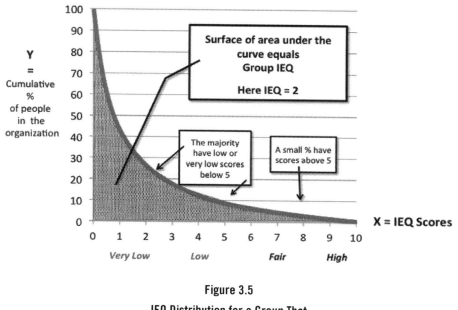
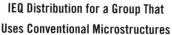

Figure 3.5

IEQ Distribution for a Group That
Uses Conventional Microstructures

IEQ of a Group Using Liberating Structures

Since Liberating Structures are easy to learn, it is simple for everybody to quickly boost his or her Engagement Expertise and bring individual IEQs above five. This makes it possible for a group of any size that chooses to use Liberating Structures routinely to flip their IEQ curve from concave to convex. In such an organization, Liberating Structures help everybody— senior leaders, managers, frontline people—to include and engage others effectively.

Figure 3.6 illustrates the IEQ for this kind of organization, where the vast majority have IEQ scores of five or above (in this example, about 88 percent) and only a small percentage have IEQ scores below five (in this example, about 12 percent). The resulting concave curve generates a large area under it and thus a high Group IEQ, in this example an IEQ of approximately eight.

With the information from individual and group IEQs, you know where you stand; you have a clear picture of what needs to be done to transform the way people collaborate, how they learn, and how they discover solutions together. As you implement changes, IEQs give you convenient metrics to track progress and identify where to focus your efforts. If people in your group start using Liberating Structures on a routine basis, you will be surprised how dramatically the group's IEQ curve will flip. This is one of the reasons why we say Liberating Structures are a disruptive innovation: no one expects such surprising results and impact on what is a massive and widespread challenge.

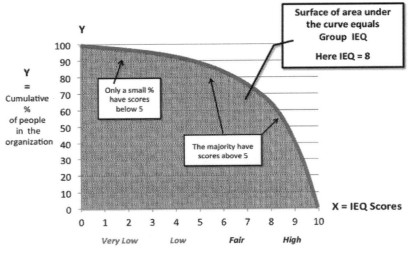

Figure 3.6

IEQ Distribution for a Group That Uses Liberating Structures Routinely

Liberating Structures And Culture Change

Dr. Michael Gardam is the medical director for infection prevention and control at the University Health Network in Toronto. In 2009, he put together an eighteen-month research project to prevent the spread of superbugs in hospitals. Here is his description of what happened.

> *"This infection control project demonstrated that fundamental change in habits, values, and beliefs can emerge from including and unleashing everyone. Liberating Structures focused attention on*

routine behaviors (e.g., hand washing, cleaning surfaces, transporting patients) and were widely employed in the study hospitals across Canada. Within a few months local solutions generated social proof, more diverse participation, and a virtuous cycle of feedback. The results were so persuasive that the project made it into popular local and national media. As the discoveries spread and generated tangible results, values and beliefs also shifted. Participants in the hospitals broke away from the values and beliefs that were, along with habits, holding them in place."

Changing culture was not a formal objective of the Canadian infection-control project. Instead, culture changes emerged without anyone "pushing" for them. First, participants decided to change some routine behaviors and habits. Then their successful new routines moved them to reconsider some of their values and beliefs and to adopt new ones. This surprised both the project organizers and participants. In the words of Dr. Gardam: "What took me by surprise was how this project fundamentally changed people's lives and how they work."

"What took me by surprise was how this project fundamentally changed people's lives and how they work." Dr. Michael Gardam

Why is this a worthwhile observation? Three reasons:

- One, culture is a big deal in organizations, either as an engine of progress or as a major source of problems or, quite often, both.
- Two, entrenched cultures are very resistant to change.
- Three, Liberating Structures offer an alternative way to influence culture that is in sharp contrast to the conventional approach.

To start with a common language about culture, let's say that culture shifts as three elements interact and co-evolve (Figure 3.7).[3] The first element in that process is the unexamined, taken-for-granted assumptions about how things really work. We'll label those **"beliefs."** The second element is the things people say they value or espouse as principles, standards, strategies, goals, and justifications. We'll call those things **"values."** Finally, there are the routine behaviors and patterns of interactions that can be observed. For purposes of our discussion here, we'll call those **"habits."**

Culture manifests itself as the sum total of all the behaviors of everybody in a particular organization or community. In a nutshell, culture is experienced and known by two catchphrases: the way we do things around here and what we expect around here. When an organization's culture changes, you can often feel it or see it before you have words to describe what is unfolding. People simplify by saying that "life is different" on the unit, in the company, or in the community. If you dig deep enough, you will find changes in behaviors and habits that are shifting in concert with more subtle changes in values and shared beliefs. To describe these changes, we use the words "more" or "less" to qualify terms like bureaucratic, entrepreneurial, risk-averse, proactive, silos, rigid, innovative, dynamic, patriarchal, "yes sir," "go-go," customer-focused, and product-focused.

In most organizations, efforts to change the culture are always top-down. They start when a leader—often a new leader—identifies an important problem that falls into the category of culture and makes a decision about the preferred future. This is new thinking, which must then be translated into new strategies, goals, incentives, and justifications for making different decisions. Sometimes this cultural wish leads to a major, abrupt change—a restructuring, for instance—that is intended to force a shift toward the desired new culture. The central assumption in this approach is that this shift in elements that we have labeled values will drive a change in beliefs and habits. The idea is that new thinking drives change. Hence the primary focus is on building a top-down, stage-by-stage logical progression from the current cultural state to the desired one. The approach focuses attention on compelling others to adopt the ideas and strategies and act in accordance to them. Transferring know-how takes the form of training and communications designed to overcome local resistance to change.

Sometimes it works, often it doesn't, and sometimes it backfires and reinforces the existing culture or pushes culture in the wrong direction.

With Liberating Structures, the focus instead is on changing **habits**, namely on changing and improving routine practices, behaviors, and patterns of interaction. The starting point is the issues or problems that the frontline people know and want to address. Changes are not forced by leaders from above but discovered and cocreated by frontline people with the support and participation of their leaders.

With Liberating Structures, the focus is on changing habits, namely on changing and improving routine practices, behaviors, and patterns of interaction.

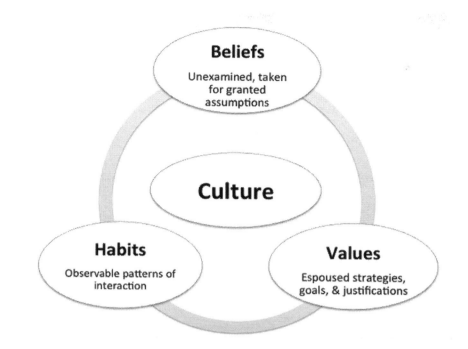

Figure 3.7
Elements of Organizational Culture

Liberating Structures are designed to help people notice the existing patterns and provide structures for including everyone in discovering more productive practices (habits) and for deciding how to shift from the old to the new. The idea here is that as self-discovered and cocreated changes in habits prove to be successful, they will gradually inspire a rethinking of what makes sense in the category of values, namely principles, strategies, and goals. Successful new habits will influence beliefs about what works and what is possible based on concrete personal and group experience. This is cultural change that grows organically as people convince themselves that those are the changes that they can and want to make based on what they have already been able to achieve with their new habits. That is why we say that it is possible to "influence culture" instead of "change culture" through the use of Liberating Structures; the word "change" implies going from A to B, which suggests that what B is has already been decided.

Successful new habits will influence beliefs about what works and what is possible based on concrete personal and group experience.

The difference between the conventional approach and the alternative offered by Liberating Structures is summarized in Figure 3.8.

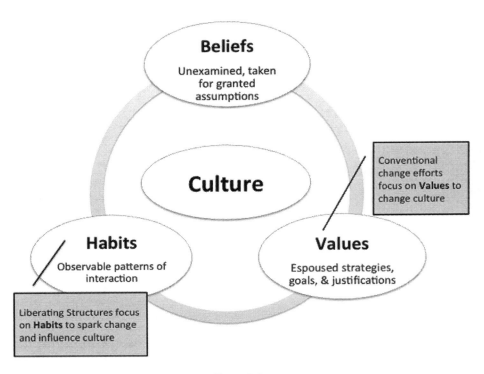

Figure 3.8

Difference in Focus for Change Efforts Supported by Liberating Structures versus Conventional Change Efforts

When people first start using Liberating Structures to address a challenge, they soon discover that they have more than the solution to a single problem. At a minimum, they quickly realize that they have found a different way to work and address challenging situations. As they expand their experiments in different directions or across functions, their successes invite them to reflect on and rethink some of their beliefs and values. This is the equivalent of a personal culture change. With that shift, even if only in a few individuals, the group and the organization's performance begin to transform.

Education is a domain where major shifts in strategy are usually controversial, costly and risky. In contrast, focusing on changing habits, improving routine practices, and altering patterns of interaction is inexpensive and low risk since the starting point is the issues or problems that educators know and want to address. Changes don't have to be forced from above but can be discovered and cocreated by the participants.

Liberating Education

If you arrive early enough for one of professor Arvind Singhal's classes you will find the usual room set up: rows of chairs, all facing forward, ready for students to sit facing the professor at the front of the room. However when students start drifting in you will surprised to see that they don't plop themselves into the chairs and open their laptops as they do in their other classes. Instead, unprompted and before professor Singhal arrives, they start moving the chairs out of their orderly lineup and into one big circular arrangement. Only then do they sit down. When professor Singhal comes in, he too takes a seat in the circle, alongside his students. As the class progresses chairs continue to be moved into other configurations depending on which Liberating Structures are used that particular day.

Professor Singhal has been using Liberating Structures for several years to the delight of his students who look very much forward to participating in his classes. As his story "Creating More Substance, Ideas, and Connections in the Classroom" in Part Three attests, there are few places where the dramatic changes possible with Liberating Structures are more quickly evident than in the field of education. "In the past eight years or so, the nature of the student feedback I hear has noticeably changed," he writes. "Qualitatively, it is deeper, more soulful. I increasingly hear: 'This class changed my life,' 'I learned so much about myself in this class,' 'I am sad that this course is ending for I will miss my classmates,' and so on. And, I have even heard students say: 'Thank you for teaching me about healthy communities. But thank you also for teaching me how to learn.'"

"I increasingly hear: 'This class changed my life,'"

The idea of using different teaching methods to foster engagement and peer-to-peer learning is obviously not new. Discussion circles and small study groups, for instance, are quite common in some schools. Yet the Big Five microstructures still dominate and constrain education, with the result that engaging all the students during their time in the classroom is a major and often insurmountable challenge. Using Liberating Structures is a simple change of habits for educators at all levels that will improve their performance quickly and easily. These new habits will also transform classroom dynamics and create the conditions students need to build a supportive community of practice.

Classrooms are privileged spaces. In an ideal world they would be used exclusively for what can be done only when students and teachers are physically together in the same place. In other words, they would be used exclusively for interactions: working together, discussing, collaborating, asking and explaining, and so forth. Thanks to modern technologies, transferring information no longer requires people to be in the same physical space. Teachers can choose to share a portion of their lectures virtually. Reducing lecture time makes space for a whole new range of interactions between students and teachers. The new challenge for teachers is making these interactions productive. Liberating Structures offer them a larger number of options to choose from, to experiment with, and to combine with whatever else becomes available from other sources.

Some educators or entire schools may choose to eliminate classroom lectures completely. Their flipped classrooms will depend even more for their success on how well the hands-on work in the classroom is organized. This will require choosing combinations of microstructures that are well adapted to the subject matter of each class. Online courses face the same challenge. They too will need interactive support structures if they are going to be more than just virtual lectures. With thirty-three different Liberating Structures an infinite number of combinations can be conceived to redesign classroom time and activities.

There is another compelling reason to use Liberating Structures in education: students need to learn how to interact, work, and collaborate effectively with other people well before they enter the world of work. This is a skill so basic and important that there is no reason not to give all students the opportunity to develop their expertise when there exists a set of methods as simple and easy to learn as Liberating Structures.

If schoolteachers and college professors use them routinely in the classroom their students will learn their value from direct experience. With a minimum of effort students will become aware of the importance of microstructures in working with others. With a little more effort they can be given the opportunity to master the use of some of the Liberating Structures before they join the workforce.

The final reason for exposing students to Liberating Structures is that most are likely to start work in a traditional organization. Therefore, for them,

Students need to learn how to interact, work, and collaborate effectively with other people well before they enter the world of work.

learning about Liberating Structures in school or college will be their only chance to discover methods that can transform their ability to succeed.

One last point: Schools and universities are just like any other organization; they too need innovative methods to address the many difficult issues, big or small, that they face outside the classroom. They need to find new ways to break down silos, overcome bureaucratic obstacles, and foster innovations. These are the never-ending challenges where methods like Liberating Structures can make a dramatic difference. Complex issues such as the problem of dropouts also demand new approaches and greater levels of engagement within the education profession and with the community. Those who use Liberating Structures in their classrooms will eventually experiment outside of them and discover that interactions among faculty, between faculty and administration, across departments, across disciplines, and with the public can also be transformed by using Liberating Structures.

What to Expect

Whether used in health-care or education, business, government, or community organizations, Liberating Structures disrupt conventional patterns in the way groups work together. They change dramatically the way results are generated **without** expensive investments, complicated training, or dramatic shifts in macrostructures. When Liberating Structures are introduced, many of the conventional approaches that people use all the time—PowerPoint presentations, open discussions, managed discussions, status reports, and brainstorms—become even less attractive than they already are or fall totally out of favor. And with that shift, everything changes.

Liberating Structures **are not** best practices imposed on a whole organization. They do not rely on expensive and lengthy efforts to change people's behaviors. They are instead a set of simple microstructures that can easily and inexpensively replace the conventional ones that are in everyday use. Individuals and groups can choose the Liberating Structures that suit their likes and dislikes then mix and match them flexibly to address their challenges. Liberating Structures are not only for leaders and change experts but for every person in the organization to use.

Caveat: Once Liberating Structures become everyday practice for your group, it's hard to go back to the way things were. Many of the Big Five conventional approaches will be eliminated from people's everyday work practices. As

Liberating Structures change dramatically the way results are generated without expensive investments, complicated training, or dramatic shifts in macrostructures.

one of our workshop participants put it: "Warning—you may never be able to tolerate another endless conference/meeting again and might feel that everyone is in 'The Matrix' except you!"

As with all disruptive innovations, no one expects what will happen. Shifts in the patterns of interaction make it possible for inclusion, trust, and innovation to come forward. Not everyone will be ready at the same time. However, some people will immediately use the freedom and responsibility unleashed to make small changes that generate breakthrough results. Immense sources of untapped knowledge, capability, and momentum are revealed. **Expect surprise! Expect smiles! Expect enthusiasm! Liberating Structures are fulfilling deep needs for meaningful and rewarding engagement present in all organizations.**

"What is accepted is no longer valid, what is valid is not yet accepted."
Jamshid Gharajedaghi

Chapter 4
Liberating Leadership
How leaders can avoid perpetuating the problems they complain about

Leaders don't purposely set out to demotivate employees or to discourage them from speaking up. They don't want to discourage cooperation. They don't want thousands of useless meetings conducted in their organization. Quite the contrary! They live with these frustrations because they see no other choice.

Enter "leadership" in Amazon's search box and you will get some ninety-two thousand results—and the number keeps climbing. The world is full of "proven" ideas on leadership. So why is it that so many fundamental issues continue to frustrate leaders everywhere?

When we ask leaders what they would like to see change in their organization, they say:

People contribute too little of their true potential, regardless of how many long hours they work.

We waste enormous amounts of energy because people don't work well together. They don't cooperate effectively, and they communicate poorly.

Internal politics keep people from pulling together with a common purpose.

Too many good ideas never come to the surface. They stay buried in people's heads and don't ever get a chance to come out.

"A leader is a person who has an unusual degree of power to project on other people his or her shadow or his or her light." Parker Palmer

Managers and their experts often operate in a world apart from the people closest to the problems. They don't understand one another or work well together. They have lost touch with the needs of clients and with the people they need to solve problems.

Relationships between people and between functions are strained. Sometimes they don't exist at all.

Too many people are doing their jobs on autopilot. They are not enthused about coming to work; they don't trust the idea of teamwork and are fed up with meetings.

Inevitable? We think not. But these issues perpetually frustrate leaders, no matter where they are in the organizational hierarchy. Plus, many of the strategies they use to mitigate these "perpetual problems" do nothing to change the situation and sometimes make it even worse.

Around the globe, leaders employ an elaborate and expensive array of countermeasures to address these frustrations. Reward programs, cross-functional incentives, change-management experts, personal coaches, and external consultants are tapped to deliver results such as:

- Build trust
- Get people to speak up
- Break down barriers between functions and levels
- Motivate employees
- Control bureaucracy
- Reduce resistance to change
- Minimize politics
- Foster cooperation
- Innovate more effectively
- Make meetings useful and productive
- Empower the frontline
- Get people to contribute their full potential

These programs and investments rarely deliver the desired results. While they have merit in some situations, these approaches don't have much influence on a main cause of the problems: how everyday work is performed. Too often, they make the problems worse and deepen cynicism in all directions.

Does any of this sound familiar in your situation?

The Bad News: Unintended Consequences and Side Effects

In spite of their good ideas or intentions, generations of leaders have been unable to turn their goals for more effective, productive organizations into reality. The bad news is that unmotivated employees, unproductive meetings, uncooperative work groups, and the rest of the problems leaders complain about are inescapable consequences of their leadership practices and of the way most organizations operate.

Here is why it happens.

Regardless of their own philosophy about leadership, people everywhere end up learning and using the same conventional top-down, command-and-control work practices—even leaders who consider themselves to be inclusive and participatory. Why? Because that is all they ever get exposed to. These conventional practices are routinely used in the vast majority of organizations, from first-level supervisor all the way to the top leadership levels. This grants top-down, command-and-control approaches unquestioned validity, and they are solidly embedded through all management layers and functions.

Traditional ways of working together exist to get things done and produce results, the underlying assumption being that they are the ones that will use the minimum amount of resources. Top-down, command-and-control practices are not designed to build trust, motivate employees, prevent silos, or address any of the other aims that elude and frustrate leaders. Instead, unwittingly, these practices combine to create a system that is perfectly designed to generate low trust, feelings of powerlessness, exclusion, frustration, and fear. The only way conventional work practices vary from one organization to the other is the leader's management style.

Leaders may be more or less inclusive, directive, or authoritarian, but they still end up using mostly the same practices. This explains why changes in leadership or organizational restructurings usually make no difference, because in most cases these routine practices remain the same: unaffected.

Over the years, the dysfunctions turn into norms; they are not seen as consequences of leadership and work practices but as standard defects of all organizations. It is quite common to explain them away by blaming "imperfect employees." Another common rationalization is, "It's the same everywhere." Without visible alternatives to inspire them, there are no discussions of what might be.

This explains why changes in leadership or organizational restructurings usually make no difference,

Patching Up the Symptoms

If/since leaders don't blame themselves, they don't feel compelled to change their ways. Instead, solutions take the form of palliative programs that attempt to improve the symptoms without addressing their root causes. For instance, programs to motivate employees, instead of fundamental changes to avoid demotivating them in the first place (none of us was born with a demotivating gene). For instance, more wall charts posted in meeting rooms about running effective meetings, instead of fundamentally changing their meeting designs and methods of participation. For instance, massive reorganizations or system-wide training programs, instead of creating structures to make it easier for everyone to contribute his or her best.

So, on the one hand, it would be fair to say that leaders are to blame for the chronic problems of their organizations since they are perpetuating the practices that caused them. On the other hand, it is also fair to say that in fact they cannot be blamed because they don't see any other practices being used around them. Everybody seems to be doing the same thing and having more or less the same problems. And lots of leaders have been quite successful and handsomely rewarded in spite of these problems. So why change? Why even bother looking for something else?

Here are some of the questions to consider.

- Does the value of your decisions depend on the input and expertise of others in your organization?
- Is your business becoming more complex and/or less predictable?
- Does your organization need to innovate or boost its rate of innovation?
- Is your competition growing stronger and changing more and more rapidly?
- Is your workforce becoming more diverse and more geographically dispersed?
- Is attracting and retaining top talent becoming more difficult?

If you answered yes to any of these questions, you need to strike at the root causes of dysfunctional teams, unmotivated employees, tedious and fruitless meetings, and other side effects of conventional work practices in your organization. Take a close look at what follows.

The Good News

The good news is that command and control is not the only game in town; there are other work practices that are much more adapted to the challenges faced by modern organizations. These alternative ways of working together are designed to get things done while overcoming typical leadership challenges. From the start and in every interaction throughout your organization, you can build trust, engage everybody to participate and speak up, break down silos, invite people to contribute to their full potential, and reduce resistance to change. Our thirty-three Liberating Structures are purposely designed to accomplish these goals. They can be used by organizations to structure a wide range of their activities, from everyday interactions, such as meetings, one-on-one conversations, and small and big projects, to strategizing, change initiatives, and customer interactions.

In Chapter 3, we outlined ten Leadership Principles that become routine practices when Liberating Structures are used on a regular basis (Table 4.1).

This is how people can choose to relate to others for the purpose of creating successful organizations where people thrive, but principles are useless unless they come with the necessary know-how to turn them into reality. Liberating Structures provide the "how-to-do-it" that makes them come alive. In our experience, even leaders who most desperately want to be inclusive don't know how to do it. When they discover Liberating Structures, they are thrilled to finally have in their hands practical ways to be the kind of leader they want to be.

Used routinely, Liberating Structures make possible the ***practice*** of a different form of leadership that can immediately yield tangible progress because it can be implemented at any level of activity. We emphasize the word "practice" because Liberating Structures are not ideas or concepts but concrete methods. With apologies for our lack of imagination, we call the form of leadership that uses these methods "Liberating Leadership." If leaders can let go of command-and-control practices, they find this form of leadership to be inclusive, adaptive, and very productive. They also discover that it is rewarding and enjoyable. The individual and the group are liberated.

*At first glance,
"including
everyone" looks
like a crazy idea*

> **When Liberating Structures are part of everyday interactions, leaders begin to:**
>
> 1. Include and unleash everyone
> 2. Never start without a clear and common purpose
> 3. Practice deep respect for people and local solutions
> 4. Build trust as you go
> 5. Learn by failing forward
> 6. Practice self-discovery within every group
> 7. Amplify freedom and responsibility
> 8. Emphasize possibilities: believe before you see
> 9. Invite creative destruction to enable innovation
> 10. Engage in seriously playful curiosity

Table 4.1
Ten Liberating Leadership Practices

The Possibilities

Let's illustrate by looking at the first principle since it is the most fundamental: "Include and unleash everyone." At first glance, "including everyone" looks like a crazy idea since it is the total opposite of what the norm is, namely "be efficient and include the minimum number of people needed." Until they see "including everyone" done with Liberating Structures and witness the benefits, the reactions we get from leaders when we talk about including everyone are raised eyebrows plus comments such as "impossible," "impractical," "would take forever to get anything done," "we'd never get everybody to agree," "would cost a fortune." They are right! This is what they have seen happen when everyone is "corralled" with traditional methods/structures to implement decisions, or when initiatives are cascaded down their organization and large groups are brought together to be convinced and trained. Corralling, cascading, convincing, and training are time-consuming and expensive at any scale, but this is what most organizations are designed to do: make decisions above and implement below.

*We always say
that leaders don't
have a choice
about whether or
not to include
everyone because
eventually
everyone that will
be affected by any
of their decisions
will have to be
included.*

We always say that leaders don't have a choice about whether or not to include everyone because eventually everyone that will be affected by any of their decisions will have to be included. Their only choice is **when** to include people and **how** to include them. Traditionally, the "when" is after the fact, when decisions have already been made and implementation has to start. The "how" consists of structures designed for convincing, training, controlling, troubleshooting, overcoming resistance—and for getting the infamous "buy-in" that is supposed to guarantee successful implementation.

The Liberating Leadership practice we advocate is to ***include people before the fact*** so that they can participate in shaping decisions and programs that affect and implicate them. It is only because Liberating Structures make it possible to do this effectively and economically that we can advocate such a practice. Once people get over the mental obstacle that including everyone is not practical or possible, the benefits of such a practice are not difficult to imagine. It is obvious that, at a minimum, commitment and preparedness for implementation will be greatly increased. Resistance to change will melt through the gradual process of cocreation. Crowdsourcing will strengthen the quality of decisions and programs. Entirely new ideas are more likely to emerge from the vastly larger number of interactions and discussions. Finally, shared ownership will get participants much better prepared for adapting decisions to changing circumstances and making course corrections as needed.

The longer-term benefits of early and systemic inclusion are easy to imagine. Entirely new professional and social connections will be built between people of different functions and levels. These will inevitably strengthen the fabric of the organization and reduce the silo tendency. With deeper and more frequent interactions, people will get to know each other much better. Trust will grow because, if for no other reason, there are many more chances for the untested assumptions that routinely get in the way to now be exposed and revised. Trust will grow because Liberating Structures constantly create a big variety of small spaces that make it easy for people to speak up and interact safely with each other, and to discover how they not only can work more effectively together but also help each other. Trust will grow because people will ***experience*** that they are more successful together than separately. Trust will grow because, with Liberating Structures, people will enjoy their time together much more than with traditional methods.

As trust grows, it creates channels for authentic feedback to flow upward and sideways. This has enormous implications for the productivity of any organization and for its ability to reduce or avoid costly mistakes. Organizations as a whole are smart and well informed about what the problems are. However, that information and intelligence is widely fragmented and doesn't flow spontaneously up to the decision makers. Liberating Structures can change that pattern.

Once people get over the mental obstacle that including everyone is not practical or possible, the benefits of such a practice are not difficult to imagine.

Liberating Structures create opportunities for many more people to make influential contributions. Anytime they do, they are acting as leaders however temporarily or briefly it may be. In that way, Liberating Structures distribute leadership without taking any of it away from the formal leaders. Instead, they reveal latent leadership that under traditional practices would not be given the opportunity to manifest itself. They liberate leadership in every person, so to speak.

The Choice

You have a choice: continue using traditional work practices and struggle with their chronic side effects or experiment with practices designed to avoid them. You can be the main force in deciding to maintain the status quo or the main force in showing and paving the way to a dramatically different set of results.

Liberating Structures are easy to learn and to use, but they require breaking some longstanding habits.

Liberating Structures are easy to learn and to use, but they require breaking some longstanding habits. Nothing particularly difficult is involved, but, still, you might have to move out of your comfort zone. For instance, in your regular meetings, there are probably established patterns about who sits where, how agenda items are handled, how discussions are directed. Liberating Structures will change these patterns. To make space for other people's contributions, your role and participation as a leader will have to change.

Getting started may feel clumsy. You will have to get up from your usual chair, move around, use different methods to energize and inspire your team. These new structures will loosen your usual level of control and invite you to become more transparent. They will mean that others have to get out of their comfort zones too. This is what Michael Gardam, Alison Joslyn, Jon Velez, and others describe in their stories in Part Three.

If you decide to change your ways, you will soon see how Liberating Structures improve your performance and the performance of the various groups that you lead or chair or participate in. Indeed, Liberating Structures will change the performance of any group by changing the quantity, quality, and depth of the interactions within it. The formula is quite simple: the same group with better interactions will perform better, often surprisingly better.

Let's face it, it's common for leaders to think that, in the short term, they are stuck with the way a team or unit is performing because they assume that the only way to improve performance is to replace people or to train them. Since both of these changes take time, and are out of the question in the moment, it's easy to understand why leaders feel stuck. Fortunately, it is possible for a group to generate surprisingly better results without replacing people or training them to change their behaviors. Changing the structures used by the group to transform the way its members interact and work together can do it. What's more, it can be done literally in the moment. Shifting structures is the only practical option for improving performance in the short term. With Liberating Structures, leaders can accomplish that shift quite easily and stop being stuck with inferior performance.

A Word to the Skeptic

At first glance, Liberating Structures may seem too easy, too simple, too straightforward, too effortless to achieve the kind of big changes that leaders are interested in, especially those in senior leadership positions. Liberating Structures may look nothing like the big, sophisticated interventions offered by famous consulting firms. Some may see them as trivial, not profound or interesting enough to warrant their attention.

Take a closer look and you will see that simplicity is the power behind Liberating Structures. Improving performance when using conventional structures is very difficult and demands lots of talent. But doing it with Liberating Structures is very easy because the structures spark improvements in performance automatically, by design. It is the structures that do the work, so to speak.

Liberating Structures produce big results easily because you do not have to depend on the talents or expertise of individuals to get engagement. You replace individual talent with microstructures specifically designed to tap into the organization's collective intelligence and get big things done. You stop trying to achieve results by dragging people along or transforming them individually. Instead, you accept people as they are and use the appropriate structures to enable them to feel eager to work and contribute their best. You discover that people transform their behaviors of their own free will in ways that no external influence, expert, or training course ever could.

Liberating Structures produce big results because they **are** simple. If they weren't simple, nobody would use them. If they couldn't fit easily within people's work, schedules, and time frames, they wouldn't be used. It is because they are simple that everybody in the organization, from top to bottom, can start to apply them in virtually all of their interactions from day one. When that happens, the cumulative impact of all these simple changes is huge.

Liberating Structures produce big results because they are simple. If they weren't simple, nobody would use them.

Think of the bamboo structures used as scaffolding for building in Asia. They appear simple and light, yet are amazingly strong; they can support putting up a skyscraper as effectively as constructing a small house. Our thirty-three Liberating Structures are like pieces of a bamboo scaffold. They can be combined and tailored for each specific construction to address any level of complexity. Learning to customize Liberating Structures designs to the specific purpose of each separate complex challenge is an art form that can be improved over a lifetime.

The Big Shift and Payoff

The big shift that comes from using Liberating Structures is more collaborative decision making and more crowdsourcing for solving problems or innovating and for developing strategies. Liberating Structures connect the doers and the deciders into productive assemblies.

With Liberating Structures, you expand the range of people included in making decisions and give a voice to those who were traditionally viewed as only "doers" or "implementers." Conventional structures mean that, as a practical matter, the number of people who can be included in shaping the future is always way too small. Liberating Structures eliminate that constraint. Liberating Structures plus the use of modern technology mean that tens, hundreds, even thousands of people—instead of a small group or task force—can now effectively contribute their knowledge and talent.

However, giving up the "convenience" of making decisions in small groups behind closed doors is a big shift from long-established habits that often go back generations. It may not be the easiest thing to do and is likely to face strong resistance by those who resent losing their traditional privileges. Some may even find it impossible to accept this new level of participation and transparency.

Leaders just live with chronic dysfunctional relationships between people or functions because they don't know how to change them.

The big payoff of course is that including a wide variety of people in day-to-day problem solving, decision making, and strategy development is the way effective leaders unleash the vast volume of contributions and innovations that lie hidden in their organizations.

The Biggest Leadership Challenge

People are the source of the greatest complexity and surprise in organizational life. Working together successfully requires all our intellectual, creative, and emotional talent.

However, the nearly universal approach to working together still revolves around centuries-old hierarchical practices. A small group decides and the vast majority is compelled to implement. Though well camouflaged in participatory jargon, authority continues to rule.

Think about why we are stuck in this way: The performance of groups of any size is determined by the quality of its members times the quality of their interactions. Leaders usually focus their attention on improving the quality of individuals. They find it frustrating and emotionally painful to deal with how individuals or groups interact with one another and therefore frequently avoid addressing frictions or conflicts.

What is difficult at the small-group level becomes excessively complex at the level of larger structures—the department, division, enterprise or block, neighborhood, community, country. That's why avoidance is such a common short-term strategy; in other words, leaders just live with chronic dysfunctional relationships between people or functions because they don't know how to change them. Common longer-term responses are to reorganize or to replace leaders in the hope that these changes will make the conflicts or dysfunctions disappear. In reality, it is impossible to know in advance what difference they will make. Too often, they don't make any difference or, worse, they destabilize the organization and amplify the dysfunctions.

Yet, to build a high-performing organization, the quality of interactions between people is at least as important as the quality of the people themselves, if not more so. Take, for example, a sports team. It is easy to see that individual talent alone does not make a successful team. The quality of interactions and relationships is displayed on the field for everybody to see. The coach and players are evaluated on their ability to execute together as a team. Chemistry matters.

In organizations, the chemistry of interactions is often concealed or hidden out of sight. When Liberating Structures are used, they not only foster a big increase in the number and quality of interactions but they also make them visible. This visibility invites participants to pay attention to them, notice the differences, reflect, and make creative adjustments. Some Liberating Structures—such as **Generative Relationships, Ecocycle, What I Need From You**—are designed to diagnose relationship issues. Many others will nearly automatically generate improvements. Changes coming from within in this way are likely to make sense, build trust, and be long-lasting.

It is easy to see that individual talent alone does not make a successful team. The quality of interactions and relationships is displayed on the field for everybody to see.

The best hope for transforming an organization is for the very people who will be implementing changes to "own" the changes, in this case the use of Liberating Structures. "Own" means that they have been included in their development, they understand them, they believe in them. They are therefore ready to implement them and to modify them as needed in the future.

Liberating Leadership Starts with You

Leadership is often a lonely spot, heavy with the weight of decisions and responsibility. It is easy to become at least partly isolated. While you cannot avoid accountability for making decisions, you can substantially change how decisions are developed and who is included in the process. Greater inclusiveness will affect the quality of your decisions and their validity. It will affect their implementation and your ability to respond quickly to the need for adjustments. It will liberate you from feeling all the weight on your shoulders. Inclusiveness will change the quality and the atmosphere of your meetings. It will change the quality of your work life. These benefits are your incentives for taking a serious look at Liberating Structures and experimenting with them.

Liberating Structures spread through personal exposure and experience.

Changing your own behavior and practices is the first step. Because it takes place when people meet and work together, using Liberating Structures is a public act and quickly visible; it will send powerful signals throughout the organization. The message will be that it is OK to replace long-held rigid traditions with some flexible new structures. When more people become included in everyday decision making and problem solving, it will be tangible evidence that "the times they are a-changin'" for real.

Liberating Structures spread through personal exposure and experience. It isn't possible to imagine what they can contribute without direct personal experience. They spread because people appreciate what they do and enjoy the dynamic conditions they create. That is true at any level, all the way to the top. Leaders shouldn't impose them or want everybody to be in lockstep. However, leaders who provide visible support and strong encouragement for the use of Liberating Structures will see them disseminate faster and more effectively and will reap the benefits of the changes they produce.

The most effective way to become aware of what is wrong with your conventional structures is to experience what happens when you use Liberating Structures instead. Just a few encounters with Liberating Structures in action make entrenched, invisible, conventional microstructures become visible by offering contrasting ways for people to work together and achieve better outcomes. This visibility is a key success factor because organizations tend to be stuck in patterns that keep reinforcing themselves, and they are rarely aware of being caught in these vicious circles. Changing those patterns requires a break, a rupture, and a successful experience that is the first step of a new virtuous circle. A success that comes as a surprise is an invitation for trying again; if more success follows, it is encouragement for taking another step in a new direction.

❖

There is only one way to learn what Liberating Structures are, what possibilities they hold, and how to use them: start experimenting with them in your everyday work. The Field Guide in Part Four is the place to begin to see what might be possible. What you can accomplish with the thirty-three Liberating Structures is limited only by your imagination. Combining many structures holds even greater possibilities. Putting them into practice today starts your journey toward liberating yourself and others around you. Part Four, Getting Started and Beyond, will make it easy for you to start to unleash the power of Liberating Structures.

PART TWO
Getting Started and Beyond

Part Two will make it easy for you to start to unleash the power of Liberating Structures. It is designed to guide your progress from using one or two Liberating Structures at a time to then stringing a few of them together and, finally, to composing elaborate storyboards for large-scale initiatives. It features:

- Getting started vignettes
- Advice for overcoming others' apprehensions and your own fears
- A one-page Menu of Liberating Structures, with abbreviated descriptions to make it easy for you to pick and choose
- Pathways to fluency in using Liberating Structures depending on your position in an organization
- A matching matrix showing which Liberating Structures are applicable to five broad goals
- Descriptions of Liberating Structures workshops
- Examples of powerful strings of Liberating Structures that match well with common challenges
- A few examples of detailed Design StoryBoards for large-scale projects or initiatives

"People tend to play in their comfort zone, so the best things are achieved in a state of surprise."
Brian Eno

CHAPTER 5
Getting Started: First Steps

Working with Liberating Structures may seem overwhelming or intimidating at first. How does one possibly master all those structures at once and know when and how best to use them? The answer is, you don't. You don't learn them all at once or ever use them all together. You learn one, you use one. You learn another, and then you might use one or the other or both. You get started with Liberating Structures the same way the old cliché tells you to eat an elephant: one bite at a time. Or, for another analogy, think of the way children master building with Lego bricks. First, they play around and learn to construct simple things like a tower or a simple cube. Then they tackle more complex structures like houses and bridges and castles. Next thing you know, they've built a whole city, or an airplane!

How you start using Liberating Structures will depend on the circumstances of your first exposure to them as well as your resources, your freedom of action, and your tolerance for uncertainty. We like the word "exposure" because Liberating Structures are like a fever. Most people who get exposed will catch the fever, and, as they use Liberating Structures in their daily work, they will expose others who will catch the fever too and spread it further. That is why the momentum of Liberating Structures can be started from any position in an organization, with or without resources, with or without position power. Here are a few vignettes to show how it can happen.

Larry was a hospital CEO who wanted to foster a dynamic and innovative culture. Since he had both authority and resources, he kick-started the use of Liberating Structures by sponsoring a two-and-a-half-day

The momentum of Liberating Structures can be started from any position in an organization, with or without resources, with or without position power.

workshop for the entire IT department plus clinical, HR, and financial leaders. All told, 180 people attended the workshop. In the three days after the workshop, Larry personally used fourteen Liberating Structures in meetings with his executive team, with physicians, and with his board.

Donia had no authority or resources; she was a market research analyst in a small department consisting of six analysts and a manager. After attending a Liberating Structures workshop, she suggested using Troika Consulting at the beginning of her departmental meeting. Her manager agreed. The Troika session was a smashing success and became the first step toward transforming the working dynamics and relationships in the department.

Vanessa was a public relations manager. She and a product manager colleague got an acute case of Liberating Structures fever while attending a Liberating Structures workshop. They decided on the spot to re-vamp an upcoming customer symposium. They generated the entire new design during the workshop and implemented it the following weekend. The feedback from participants was so enthusiastic that it convinced Vanessa to start using Liberating Structures in day-to-day work.

Arvind is a communications professor. After attending a conference where he witnessed the use of the Fishbowl structure, he started ex-perimenting with it in his own class. Students responded so positively that Arvind never looked back. He gradually became a routine user of other Liberating Structures and then started to deliberately spread them to students and other professors by publicizing his work and or-ganizing workshops. He now calls himself a Liberated Professor. (You can read his article at: http://www.liberatingstructures.com/stor-age/articles/Liberated%20Professor%20Speaks.pdf).

Sherry is a nurse committed to patient safety. She started using TRIZ with her hospital unit to engage everyone in a seriously fun way to pre-vent infections. She asked them, "How can we make sure that we expose every patient to a superbug during their visit?" Everyone got the mes-sage and started making changes that generated safer practices.

Neil is an OD consultant. He experienced two Liberating Structures at a national conference and immediately started to bring them into his consulting practice. With a little coaching over the phone, he soon had applied twenty-five or more Liberating Structures with different client groups.

Menu of Liberating Structures

When asked for a simple way to match Liberating Structures to a particular challenge, we often say, "If your goal is to engage and unleash everyone in generating great results, *any* Liberating Structure will be better than a conventional approach."

A more serious answer is, "Matching your challenge to a Liberating Structure depends on you and the details." A good match requires a sense of local context and a good feel for the history of the group you are working with. Liberating Structures are flexible enough to be used with your everyday team, a group organized for a special purpose, or a widely distributed set of participants, but each use benefits from thoughtfully matching the potential structures to your goal.

Look at the Menu of Thirty-Three Liberating Structures (Figure 5.1) and use the descriptions to clarify the first step in reaching the goal you have in mind. Ask questions like these: What's our first step? What do we need to start with? Who needs to be involved? What kinds of Liberating Structures can accomplish what we want? Where would each one get us, and what would we do next? Then pick one of the structures that match the purpose of your first step toward your goal. Check out the more detailed description in Part Four: The Field Guide to Liberating Structures or on the website **(www.liberating-structures.com/menu).**

Don't think too hard about choosing the right Liberating Structure from the menu. Just begin with your favorite structure or with one that seems easiest or most comfortable. Most people get started by using one or more favorite Liberating Structures in a variety of situations, from routine meetings to resolving conflicts within their work team. From their initial successes, they start experimenting with others and expand their repertoire over time. Don't worry about finding the perfect choice; there are always several Liberating Structures that can help your progress if your purpose is clear (see Figure 5.2, the Liberating Structures Matching Matrix). And remember that *any* Liberating Structure will be better than a conventional approach.

Just begin with your favorite structure or with one that seems easiest or most comfortable.

Impromptu Networking
Focusing on People, Purpose & the Power of Loose Connections

 TRIZ
Designing a Perfectly Adverse System to Make Space for Innovation

 What, So What, Now What? W³
Reflecting on Your Progress and Making Adjustments-As-You-Go

 Conversation Café
Making Sense of and Forming Consensual Hunches about Challenges

 Appreciative Interviews
Discovering & Building On the Roots Causes of Success

 1-2-4-All
Conversing in Cycles: Self-Reflection, Pairs, & Small Groups

 9 Whys
Becoming Clear About Purpose

 15% Solutions
Noticing the Influence & Discretion You Have Now

 Ecocycle
Engaging Groups in Growing and Sifting Their Portfolio of Activities

 Shift & Share
Spreading Good Ideas from the Grass Roots Up & the Fringe In

 25-To-10 Crowd Sourcing
Vetting Powerful Ideas and Igniting Action

 Min Specs
Unleashing Innovation by Specifying Only "Must-do's" & "Must-not-do's"

 Wise Crowds
Tapping the "Wisdom of Crowds"

Wicked Questions
Framing a Paradoxical Challenge That Engages Everyone's Imagination

Purpose-To-Practice
Designing for Shared Ownership, Adaptability, and Resilience

  Improv Prototyping
Developing Inventive Solutions to Chronic Challenges

 Agreement-Certainty Matrix
Matching Approaches to Your Different Types of Challenges

 **What I Need From You**
Surfacing Needs and Working Across Silos

Heard, Seen, Respected
Practicing Deeper Listening and Empathy

Social Network Webbing
Drawing Out Informal Connections & Adaptability

Design StoryBoards
Detailing Design Elements for Meetings & Innovation Efforts

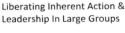 **Open Space**
Liberating Inherent Action & Leadership In Large Groups

 Discovery & Action Dialogue (DAD)
Discovering Solutions To Big Challenges In Plain Sight

 Integrated~Autonomy
Moving from *Either-Or* to *Both-And* Creative Solutions

 Generative Relationships
Understanding Patterns in Relationships that Create Surprising Value

 Critical Uncertainties
Preparing and Practicing Strategy-Making for Surprising-Yet-Plausible Futures

 User Experience Fishbowl
Sharing Insights Gained from Field Experience with a Larger Community

 Drawing Together
Drawing Out Insight that Precedes Logical Understanding

 Panarchy
Spreading Your Innovation or Good Idea At Many Levels Simultaneously

Troika Consulting
Guiding Your Next Steps with Colleagues

Celebrity Interview
Exploring Big Challenges with an Expert or Leader

 Helping Heuristics
Practicing Progressive Methods for Helping Others and Asking for Help

Simple Ethnography
Making Field Observations of User Experience

Figure 5.1

Menu of Thirty-Three Liberating Structures

Goal Microstructure	Discovering Everyday Solutions	Noticing Patterns Together	Unleashing Local Action	Drawing Out Prototypes	Spreading Innovation
1-2-4-All	✓	✓	✓	✓	
Impromptu Networking	✓	✓			
Nine Whys	✓	✓		✓	✓
Wicked Questions	✓			✓	
Appreciative Interview	✓	✓	✓	✓	
TRIZ	✓	✓	✓		✓
15% Solutions	✓	✓	✓	✓	✓
Troika Consulting	✓		✓	✓	
What, So What, Now What?	✓	✓	✓	✓	
DAD Dialogue	✓	✓	✓	✓	✓
25/10 Crowd Sourcing	✓	✓	✓	✓	
Shift & Share	✓	✓		✓	✓
Wise Crowds	✓	✓		✓	✓
Conversation Café	✓	✓			
Min Specs	✓	✓		✓	✓
Improv Prototyping	✓	✓	✓	✓	✓
Helping Heuristics	✓	✓			
User Exp Fishbowl	✓	✓	✓	✓	✓
Heard, Seen, Respected	✓	✓			
Drawing Together	✓	✓		✓	
Design StoryBoards	✓			✓	✓
Celebrity Interview	✓	✓			✓
Social Network Webbing		✓	✓		✓
What I Need From You	✓	✓	✓		
Open Space		✓	✓	✓	✓
Generative Relationships		✓	✓		
Agreement-Certainty		✓			
Simple Ethnography		✓		✓	✓
Integrated ~Autonomy			✓		✓
Critical Uncertainties		✓	✓		
Ecocycle Planning		✓	✓		✓
Panarchy		✓	✓		✓
Purpose-To-Practice		✓			✓

Figure 5.2

Liberating Structures Matching Matrix

In the matrix, the strengths of each Liberating Structure are arrayed according to common goals for groups. The five common goals are:

- Discovering everyday solutions (problem solving + coordination in meetings and regular interactions)
- Noticing patterns together (looking for ways to explain or make sense of changes)
- Unleashing local action (getting each person engaged in taking action)
- Drawing out prototypes (quickly developing small pieces or chunks of solutions that can be refined and combined later)
- Spreading innovation (spreading ideas/services/products out and scaling up to higher levels)

Match your group's goals to Liberating Structures with particular strengths.

Safety First

To get started with Liberating Structures, select a safe place for your first attempts. Of course, whether an experiment feels safe or not is different for each person. Larry, the hospital CEO, not only had resources and authority but also was personally very confident. So he jumped into using Liberating Structures immediately after the workshop; nothing held him back from having every meeting be an opportunity to try as many of them as possible. Someone else may feel more comfortable starting with only one of the easier Liberating Structures, such as **1-2-4-All** or **Troika Consulting**. Some may prefer to start with a small group of trusted colleagues as a safe way to get their feet wet and gain both confidence and support. There are no rules, no right or wrong way. All that is needed is to experiment and experience the results. As we have said so many times, practice is the only way to learn *and* to discover what each Liberating Structure makes possible.

We strongly recommend, if at all possible, that you begin your early experiments with a partner. It is much easier to decide which Liberating Structure to use via a conversation with a trusted partner than talking about it alone in your head. You will feel much more relaxed knowing that your partner can jump in to support you. A partner who observes and helps you debrief after each experience is the quickest way to learn and it's much more fun than practicing alone. Also, a partner will inevitably notice important details that you will miss. Invite your observer-partner to pay special attention to your concerns and fears. This may include how you clarify purpose, invite participation, react to dynamics among group members, respond to insights and actions that emerge, and adapt as deviations from your plan unfold.

If you decide to work with a partner when getting started with Liberating Structures, choose someone who will not be shy about giving you honest and direct feedback about your performance. Any trusted colleague, regardless of Liberating Structures expertise, who will be an interested and alert observer is preferable to "working without a net."

Breaking with Tradition

Regardless of an organization's mission and geography, Liberating Structures are usually a striking departure from its habits, traditions, and culture. For new users, people not familiar with Liberating Structures and the outcomes they produce, this break with convention can be a source of anxiety or fear. When working with new users, you need to be mindful of their apprehensions. For example, you may be warned that people will become confused or simply refuse to participate. You may be told that "it" will not work here, not in "this" culture or with "these" people.

You may be told that "it" will not work here, not in "this" culture or with "these" people.

Our experience says otherwise. While in Belgium, we proposed using **Impromptu Networking** to start a workshop with fifty Flemish cardiologists who were standing in a large room having a drink before dinner. We were told this approach would never work, not with this group of high-level specialists. "Flemish cardiologists will fold their arms, stare you down, and write you off." The message was sharp and clear: "Don't do it, you will embarrass yourself and us!"

We insisted and, no surprise to us, the cardiologists loved **Impromptu Networking**. In fact, it was difficult to get them to stop talking to each other and sit down for dinner. It was a perfect beginning for a meeting designed to spark more collaborative action. They engaged immediately into shaping their next steps with newfound trust and connection.

Clearly, as one should expect, breaking with tradition evokes both excitement and fear. That is what we have found in multiple countries and in all types of organizations. Some people couldn't wait to start using Liberating Structures, while others worried about acceptance and how their boss, colleagues, students, or clients might judge them if they moved away from conventional methods. You may encounter the following:

- Concerns that the outcome isn't predictable
- Resistance to the risk of having to step beyond one's area of expertise because Liberating Structures will cut across boundaries
- Fear that more diversity of perspectives than what is welcome will be revealed
- Fear of losing control or of ending with the "wrong outcome"
- Unspecified fear of the unknown and/or uncertainty

Fortunately, such fears dissipate quickly since Liberating Structures invariably generate much more satisfying and energizing interactions than participants experience with familiar conventional structures. With Liberating Structures, outcomes are not predictable in detail, but high levels of engagement always materialize regardless of context or culture. So while it is normal for new users to be anxious, you can relax knowing that Liberating Structures will deliver better-than-expected results. Those experiencing Liberating Structures for the first time will soon see for themselves that the possible outcomes easily allay any lingering anxieties.

Your Own Fears

What about your own doubts or fears about introducing Liberating Structures into your organization? It's common for people to feel uncertain when getting started with Liberating Structures. *"I don't want to look like I don't know what I'm doing"* and *"I worry that people will think I'm overreaching my expertise or responsibilities"* and *"I'm afraid that this all might look trivial or touchy-feely"* are some of the apprehensions we have heard. Others have expressed concern that using Liberating Structures in their organizations might reveal awkward differences of opinion. We have heard about how uncomfortable it is to stray from the usual approach to problem solving: bring in the experts. People worry that by using Liberating Structures they will initiate unproductive, uncontrollable chaos. And then there's the age-old fear of learning and doing something new, venturing into something unfamiliar and unexpected.

To all of them, we must say, *Just do it*. There is no better way to overcome your apprehension than to dive right in and put your first Liberating Structure to work for you immediately. As we have said, it matters not which Liberating

Structures you start with. If you are like most people, you will begin by using a few favorites and expand your range over time. As you gain more experience, the particular strengths of each Liberating Structure in particular circumstances will become clear and you will see how you can combine them into powerful sequences. You will be learning a new language, saying things like "Let's do a **TRIZ**!" As you become more fluent, your ability to improvise will grow. You will be able to decide in the moment to use a particular Liberating Structure or to substitute one for another in response to what is happening in the moment.

As you grow more and more confident about your ability to be successful with Liberating Structures, your fears will lessen but never completely recede because unpredictability never goes away: your success will always come with many surprises. These are a big part of the satisfaction you will derive from using Liberating Structures. As you gradually push the envelope by including more people, more functions, and more levels, and by embracing more diversity, more surprising and exciting results will emerge.

Three Pathways to Fluency and Routine Use

Where you sit in an organization influences not only your first steps but also the subsequent paths you can take to develop fluency in the use of Liberating Structures.

For Senior Leaders

Senior leaders with resources can quickly engage many other people with workshops for some two hundred people at a time (see Immersion Workshops below) and they can also put in place mechanisms to encourage dissemination and to support a growing number of applications. A senior leader who personally becomes a visible regular user sends a powerful **invitation** to the entire organization to join in the experiment. From this, a critical mass can emerge to overcome the huge inertia of conventional practices that dominate existing work systems.

We use the word "invitation" purposely because we believe that it is not a good idea for leaders to use their authority to impose Liberating Structures. Instead, we advise creating opportunities for people to learn and allowing them to implement at their own pace and at their own level of comfort. We believe that the use of Liberating Structures will best flourish when it is left to grow through the enthusiasm and energy of spontaneous adopters. So the role of leaders is not to impose but to provide lots of support where it is wanted and welcomed. In addition, they need to be regular users themselves for there is absolutely no other way for them to fully make sense of what Liberating Structures can contribute to the performance of their organization.

Leaders have many opportunities every day to start practices that can easily be copied by others in their organization. For instance, replacing conventional meeting agendas with "storyboards" will inevitably support the use of Liberating Structures since they always specify for each session not just its purpose but also the detailed structure that will be used to achieve the purpose.

The use of Liberating Structures spreads most effectively when people experience and discover what they make possible. For leaders, this means creating opportunities for people to be exposed to Liberating Structures in workshops or making it easy for people to learn them in partnership with others. It means supporting the development of communities of practice in all organizational functions so that people can easily network and learn peer-to-peer. It means encouraging experiments and disseminating news of both successes and failures.

Managers, Individual Contributors, Solo Practitioners

In contrast to senior leaders, managers, frontline workers, and professionals such as educators or nurses are unlikely to have access to a lot of resources. So their starting point will not be a workshop but a single application of one Liberating Structure or a small number of structures in connection with a meeting with their team or colleagues. In our experience, small but frequent steps, with a thorough debrief after each step, are the most effective way to proceed. We always advocate working with a partner as it makes the learning process so much more effective, faster, safer, and fun.

Don't try to convince anybody, words will not do it but experiences will.

We are frequently asked, "I want to start using Liberating Structures myself, but how can I convince the people around me to start using them?" Our answer always is, "Don't try to convince anybody, words will not do it but experiences will." In other words, just use a Liberating Structure at your first opportunity and let those who like it learn from you. Then use your next opportunity, and the next, and so on. Let people discover and convince themselves of the value of Liberating Structures through the experiences you create.

Remember too that all new users of Liberating Structures have the potential to initiate a community of practice if they choose to. It starts with getting one partner and then being deliberate in attracting and supporting new users by offering assistance or by inviting them to observe. We have seen many instances where adopters of Liberating Structures have been asked to run small workshops as a way of spreading the practice—for example, two to three hours covering a few basic structures. Or they were asked to help with designing or facilitating a meeting. Spread can be spontaneous or planned.

Internal or External Consultants

For internal or external consultants with influence but limited resources, starting to use Liberating Structures in work with their closest clients is the most effective way to get started. As their experience builds, they will soon have to make a choice between keeping their new expertise for their own benefit or turning as many of their customers as possible into users. The latter obviously is the more powerful strategy, but it requires that the consultant become a coach and teacher in addition to a being a proficient user. This will translate into codesigning and co-facilitating with individual clients and will likely require eventually going beyond individual coaching by organizing workshops for small or large groups.

As the work progresses, it is likely to involve navigating up the organization in order to engage and get the support of leaders in more senior positions than one's initial clients. It may not be an easy transition for a consultant to, as quickly as possible, hand off responsibilities for facilitating Liberating Structures to others. After all, this is like giving away one's reason for existence and looks like a lousy business model. Who is going to need you if at every step you share your experience and invite new users to take over and expand their practice? While this may sound like a legitimate concern, the scope of what needs to be accomplished to help an organization get the full benefit of Liberating Structures is so vast that no single consultant is likely to run out of work. Expansion or promotion is the much more likely scenario. Ripples will turn into waves.

Especially for anybody who learns Liberating Structures by reading instead of direct experience, **1-2-4-All** is a very good place for a safe start (see description in the Field Guide or in Chapter 3). It is such an effective structure that any meeting would have to be exceptionally unusual not to offer at least one opportunity for using **1-2-4-All** to good advantage. So start with this structure, and when you feel comfortable, try another. There are more than a dozen easy structures that are sufficiently simple to jump into and try out—for instance, **Troika Consulting; Impromptu Networking; Appreciative Interviews; What, So What, Now What?; Conversation Café; Nine Whys; Wise Crowds; 15% Solutions**. Table 5.1 shows options for getting started from various organizational positions. See the Menu earlier in this chapter (Figure 5.1) for a quick overview of these Liberating Structures and then follow the discussion in the Field Guide or on www.liberatingstructures.com to translate into action.

The next step is for you to move up the boldness ladder by combining two or more structures. Then find others who love the work and share stories with one another. Experiment with Liberating Structures in as many aspects of your life as you dare to; they not only have a place at work but also at school, in your family, and in your social circles.

Leader with Resources to Engage Many Others	Manager, Individual Contributor, or Solo Practitioner	Internal or External Consultant
1. Sponsor an immersion workshop.	1. Try a basic Liberating Structure like **1-2-4-All** or **TRIZ** in routine work.	1. Try a basic Liberating Structure like **1-2-4-All** or **TRIZ** in routine work.
2. Sponsor follow-up learning groups (communities of practice) for people in your unit or business.	2. Attend a workshop or shadow someone with experience to build your portfolio. Find a partner.	2. Attend a workshop or expand experience on your own. Propose and organize a first workshop for clients.
3. Encourage use in your own leadership team meetings and in projects.	3. Try new Liberating Structures and invite others in your group or community to shadow you.	3. Expand experience with a project, start coaching leaders to design and facilitate with Liberating Structures.
4. Begin use in strategy development and design work.	4. Look for places to insinuate Liberating Structures in meetings and projects outside your group.	4. Form informal learning groups, invite leaders to join, launch evaluation efforts.
5. Expand into an organizational strategy.	5. Offer coaching or small workshops to colleagues and managers.	5. Invite users and nonusers to a series of small workshops.

Table 5.1

Five Ways to Get Started, No Matter What Your Position

Immersion Workshops

Clearly, there are many ways to learn Liberating Structures and get started using them. We believe that one of the most efficient and effective ways—if it is possible—is to experience an Immersion Workshop. A Liberating Structures Immersion Workshop is like a foreign-language immersion course that temporarily relocates you away from a familiar culture. In an Immersion Workshop, you experience nothing but the language and practices of Liberating Structures. There are no presentations, facilitated discussions, updates, brainstorms, or open discussions. Having a team of people from your organization participate in an Immersion Workshop—or, even better, when the organization holds an Immersion Workshop in house—makes it possible for a critical mass to form around Liberating Structures, making it more likely that they will take hold and spread.

Liberating Structures are not difficult to learn, but *they need to be experienced* at least once to understand and believe what they can achieve. The reason is that their impact is counterintuitive because it cannot be explained by the logic of top-down command and control that dominates organization cultures. Fortunately, you can develop a practical understanding of most individual Liberating Structures in less than an hour each, enough to grasp them and then try them out with little risk. Taking this approach, Immersion Workshop participants repeatedly act their way into new thinking as they witness what can be accomplished when letting go of control with the support of simple but clear structures. Practice and debriefs with peers generate more confidence in the new methods. The participants discover the validity of the Liberating Structures principles personally rather than being told about them.

Liberating Structures are not difficult to learn, but they need to be experienced at least once to understand and believe what they can achieve.

What's the Purpose?

The purpose of an Immersion Workshop depends in part on whether participants are all from the same organization or come from different ones.

For Participants from the Same Organization

For participants from the same organization, these are typically the objectives:

- To have people experience and learn together what they will need to practice together on the job

- To work on real-life challenges and issues that are common concerns to all participants
- To discover what can be accomplished when leaders and frontline people work together and a diversity of functions are included
- To create enough critical mass to allow Liberating Structures to easily take hold and spread within the organization

By design, the Immersion Workshop is a quick, compressed model of all of the Liberating Structures principles. For example, one way that Principle #1, "Include and unleash everyone," is brought to life is with the structure of the participant group: the workshop includes people from all layers of the organization and from the complete range of organizational functions. The makeup of the workshop group consciously mirrors what participants might want to emulate on the job when they start using Liberating Structures in their everyday interactions.

For Participants from Different Organizations

The purposes of an Immersion Workshop for people from many different organizations are:

- To experience many different Liberating Structures in a short time
- To appreciate how universally useful Liberating Structures are
- To discover what is possible when a group of very diverse people work together

With various organizations represented in the room, participants are exposed to many different ideas and to people who come from a variety of positions and fields. Unlike other types of public workshops, Immersion Workshops are not tailored for a particular audience, such as leaders or managers or HR professionals. Instead, they are constructed so that everybody can bring his or her challenge, with the idea that the more diversity in the participant group, the richer their experience.

In a multi-organization workshop, people see for themselves what can be accomplished in very diverse groups. Also, participants have a unique opportunity to enlarge their network of connections and find support for using Liberating Structures back in their own organizations. On the other hand, they miss out on key benefits of same-organization workshops: they must return to organizations that have not experienced the power of Liberating Structures and will have to build credibility and critical mass to realize what might be possible in their actual work groups. A big plus, though, is that they learn how other organizations are experiencing and addressing the same chronic problems.

Whom to Include

Liberating Structures are about working together and they are best learned together. For an in-house workshop, include a diverse mix of leaders, managers, and frontline workers with shared interests. As long as a representative sample of the whole organization plus the entire management layer is included, it is possible for a group of any size to learn rapidly the approaches together—we have worked with close to two hundred participants in the same room. A typical invitation plan is illustrated in Figure 5.3.

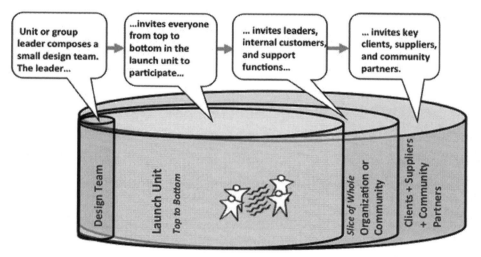

Figure 5.3
Liberating Structures Immersion Workshop Invitation Plan

The reasons for including the front line along with leaders is that most organizational issues of any importance involve multiple functions, levels, and disciplines, and the place where things get done is on the front line, not in the management ranks. Putting them in the same room to learn together new methods of working together creates the opportunity to have them discover what they can do together to address their challenges. Learning together is a powerful way to discover how Liberating Structures generate better-than-expected outcomes. Including multiple layers and diverse functions in the workshop experience also promotes the communities of practice that can launch Liberating Structures quickly throughout the organization or community. Confidence builds when everyone starts on an equal footing and there is no waiting for permission.

It's a liberating experience for an organization's leaders to be part of an Immersion Workshop: they discover that they don't have to be in control. As frontline people find their voice and become more and more assertive about participating and contributing in the workshop activities, leaders become less and less concerned about being in charge. It's as energizing for the organization's front line as it is for management to experience together and in the moment how leadership and letting go can be compatible and complementary.

What Leaders Should Expect

Leaders who sponsor and participate in the first Immersion Workshop in their organization can expect a surprising, unnerving, exhilarating, or reassuring experience—or all of the above. A large workshop is likely to be the first time that so many layers and functions are gathered in the same space to work together in a variety of configurations on resolving issues, and so the discovery of what is possible is likely to be a surprising experience. Letting go of control, as Liberating Structures require, can be unnerving at first. Fortunately, benefits become quickly visible, providing reassuring evidence that letting go of control can be a responsible choice. As more and more participants gain confidence and contribute, the shared experiences can be exhilarating: Wow! An Immersion Workshop is particularly attractive for leaders who are frustrated with traditional approaches and are looking for innovation; it is rewarding and reassuring to experience the concrete outcomes from the wide range of activities that include and engage everyone in the workshop.

Key Elements of an Immersion Workshop

Since 2004, Immersion Workshops have been conducted in some twenty different countries across Latin America, Europe, Canada, and the United States. Organizational settings have included multinational business, hospitals, government, schools, and nonprofit organizations. It's remarkable that similar impacts have been achieved in all those spheres, around the world, regardless of cultural differences.

A three-day Immersion Workshop may feature the themes and methods shown in Figure 5.4. Each session is designed to address customized organizational needs, specific innovation opportunities, and shared challenges. After the workshop, one-on-one consulting sessions are the most effective way to translate into immediate action what has been experienced during the workshop.

Immersion Workshops are designed to introduce participants to a large number of Liberating Structures very rapidly—it's a fast "do one, do another one" method of learning. The idea is to create awareness of the range of possibilities that Liberating Structures open up. Also, covering a wide variety of structures underscores the notion that there is no single way to address any particular challenge. Another message that Immersion Workshop participants get loud and clear: you learn by doing; once you've seen a Liberating Structure in action and practiced doing it in the workshop, you can do it back home.

An Immersion Workshop treats each Liberating Structure separately. A design team from the organization helps to identify current issues and problems that matter to participants and designs workshop experiences to address those real-life challenges. By covering so many so fast, the workshop demonstrates that the Liberating Structures playbook has something for everybody and everything. Every participant learns that there are several Liberating Structures from which to choose to deal with most situations. In our experience, different people, for whatever reason, are attracted to different Liberating Structures. An Immersion Workshop virtually guarantees participants will experience at least one structure that they like and that will be appropriate for their challenges.

DAY 1

 Impromptu Networking
Rapidly share challenges and expectations, building new connections

 1-2-4-All
Engage everyone simultaneously in generating questions/ideas/suggestions

 Appreciative Interviews
Discover & build on the root causes of success

 Min Specs
Specify only the absolute "Must do's" & "Must not do's" for achieving a purpose

 TRIZ
Stop counterproductive activities & behaviors to make space for innovation

 15% Solutions
Discover & focus on what each person has the freedom and resources to do now

 Troika Consulting
Get practical and imaginative help from colleagues immediately

 What, So What, Now What?
Together, look back on progress to-date and decide what adjustments are needed

DAY 2

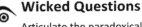 **Social Network Webbing**
Map informal connections & decide how to strengthen the network to achieve a purpose

 Wicked Questions
Articulate the paradoxical challenges that a group must confront to succeed

 Improv Prototyping
Develop effective solutions to chronic challenges while having serious fun

 User Experience Fishbowl
Share know-how gained from experience with a larger community

 Drawing Together
Reveal insights & paths forward through non-verbal expression

 Celebrity Interview
Reconnect the experience of leaders and experts with people closest to challenges

 Conversation Café
Engage everyone in making sense of profound challenges

 Open Space
Liberate inherent action and leadership in large groups

 25/10 Crowd Sourcing
Rapidly generate & sift a group's most powerful actionable ideas

DAY 3

 Discovery & Action Dialogue
Discover, spark & unleash local solutions to chronic problems

 9 Whys
Make the purpose of your work together clear

 Generative Relationships
Reveal relationship patterns that create surprising value

 What I Need From You
Surface essential needs across functions and accept or reject requests for support

 Critical Uncertainties
Develop strategies for operating in a range of plausible yet unpredictable futures

Purpose-To-Practice
Define the five elements that are essential for a resilient & enduring initiative

Ecocycle Planning
Analyze the full portfolio of activities & relationships to identify obstacles and opportunities for progress

 **DAYS 4 and 5**
Coaching + design sessions for individuals and teams that ask for help with a challenge. Together, we develop concrete next steps.

Figure 5.4
Sample Three-Day Immersion Workshop

Shorter Immersion Workshops

Since it is obviously not always possible to organize a three-day-long workshop, series of short workshops are effective alternatives as long as the following objectives guide their design:

- Illustrate how Liberating Structures are useful for a wide range of challenges
- Ensure that every person is likely to find one or more microstructures he or she wants to start using immediately
- Help participants gain confidence together via practice on diverse issues
- Show how Liberating Structures enable new ideas and answers to repeatedly emerge bottom up
- Illustrate how Liberating Structures methods are modular and can be mashed up easily
- Demonstrate how easy it is to generate results with Liberating Structures
- Duplicate the speed of frontline working conditions

As a rough guideline, three-hour workshops can include four to five Liberating Structures and whole-day workshops twice that many. Inside an organization, experienced users can also arrange series of miniworkshops that cover only one Liberating Structure at a time and where participants can also share their experiences. Agendas, presentation materials, and notes on process and outcomes from some of our public workshops are available on our website http://www.liberatingstructures.com/news-and-events/.

Liberating Structures Coaching

The purpose of coaching sessions is to make it easy for participants to take their first steps toward having Liberating Structures be an everyday practice. Participants sign up for one-hour sessions to work on some challenging problem or goal alone or with colleagues. The objective is to design a sequence of Liberating Structures that will help them address their challenge. A typical session would begin with a series of questions to clarify the issue or bring to the surface the deeper problem. It would continue with more questions about who needs to be involved, what is the common purpose, what resources or restrictions exist, what end result is hoped for, and so on. Along the way, possible steps are identified as well as the Liberating Structures that could be used to support each of those steps. Participants are encouraged to come up with their own ideas and preferences about which Liberating Structures to use. The session ends with at least one concrete design that participants can start implementing immediately. The strings that are described in the next chapter are examples that illustrate the kind of designs that may emerge from a coaching session.

People walk out of a coaching session knowing what they can do, if they want to, to achieve the outcomes they want. They are quite clear on what to do and what to expect when they "bring it all back home." The next step is to fly solo or to work with some partners in order to apply the same process to another challenge, and another, and another.

Chapter 6
From First Steps To Strings

Learning to use Liberating Structures is like learning a new language. First you learn individual words. Then you put them together into a simple sentence and soon you are speaking series of sentences in the new language.

In the Liberating Structures Menu in Chapter 5, each structure is described by a single sentence, there to help you decide when to use it. When one Liberating Structure is sufficient for handling a small routine situation, that single sentence will capture and communicate the essence of what will happen. As you progress from simple applications to attacking more sizeable projects or more ambitious goals that require more steps, you will need to connect several sentences to describe and think through what will happen. In other words, you will need not one or two Liberating Structures but a sequence of them. We call these sequences **strings**. Constructing strings that are adapted to your challenges and have a powerful impact is your second step in mastering the language of Liberating Structures.Making strings is serious fun and invariably stimulates a group to discover innovative ways to solve problems or exploit opportunities. To facilitate this task, we have created a set of Liberating Structures Design Cards that make it easy to quickly come up with many combinations. Or you can simply use the Liberating Structures Menu for inspiration on which structures to include in your strings.

Composing strings is particularly useful when done with a partner or in a group/design team. This approach is always a rewarding investment since it automatically clarifies the true nature of your challenge and what steps are required to address it properly. With **1-2-4-All**, it is quite easy to engage a

"If you truly want to understand something, try to change it." Kurt Lewin

large group in generating many alternative strings simultaneously and then selecting the most attractive one. Including others in composing and selecting strings not only gets everybody on the same page, it dramatically improves the group's capacity to improvise and adapt quickly.

This chapter offers advice about composing strings and provides a number of examples. We like to call this activity *composing* because its purpose is to create an interdependent whole greater than the mere sum of a few Liberating Structures. The goal always is to create results that are much better than could be expected from conventional structures and to build capacity for rapid adaptations.

Matching A Challenge with Specific Liberating Structures

Composing always starts with a series of questions such as, "What are we trying to accomplish? Why is that important? Why? Why? Why? Is the true purpose and deepest need for our work clear? Who is going to be affected?

Identifying which Liberating Structures can be useful for addressing a challenge can't begin without a fair amount of clarity about the nature of the challenge and the deeper purpose of what needs to be accomplished. Therefore, composing always starts with a series of questions such as, "What are we trying to accomplish? Why is that important? Why? Why? Why? Is the true purpose and deepest need for our work clear? Who is going to be affected? Is the purpose unambiguous and common to all concerned?; if not, what are we going to do? For whom is it particularly important? Who else could contribute? Are some people ahead of the game? When this work is done, what will be different? What connections up, down, and out across what boundaries could make a difference? What are the main obstacles? How would such a challenge normally be handled? What conventional approaches would be used? What first step(s) make the most sense? Then what are logical second and third steps?"

With the answers to such questions clarified, it becomes pretty easy to compose one or more strings of microstructures that fit the challenge. If responses

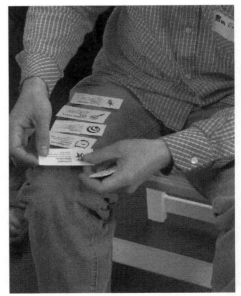

Composing a string with Liberating Structures Design Cards

are inadequate or lacking, it is a sign that one or more Liberating Structures are needed up front to generate more clarity. For instance, if your purpose is not sharp, consider including **Nine Whys** in the early portion of your string. Use the verbs and words in the Liberating Structures Menu and/or the Design Cards to spark your memory and intuitive thinking. Terms like "connect," "debrief," "make space," "uncover," "success," "generate ideas," "share experiences," "first steps," "help each other," "reflect," "crowd wisdom," "spark action," and "spread ideas" will trigger different reactions and ideas from situation to situation. Going through this experience will provide useful hints on structures that may need to be included in your design.

Additionally, each situation you face may evoke a *diagnostic trigger* in your mind, a key aspect or condition that will point toward using specific structures. Unproductive meetings, groups feeling stuck in a rut, underperforming products or services, and "analysis paralysis" are examples of *triggers* that indicate a particular Liberating Structure or some string of structures would be in order. Keep a sharp eye out for these useful hints.

Finally, for the first structure of your strings, choose one that you are comfortable with, that you like, and that you think will draw a positive response from participants.

Five Sets of Strings

From the thousands of combinations that thirty-three different structures make possible, we selected a few examples that will quickly give you a good idea of what you can construct yourself. We grouped them into five broad scenarios. The sample strings outlined below will get any number of participants started, whether a large group or one as small as two people. Don't hesitate to make up your own pattern of strings!

Goal 1: Finding Everyday Solutions

Look for triggers such as these: meetings are rote or uninspiring, people spend more time presenting than doing, rigid practices get in the way, top-down initiatives have no buy-in, imported best practices are not welcome. Any of them is a clear signal that there is a need for changes such as stopping unproductive activities, tapping tacit know-how to stimulate new ideas, discovering local solutions, building trust, and coordinating action.

Sample Strings

TRIZ + 1-2-4-All + 15% Solutions + Troika Consulting

Make space for new ideas with **TRIZ** by stopping unproductive activities or rigid behaviors. Invite everybody to generate new ideas with **1-2-4-All**. Ask all participants to identify what they can do immediately, what their **15% Solution** is, and then invite them to help their peers expand and enhance their own 15 percent in a **Troika Consulting** session.

Nine Whys + 1-2-4-All + 15% Solutions + 25/10 Crowd Sourcing (for groups larger than fifteen)

Clarify purpose with **Nine Whys**. With **1-2-4-All,** invite all participants to generate **15% Solutions** that they can act on without additional resources, detailed planning, or special approvals. Then invite all participants to propose bold solutions that require more resources. With groups of more than fifteen people, sift the solutions with **25/10 Crowd Sourcing**.

Drawing Together + 1-2-4-All + 15% Solutions + Troika Consulting

Invite everybody to access and reveal hidden insights and solutions to a shared challenge through nonverbal expression. Create shared images via **Drawing Together**. With **1-2-4-All,** interpret the drawings and sift and sort emerging solutions and first steps. Ask all participants to identify what they can do immediately, "What is your **15% Solution**?" Then invite them to help their peers expand and enhance their own 15 percent in a **Troika Consulting** session.

Users Experience Fishbowl + 1-2-4-All + Wicked Questions

To pave the way for others to learn and adapt, ask for a few volunteers to share in a **Users Experience Fishbowl** their experiences and behaviors while facing a complex challenge. With **1-2-4-All,** invite everybody to generate **Wicked Questions** that reveal the paradoxical goals that the group must absolutely address with its next steps.

Goal 2: Noticing Patterns Together

Look for triggers such as these: group members are cynical, people no longer see opportunities for positive change, the group feels stuck in a rut, a surprising or shocking event has thrown off expectations or disturbed the market. Any of them is a signal that there is a need for changes such as finding new ways of understanding a complex challenge; expanding the boundaries for solutions;

determining multiple actions by including many in finding and diagnosing patterns together; and clarifying requirements for system-wide coordination.

Sample Strings

What, So What, Now What? + Appreciative Interviews + Min Specs

With **What, So What, Now What?** clarify the current reality (where the group is starting, really), what it means, and what actions this suggests. Uncover with **Appreciative Interviews** the patterns and conditions that made past successes possible. Reduce the list through **Min Specs** down to the absolute must dos and must not dos for moving forward successfully. Revisit the Now What? opportunities for action and identify those that meet the Min Specs.

Shift & Share + Wicked Questions + 1-2-4-All

Draw a wide variety of innovative activities out into the open with **Shift & Share**. Illuminate the narrow path to more success and novel mash-ups with **Wicked Questions**. Sort the follow-up activities or widen the path with **1-2-4-All**.

Conversation Café + What, So What, Now What? + ... Next string

Following a surprising or shocking development, engage everybody with a **Conversation Café** to reflect on and make sense of the new situation. Share the facts and insights to decide on the next steps with **What, So What, Now What?** Compose a string for making progress on the next steps.

Impromptu Networking + Generative Relationships + 1-2-4-All

Stimulate sharing, reflection, and a few new connections with **Impromptu Networking**. With **Generative Relationships**, jointly diagnose the interaction patterns that are inhibiting the group's performance and identify what each person and formal leaders can do to remedy the situation. Use **1-2-4-All** to generate next steps.

WINFY + What, So What, Now What? Debrief + Wise Crowds in Fishbowl

Use **WINFY** to invite participants to clarify their group's strategic needs for working effectively with all other functions and to find out what support each group can or cannot expect to receive. Follow with each group doing a **What, So What, Now What?** Debrief to decide their Now What?

End with all the groups' spokespeople participating in a **Wise Crowds** consultation session to spark better relationships and coordination. Do the Wise Crowds in a **Fishbowl** to get everybody on the same page.

Goal 3: Drawing Out Prototypes

Look for triggers such as these: current activities, services, or products are not performing well; creative individuals are frustrated or isolated; there are no clear paths for new ideas to attract investment; important client needs are ignored; patches to current offerings are expensive. Any of them is a signal that there is a need for changes such as: revealing and making explicit what is already working while inviting something new to emerge; drawing out successful "chunks" of what's working and combining them in new ways; unleashing everyone in building prototypes; accelerating coordination, progress, and spread dramatically.

Sample Strings

Appreciative Interviews + TRIZ + Ecocycle
With **Appreciative Interviews**, uncover the patterns and conditions that made past successes possible. Destroy barriers to innovation with **TRIZ**. Clarify the status of all products/services in the portfolio with the **Ecocycle** and identify opportunities for immediate action.

Users Experience Fishbowl + Simple Ethnography + Improv
Illuminate the limits of what is known about handling a challenge by asking the most knowledgeable people to share their experiences in a **Fishbowl**. Use the information generated to guide the collection of observations through **Simple Ethnography**. Use this to create scenarios for **Improv Prototyping**.

Simple Ethnography + What, So What, Now What? Debrief + Design StoryBoard
Use observations gathered with **Simple Ethnography** to identify opportunities for prototyping. Review opportunities through the three steps of a **What, So What, Now What?** Debrief. Sketch out detailed plans for field testing and adaptations with **Design StoryBoard**.

DAD + 1-2-4-All + Design StoryBoard

Bring hidden solutions to chronic challenges into focus via a series of **DADs**. The dialogues will also invite peers to begin adapting successful behaviors in their own settings. Use **1-2-4-All** to review individual and group successes in order to reveal what higher-level solutions emerge. Sketch out the path for determining how to coordinate across groups or units via a **Design StoryBoard**.

Goal 4: Unleashing Local Action

Look for triggers such as these: people are not taking risks; people are waiting for permission to act; layers of red tape stifle creativity; more time is spent presenting than acting; "analysis paralysis" has taken over. Any of them is a signal that there is a need for changes such as: unleashing purposeful action in large groups without detailed plans or elaborate budgeting; boosting freedom and responsibility with a minimal set of enabling constraints; improving coordination of diverse activities.

Sample Strings

Open Space + Min Specs + 25/10 Crowd Sourcing

Unleash a wide array of local actions with **Open Space**. Then, within the well-defined boundaries of **Min Specs**, identify bolder initiatives with **25/10 Crowd Sourcing** and invite volunteers to move them forward.

Nine Whys + Improv Prototyping + Design StoryBoard

Clarify with participants the deepest purpose of their work together with **Nine Whys**. Use **Improv Prototyping** to reveal what challenges emerge when addressing this larger purpose and what solutions emerge out of diverse participation. Put the pieces together in a **Design StoryBoard** for moving forward.

Critical Uncertainties + Wise Crowds + 15% Solutions

Generate robust stress-tested strategies for an unpredictable future with **Critical Uncertainties.** Use **Wise Crowds** and **15% Solutions** to provide interdisciplinary advice to each individual about their implementation.

Goal 5: Spreading Innovation by Scaling Out and Up

Look for triggers such as these: innovations do not spread to other groups; specifications for adopting an innovation do not fit diverse operating realities; solutions at the local level do not scale up; formal efforts to standardize innovative practice are "gamed" or ignored by local units. Any of them is a signal that there is a need for changes such as: spreading ideas or innovations *out* across groups or units; scaling *up* from local application to regional, global, or policy levels; fueling movements and transformations across boundaries.

Examples of Powerful Strings

Nine Whys + Min Specs + Ecocycle + Panarchy
Clarify how your work is justified to the larger community (purpose) with **Nine Whys** and specify the must dos and must not dos with **Min Specs.** With the **Ecocycle**, clarify the status of your portfolio of activities and relationships at the level of your organization. Use **Panarchy** to clarify activities and relationships at all the other levels that affect your initiative and identify opportunities for actions.

Nine Whys + Social Network Webbing + 15% Solutions + Troika Consulting
Clarify purpose with **Nine Whys.** Then, with **Social Network Webbing**, identify all the individuals and groups that can be attracted to the work with formal or informal ties. With **15% Solutions**, everybody decides what he or she can do immediately to strengthen and develop the network. Continue with **Troika Consulting** for each person to receive further advice on what to do and how.

Celebrity Interview + Min Specs + Ecocycle
Build deeper understanding and trust with formal leaders via a **Celebrity Interview**. Use **Min Specs** to identify the must dos and must not dos for spreading change. Draw the status of activities and relationships on the **Ecocycle** and identify opportunities for changes.

DAD + 1-2-4-All + Panarchy + Design StoryBoard

Use series of **DADs** to discover *hidden* solutions to chronic challenges and then **1-2-4-All** for all participants to decide how to adapt successful behaviors to their local settings. Brainstorm how to insinuate the success at other levels with **Panarchy**. Sketch out pathways for coordinating up, down, and out via a **Design StoryBoard**.

Purpose-To-Practice+DrawingTogether+Integrated~Autonomy

Create an organizational design based on shared ownership with **Purpose-To-Practice**. With **Drawing Together**, spark imaginative solutions to the challenges of integrated yet autonomous operations. Spell out the specifics of working across widely distributed sites with **Integrated~Autonomy**.

These few string examples illustrate how much you can accomplish in a short time—often less than one hour or ninety minutes—and how easy it will be for you to compose many others based on the specifics of your own challenges. Be prepared to be pleasantly surprised! As a rule, we compose strings that include much more than we imagine can be accomplished in the time allotted. When we do not complete the entire string, there is a basis for planning next steps with the group. Be sure to keep records of your strings to share with others.

Chapter 7
From Strings To Storyboards

A project or a transformation initiative that is too big to be supported by a single string of Liberating Structures calls for a comprehensive design, which is simply a series of strings and structures linked together in a logical progression. This chapter describes three examples that are typical of our experiences in the field:

1. Launching a multi-stakeholder collaborative project via a meeting
2. Developing strategy and building a new leadership team via a retreat
3. Advancing a broad movement across many regions via a summit

"Any sufficiently advanced technology is indistinguishable from magic." Arthur C. Clarke

As you will see, the designs for some situations can be fairly simple while others require detailed storyboards.

At first glance, these designs may seem far too ambitious or idealized. We ask you to suspend your judgment: we have found that as the participants become more familiar with Liberating Structures, the speed and depth of their ideas and activity increase. Liberating Structures make much more possible. The experience can be breathtaking—almost too good to be true. With increasing inclusion comes more trust. With more trust, it is possible to *believe before you see*. With shared beliefs, it is possible to take bigger leaps and move boldly forward together. This is what we have seen happen time after time after time.

Launching a Multi-Stakeholder Collaborative Project

Twenty-five leaders from a variety of organizations—schools, small non-profits, and business—are starting to work together to attract funding from a large foundation for a community-wide initiative. Their goal is to build a healthier and more vibrant community, but they need a "big idea" to inspire collaboration and spark a community movement. A funder has expressed strong interest. The pressure is on.

The design for the meeting is intended to help the whole group arrive step by step at a well-thought-out big idea. It consists of a logical sequence of seven stages each with its own purpose and supported by a specific Liberating Structure. In the agenda below, the questions used to spark engagement and idea generation appear below each Liberating Structure in the design. *Notes regarding important transitions for the facilitator are italicized.*

All designs consist of a logical sequence of stages, each with its own purpose and supported by a specific Liberating Structure.

The logical sequence for the design is as follows:

- Connect participants with each other
- Discover what participants have in common and what's different
- Find the themes and patterns that cut across all of their interests
- Extract all the big ideas that these themes and patterns inspire
- Determine the most attractive ideas
- Dig deeper to find the one with the greatest benefit to the community and that will attract the most support
- Clarify what participants must absolutely not do as a group to make it possible for their big idea to become reality
- Identify who else must be included
- Decide on their next steps

Since the twenty-five leaders don't all know one another, the first step in the agenda is designed to help them build new connections that will serve them down the road. The second purpose is to reveal which challenges and expectations they share and which ones are different. **Impromptu Networking** is selected for this first step in the agenda as follows:

Step 1. Impromptu Networking (fifteen minutes)

- What is a challenge you would like our big idea to address? What can you give and get from a new community initiative?

In step 2, the participants use **1-2-4-All** to identify the themes and patterns that cut across their wishes as follows:

Step 2. 1-2-4-All (one or two rounds) (ten to twenty minutes)

- What will be different as a result of our work together? Be as concrete as you can about behaviors and tangible health or economic outcomes.

  *Look for two or three themes to emerge out of the individual contributions. One round of **1-2-4-All** may be enough if responses are tangible and compelling through the eyes of participants.*

In step 3, the best ten bold ideas are sifted with **25/10 Crowd Sourcing** as follows:

Step 3. 25/10 Crowd Sourcing of Bold Ideas (fifteen minutes)

- If you were ten times bolder, what would you do? What first step will get the ball rolling?

  Call out the top ideas and post on a large wall chart.

In step 4, the participants identify the most promising idea with **1-2-4-All** as follows:

Step 4. 1-2-4-All (ten minutes)

- Which ideas do you think will make a big difference in the community? Is there one that stands out? Can you and your organization support and move forward with this idea?

  Look for one idea to emerge above all others.

In step 5, participants then clarify what they must absolutely not do.

Step 5. TRIZ to Make Space for Innovation (fifteen minutes)

- How can we make sure that we act as a collaborative community group in name only... without having the back of anyone but ourselves?

Looking forward to a successful proposal, start to establish a productive pattern of behavior among participants.

In step 6, they identify who else must be included as follows:

Step 6. Social Network Webbing (twenty minutes)

- Who are the people we need to attract to this initiative? Who are the people we need to start the work? Who can block and who can enable fast progress? Who are experts on the periphery of this social network we need to tap?

Make it real by naming names.

In the final step, the participants agree on their next steps by clarifying the five components of their next task (Purpose, Principles, Participants, Structure, and Practices) as follows:

Step 7. Next Steps
- Writing up the proposal.

- **Purpose-To-Practice** to clarify how the proposal will be readied.

Purpose-To-Practice will deepen the group's readiness to hit the ground running when the work to write the proposal starts.

At the end of an intense but short three-hour session, the twenty-five leaders were surprised by their experience using Liberating Structures and delighted with the outcome. They had their big idea, which was the fruit of their common labor, and they felt clear and prepared for what to do next.

Developing Strategy and Building a New Leadership Team

A newly appointed system CEO is convening a handpicked executive "dream team." The execs and their direct reports (thirty people) are invited to a one-and-a-half-day strategy retreat. Goals for the retreat include coming together as a team, developing a more innovative way of working together, and reviewing and generating market strategies. The organization is well positioned to make fast progress in its market.

Here is a storyboard agenda in four parts, each supported by its own tailored string of Liberating Structures.

Time & Topic	Goal	LS	Why this method?	Steps / Timing
7:30am Continental Breakfast 8:00 am **Welcome**	Get acquainted; hear multiple views of participants; start to co-create the boundaries; form loose connections across functions.	**Impromptu Networking**	Signals that everyone is invited & unleashed to join in the transformation work; the solutions are widely distributed (we don't know the local solutions in advance).	3 rounds in pairs, (5 minutes for each exchange); 5 minute debrief. *What big challenge do you have? What do you hope to give to and get from this team?*
8:20am Sponsor **Welcome + Stage Setting**	State of the union & get the hard questions out on the table immediately.	**Celebrity Interview (CEO)**	Creates a nuanced & personal view of challenges & strategy in an entertaining format.	*Formulate tough questions in advance to prepare the CEO* 25 minutes for the interview
8:50am **Clarity of purpose**	Sharpen individual and team purpose	**Nine Whys**	Invite every individual and the group as a whole to own their work & set boundaries together. A powerful purpose generates self-organization & attracts people to the work.	*Why is your work on this team important?* In 5 minute paired interviews. *Is a justification for the work coming into sharper focus?* In fours

Figure 7.1

Leadership Team Retreat StoryBoard: Part 1

The purpose of Part 1 (Figure 7.1) is to signal that each person is invited to shape the next steps for coming together as a team and to set the stage for developing bold strategies. Starting with **Impromptu Networking**, this series of Liberating Structures is a dramatic shift from the more controlling practice of starting with a series of presentations. Immediately, individuals feel more connected and able to make contributions. The CEO **Celebrity Interview** opens the door further by laying out the big challenges that must be addressed by everyone together. The clear message here is that the boss does not know the answers in advance of the work being done. Clarifying purpose with **Nine Whys** underlines the importance of the group to the larger company and community. With relationships affirmed and the group's purpose in sharper focus, the stage is set for bold action ... *before the first coffee break!*

Time & Topic	Goal	LS	Why this method?	Steps / Timing
9:25am **Spark more innovation**	Create an environment where innovation thrives	 **TRIZ + 1-2-4-All**	TRIZ is a seriously fun way to engage in the very hard work of *creative destruction.* Innovation needs open space to take root!	3 10-minute segments *How can we reliably create a team in which leaders take very few risks to move away from current reality toward the future... and we don't have each other's back?*
10:20am **Develop strategy**	Include everyone in clarifying strategy and next steps. Together, start work toward similar answers among all members (new and ongoing).	 **Mad Tea + Strategy Safari**	Focusing attention (and avoiding paralyzing over-analysis) on the *big five* questions that can quickly generate shared understanding of strategy and next steps.	In pairs, finish 14 open sentences via Mad Tea... with these themes: •• What is happening around us that demands adaptation? •• Where are we starting, honestly? •• Given our purpose, what seems possible now? •• What is at stake if we do not change? •• How are we moving away from the current state toward the future?
11:30am **Debrief** 12:00 Noon Lunch	Gather insights and actions for each person and the team as a whole.	 **What³ debrief**	Enables every voice to be heard, eliminates unproductive arguments, continues to build action.	*10 minutes each in this order:* *What?* *So What?* *Now What?*

Figure 7.2
Leadership Team Retreat StoryBoard: Part 2

The purpose of Part 2 (Figure 7.2) is to engage each person in starting to articulate actions and strategies. Again, this is a dramatic shift since participants have not been fully included in the past. **TRIZ** makes space for new ideas to take hold by identifying actions or behaviors to be stopped or creatively destroyed. Deciding that big obstacles will be removed often results in a giddy enthusiasm for launching innovations.

To temper jumping in too quickly, the **Mad Tea + Strategy Safari** activities help to quickly create a bigger context in which new strategies will need to operate.

In the Mad Tea activity, participants form two circles, one inside the other. Each person faces one other person and completes an open-ended sentence in less than thirty seconds (see box). When time is up, participants are invited to move to their right so that they are in front of someone else to complete the next sentence, and so on. The unfinished sentences focus attention on every individual and the group answering the Safari questions together (e.g., If we do nothing, the worst thing that can happen for us is...). In a seriously fun way, Mad Tea quickly provokes a deeper set of reflections and strategic insights. Then the big five Strategy Safari questions focus attention and produce shared understanding of strategy and next steps.

Mad Tea Open Sentences

1. What first inspired me in this work is...
2. Something we must learn to live with is...
3. An uncertainty we must creatively adapt to is...
4. What I find challenging in our current situation is...
5. Before we make our next move, we cannot neglect to...
6. Something we should stop doing (or divest) is...
7. What I hope can happen for us in this work is...
8. A big opportunity I see for us is...
9. If we do nothing, the worst thing that can happen for us is...
10. A courageous conversation we are not having is...
11. An action or practice helping us move forward is...
12. A project that gives me confidence we are transforming is...
13. A bold idea I recommend is...
14. A question that is emerging for me is...

The Big Five Strategy Safari Questions

1. What is happening around us that demands adaptation?
2. Where are we starting, honestly?
3. Given our purpose, what seems possible now?
4. What is at stake if we do not change?
5. How are we moving away from the current state toward the future?

Table 7.1
Mad Tea + Strategy Safari Activities

With action ideas in mind and a strategic context outlined, **What, So What, Now What?** is used for the participants to start harvesting the best ideas for moving forward well before the end of the retreat. This gives more time for everyone to contemplate the mix of actions and ideas being unleashed. Again, every voice is included in making sense of all the possibilities, and surprising insights will emerge from many participants.

Time & Topic	Goal	LS	Why this method?	Steps / Timing
1:00pm	Together, deepen action strategies	**Wise Crowds**	Boosts individual action & helping skills	Groups of 4 to 7: each person asks for and receives a consultation
Advance strategic thinking and action	Build confidence tapping & sifting group wisdom	**25/10** **25/10 Crowd Sourcing**	Generates and sorts inspiring strategies	Bold action ideas are proposed & sorted by everyone in the crowd in 20 minutes
	Together, see the forest **and** the trees	**Ecocycle Planning**	Advances the portfolio of strategic relationships & product-service offerings	Strategic relationships & offerings are sorted into stages: birth, maturity (rigidity trap), creative destruction, renewal (poverty trap)
	Together, enhance coordination across boundaries	**WINFY fishbowl**	Helps to *work out the knots* across functional boundaries	**WINFY functional leaders:** •• Strategy •• Operations •• Subsidiary Exec •• Philanthropy •• System Exec •• Finance
5:00 pm **Day 1 Debrief** **5:30pm**	Gather insights and actions as they unfold	**What³ debrief**	Enables every voice to be heard, eliminates unproductive arguments, continues to build action	*10 minutes each in this order:* *What?* *So What?* *Now What?*

Figure 7.3

Leadership Team Retreat StoryBoard: Part 3

The purpose of Part 3 (Figure 7.3) is to build on the foundation of the first two parts and move deeper into solutions for individual and group challenges. **Wise Crowds** and **15% Solutions** start the work by focusing on individual concerns first. Peer-to-peer consults build internal confidence and spark practical action. With more individual confidence in hand, **25/10 Crowd Sourcing** generates bold strategies for the group as a whole. Stepping back to see the forest and the trees, all the new and existing strategies are put into context with the **Ecocycle**.

The whole portfolio of strategies comes into view, and each item on the **Ecocycle** suggests a type of action to move the work forward. To build immediately toward practical results, **What I Need From You (WINFY)** is used to focus attention on one big challenge that requires a high level of cross-functional cooperation. Working out the knots across boundaries for a single strategy will help with many others. Creative tension builds as group members see and feel opportunities for advancing their work.

With **What, So What, Now What?** to end the day, everyone (especially the more deliberate thinkers) has time to contemplate the day's action, moving closer to shared ownership of strategy making and implementation. The group will be exhausted *and* exhilarated after a day like this. An evening full of fun is needed to decompress.

Time & Topic	Goal	LS	Why this method?	Steps / Timing
8:00 am **Opening Reflection**	Refine the agenda for the day	**1-2-4-All**	Includes everyone in shaping the agenda for the day	Ask, "What can we do today to move the team & our strategy forward?
8:20 am **Move to action**	Spark action on strategies that matters most to participants	**Open Space Technology**	OST boosts freedom and accountability. Because participants create their own agenda, follow-through is enhanced.	Theme: What do we need to do or stop doing to move forward with our purpose? Two 60- minute parallel time blocks.
10:30 am Prepare for surprise	Creatively adapt with agility and speed as surprises unfold	**Critical Uncertaintie**	Imagines plausible market scenarios to test current strategy & quickly adapt to shifts in the market.	Four plausible scenarios are created. Then, *robust and hedging* strategies are shaped to operate successfully in each future scenario.
11:30 pm **Debrief** 12:00pm Adjourn	Gather insights and actions as they unfold	**What³ debrief**	Enables every voice to be heard, eliminates unproductive arguments, continues to build action	*10 minutes each in this order: What? So What? Now What?*

Figure 7.4
Leadership Team Retreat StoryBoard: Part 4

The purpose of Part 4 (Figure 7.4), the next morning, is to plunge the group into action and set the stage for future work. The group focuses on action and tactics via **Open Space**. Building on the ideas from the previous day's **Ecocycle, 25/10 Crowd Sourcing,** and **WINFY, Open Space** now concentrates attention on how to advance single strategies. Session conveners facilitate the group's work to generate action plans.

Using **Critical Uncertainties**, the group evaluates how useful each strategy would be in four future operating environments. The gaps and innovation opportunities revealed in this activity will be addressed in the next retreat. This provides creative tension for the group's ongoing work.

A final round of **What, So What, Now What?** to end the retreat is used to draw out all the feelings of camaraderie, accomplishment, and momentum that have emerged. Detailed action plans and next steps will be compiled in a proceedings document with a small amount of additional effort. Output from the **Ecocycle, WINFY, Open Space,** and **Critical Uncertainties** will be particularly helpful for immediate follow-up and for preparing for the next retreat.

Advancing a Broad Movement across Many Regions

Two years after launch, sponsors of a national movement invite four hundred leaders from all fifty states to a summit in the nation's capital. Some states are functioning at a high level while others are just getting off the ground. The goals are to galvanize more diverse participation in each state, restore hope for transformative change, and ignite bold action while deepening strategic thinking. Teams from each state will learn and share over two days.

The storyboard for the summit is in three parts.

Time & Topic	LS	Why this method?	Steps / Timing	Notes * Part of Proceedings doc
8:00 am **Community Welcome**	**Impromptu Networking**	Signals that everyone is invited & unleashed to join in the transformation; the solutions are widely distributed (we don't know the local solutions in advance)	3 rounds in pairs, (5 minutes for each exchange); 5 minute debrief. What big challenge do you have? What do you hope to give to and get from this community of leaders?	Facilitator All participants Mixed participation
8:15am **Sponsor Welcome + Stage Setting**	**Celebrity Interview**	Creates a nuanced & personal view of challenges and strategy in an entertaining format.	*Brief intro and welcome.* *Interview of transformational leader.* *Formulate questions in advance.*	Sponsors Celebrity & Host Synthesizers In regional teams * Leadership Insights
9:00am **Clarity of purpose**	**Nine Whys**	Invite every individual and the group as a whole to own the transformation & set boundaries together. A powerful purpose generates self-organization	*Why is your transformation work is important?* In 5 minute paired interviews *Is a justification for the work coming into sharper focus?* In fours See detailed description	Facilitator Synthesizers & Harvesters Graphic Recorders *In regional teams* * Purpose Statements
9:25 am Spark more innovation Break	**TRIZ**	TRIZ is a seriously fun way to engage in the very hard work of creative destruction. Innovation needs open space to take root!	*3 10-minute segments* *How can we keep doing the same things and expect different results?*	Facilitator Harvesters Synthesizers Graphic Recorders *Mixed participation* * Stop Doing Actions

Figure 7.5
National Summit Storyboard: Part 1

The purpose of Part 1 (Figure 7.5) is to signal that each person is invited to shape next steps for promoting more diverse participation and stimulating bold action and deeper strategic thinking. Beginning with **Impromptu Networking**, this series of Liberating Structures is a clear shift from starting with a presentation or some other more controlling or unintentionally exclusive conventional practice. Individuals immediately feel more connected. The **Celebrity Interview** of one of the sponsors' leaders opens the door further by laying out the big challenges that must be creatively addressed by everyone together, particularly those closest to the challenge; the clear message here is that even an expert national leader does not know the answers in advance of the work being done.

Including everyone in clarifying purpose with **Nine Whys** underscores the importance of having diverse individuals and all regions contribute to the larger national movement. More importantly, the purpose must be powerful to attract broad participation—the lifeblood of a successful movement. With relationships affirmed and a more focused purpose established at each level, the stage is set for bold action. **TRIZ** unleashes "stop-doing" actions. Seeing that big obstacles will be removed inspires ideas for transforming the future.

Throughout the summit, as shown in the Notes column in the storyboards, facilitators, sponsors, graphic recorders, and participants themselves work on harvesting, synthesizing, and publishing all the wisdom unleashed from this large group of four hundred. As the summit progresses, insights and action ideas are collected for a proceedings document to be published by the end of the meeting.

The purpose must be powerful to attract broad participation—the lifeblood of a successful movement.

Time & Topic	LS	Why this method?	Steps / Timing	Notes * Part of Proceedings doc
10:30 pm Success stories	Appreciative Interviews	Positive stories attract more success & help identify effective investments.	In pairs, groups of four, and then the whole room. Conditions and Assets collected across different states.	Facilitator *Mixed participation* * *Root causes of success*
11:30am Action planning Lunch	Graphic Gameplan	GGs make the strategic context and action visible to everyone involved in the movement. Updating with GG can help coordinate the work as it unfolds	Provide Graphic Gameplans in participant packets + oversized team "placemats." Mix in national gurus to provide light coaching or simply participate in regional team planning.	Facilitator, Coaches *In regional teams* * Highlight 2 Gamplans on big screen
1:00 pm Open Space unconference	Open Space Technology	OST boosts freedom and accountability. Because participants create their own agenda, follow-through is enhanced.	*Theme: What do we need to do or stop doing to advance the transformation?* Participants generate & convene sessions. Two 60- minute parallel time blocks starting at approximately 1:30pm, ending at 3:30pm	Sponsor shares Min Specs Facilitator Opens Space *Mixed participation* * OST Topics Schedule
3:45 pm Develop shared understanding of next steps	Mad Tea + Strategy Safari	Focusing attention (and avoiding paralyzing over-analysis) on the *big five* questions can quickly generate shared understanding of strategy and next steps.	In pairs, finish 15 open sentences via Mad Tea format. Sort and sift in mixed groups, then in teams. Project a handful of the top scoring answers one the big screen. Harvesters collect and confer with Synthesizers.	Facilitator, Synthesizers *Mixed, then in regional teams with coaches*
4:30pm Day 1 Closing	What³ debrief	Enables every voice to be heard, eliminates unproductive arguments, continues to build on Gameplans.	*10 minutes each in this order:* *What?* *So What?* *Now What?*	Facilitator *In regional teams* * Top 5 Answers to Strategy Questions

Figure 7.6
National Summit StoryBoard: Part 2

The purpose of Part 2 (Figure 7.6) is to engage each person in generating action as well as regional strategies. Again, this series of structures is a shift since participants have not been fully included in the past and have waited for direction from the center or top. In order to move deeper into solutions for individual and regional group challenges, **Appreciative Interviews** start the work by focusing on the root causes of success, shared through storytelling. Every person is invited to share a success story with a person from another state. Paired interviews will build internal confidence and spark practical action within and across coalitions.

With peer learning unleashed and action ideas in mind, Graphic Gameplans are used to begin harvesting the top ideas for moving forward in each regional team. Visual tools like the Graphic Gameplan (Figure 7.7) make the work on strategy through the rest of the day explicit, inviting, and transparent to all. Individually and together, participants are able to make sense of the mix of actions and ideas unleashed throughout the morning. Again, every voice is included in figuring out all the possibilities for advancing his or her region and the national transformation strategy.

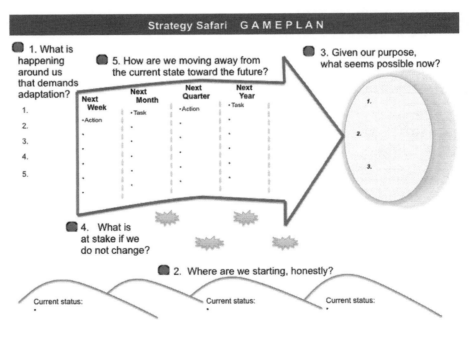

Figure 7.7

The Strategy Graphic Gameplan

After lunch, the group moves more deeply into action and tactics via **Open Space**. With insights from the **Celebrity Interview**, **Nine Whys**, **TRIZ**, and **Appreciative Interviews** in the morning, **Open Space** focuses attention on what each region can stop or start to advance the transformation. Conveners facilitate the group during the session, take notes about follow-up, and possibly lead the group after the summit if needed. Concrete action plans are generated.

Mad Tea + Strategy Safari are then used to add serious fun and strategic context to the tactics emerging. The Mad Tea open sentences provoke a lively, wide-ranging, and cathartic conversation, with novel ideas and deeper insight popping out as the Mad Tea unfolds. The big five Strategy Safari questions focus attention and produce shared understanding of strategy and next steps. (The Mad Tea + Strategy Safari trigger items are listed in Table 7.1.)

To bring the day to a close, **What, So What, Now What?** continues the harvest of best ideas for moving forward. This debrief happens well before the end of the summit. More deliberate thinkers in each regional group have time to contemplate the mix of actions and strategies unleashed throughout the day. Again, every voice is included in making sense of all the possibilities for advancing his or her region and the national transformation strategy.

Throughout the summit, visual methods like the Strategy Gameplan (Figure 7.7) make it possible to quickly synthesize, harvest, and publish wisdom from this large group of four hundred. As the summit progresses, insights and action ideas are gathered by staff for a proceedings document to be published by the end of the meeting. Large wall charts record the work in progress. Everyone can see how his or her contributions are informing the others and the national transformation. This is hard work and a little weariness is to be expected. An evening full of fun is needed to relax and unwind.

Everyone can see how his or her contributions are informing the others and the national transformation.

Open Space continues through the morning of the second day of the summit (Figure 7.8). With even more action and momentum unleashed, **25/10 Crowd Sourcing** generates and ranks bold strategies in each region and the nation as a whole. Participants sense that much more is possible—and that it is within their grasp—locally and nationally. To help participants from each region hit the ground running on their return home, Graphic Gameplans again capture the top strategies and the actions that will attract diverse participation in their state.

Time & Topic	LS	Why this method?	Steps / Timing	Notes * Part of Proceedings doc
8:30am **Open Space** **Unconference**	**Open Space Technology**	OST boosts freedom and accountability. Because participants create their own agenda, follow-through is enhanced.	*Theme: What do we need to do or stop doing to advance the transformation?* Participants generate & convene sessions.	Graphic Recorders Harvesters Editors, Synthesizers *Mixed Participation*
11:15am **Generating & prioritizing** **BIG IDEAS**	**25/10** **25/10 Crowd Sourcing**	Quickly engages the whole group in owning and prioritizing strategy	Two 60-minute time blocks Bold ideas + first steps circulated & scored on index cards	* News Wall of 60-80 Convener Reports * Top 10 Bold Ideas
12:00 Lunch			Breakdown OST room	
1:00pm **Action planning**	**Graphic Gameplan**	Gather the energy and momentum unleashed by OST. GGs make the strategic context and action visible to everyone involved.	Continue with Graphic Gameplans on oversized team "placemats." Mix in national gurus to provide light coaching or simply participate in regional team planning	Coaches Harvesters & Synthesizers *In regional teams* * Project 2 Gameplan examples on screen
1:45pm **Strategic action**	**Ecocycle** **Portfolio review**	Everyone can sift, prioritize and advance relationships with diverse coalition members	Strategic relationships are sorted into stages: birth, maturity (rigidity trap), creative destruction, renewal (poverty trap)	Facilitators Synthesizers & Harvesters *In teams, then Mixed* * Ecocycle Portfolio Map
3:00-3:30pm Debrief and Closing	**What³ debrief**	Final build on Gameplans & summing up take-home insights & actions	*10 minutes each in this order:* *What? So What? Now What?*	Facilitator * Publish Summit Proceedings

Figure 7.8

National Summit StoryBoard: Part 3

Stepping back to see the forest and the trees, all the new and existing strategies are put into context with the **Ecocycle**. Each regional group completes its local portfolio map and contributes to a national map of key strategic relationships. Synergies and gaps between regional and national activities come into view. Forging new relationships and attracting diverse participation are some clear challenges that emerge. National and state leaders gain fresh perspectives on their accomplishments and the path ahead.

In closing this summit of the people, by the people, for the people, **What, So What, Now What?** brought out feelings of new camaraderie, confidence, accomplishment, and momentum. There was a standing ovation and copies of the proceedings were distributed for everyone to take home.

Composing for Large-Scale Projects

However powerful the sample strings and detailed storyboards described above may be, we do not want you to copy them. They are not recipes or best practices. Each of these compositions was matched to a local context and unique user needs. Composing with Liberating Structures begins and ends with understanding the needs of users.

Composing for ambitious goals and large-scale events—similar to the example above about advancing a movement—may look complicated, but it's not. The process is actually a simple one: you draw out the deepest needs of users via a clear purpose and match it with congruent microstructures. A simple agenda, as in the community-wide meeting example above, might specify only the structures to be used, the questions designed to spark idea generation, and the time allotted to each plus notes on key issues to pay attention to in the transition from one structure to the next.

The more detailed storyboard approach has you carefully define all the micro-organizing elements needed to achieve your purpose: a structuring invitation, space, materials, participation, configurations, facilitation, and time allocations.

Composing Overview

In brief, composing an agenda or a design storyboard for an activity, meeting, or initiative involves a preparation phase and then a four-step composition process.

Preparation

Clarify purpose by asking why, why, why: why is this meeting or project or initiative important? Ask, "What will be different after this experience? What should we start doing and what should we stop doing?" Keep going until you can go no deeper.

Composition

Choose appropriate Liberating Structures that will help you achieve your purpose or goals step by step, preferably working with a partner or a diverse design group (see Chapter 5). For bigger projects that unfold over long periods of time, working with design groups is highly recommended. For each goal or challenge standing between where you are now and the desired end result, you puzzle out answers to the following questions:

1. What Liberating Structure fits this challenge?

Sift and sort through options. Use the Liberating Structures Menu in Chapter 5 and the *What Is Made Possible* descriptions in the Field Guide. Many Liberating Structures are suited perfectly to mash-ups. Post-it notes can help you arrange and rearrange with creative abandon.

2. What insights or outcomes may emerge from this activity?

If needed, reread the Liberating Structures Menu and the *What Is Made Possible* descriptions, anticipating positive and rapid movement among group members. What has slowed progress in the past may evaporate very quickly. Break up your outline into steps or chunks that can be designed and can function independently (don't try to put together a comprehensive design from the start).

3. What is made possible now?

Try to anticipate leaps in understanding and readiness to take action. Believe before you see. Liberating Structures will build "group genius" and velocity. If possible, pretest elements of your design. Try out your questions or invitations with a design partner or a sample of people who will be in the group meeting or event. Consider testing and vetting in waves and in different configurations. Tap your design team members to do the work.

Bring your experience into your next steps.

4. What next step or activity can follow to build momentum, breadth, and depth among group members?

Repeat the steps above.

You will make discoveries and create adaptations as you go. Puzzling out the order and timing may flow quickly or it may require multiple sessions. Composing is not an exact science; the abbreviated descriptions here simply show the kind of things to consider for producing a workable design.

It will not matter if one of the activities in your design ends up looking like it was not the right choice. A Liberating Structures composition is intentionally modular: when an activity doesn't work, doesn't produce the intended results, improvise; pick another structure and move on. Repeating the design cycle, whether in advance or in the moment, starting with preparation and moving through follow-up, will improve your skills very quickly.

PART THREE
Stories From the Field

We have found people all over the world using Liberating Structures for anything and everything. There are seemingly no limits to the ways Liberating Structures can be put to work to achieve dramatic results—from outcomes as simple as transforming the way a task force conducts its meetings to turning an entire enterprise around. In our experience, there is no place or situation where Liberating Structures cannot be useful. The only limits are your imagination and your willingness to experiment with new and different structures for your interactions with others.

In the case examples here, you will meet a lawyer, a business executive, a professor, a legislator, a nurse, a doctor, a student, and others who discovered how to put Liberating Structures into practice and accomplish extraordinary results. Their stories were chosen to show how simple it might be in your situation to choose one or more Liberating Structures to introduce into your daily work and reap the benefits of broader inclusion and greater collaboration with people at all levels of your organization.[1]

As you will see, these stories unfold in all types of organizations, ranging from health-care, academic, and military organizations to global business enterprises, local judicial and legislative systems, and national and international R&D efforts. They illustrate the depth and breadth of what Liberating Structures can make possible in a broad variety of situations.

Each story shows how a leader applied Liberating Structures to help achieve an ambitious goal—from passing legislation to preventing deadly infections to turning around a business. Despite hosts of obstacles and

"It is not because things are difficult that we do not dare; it is because we do not dare that they are difficult." Seneca

naysayers, these leaders summoned the energy and courage needed to beat a path forward where there was none. Experimenting with Liberating Structures, they successfully included many others in shaping next steps. Along the way, they discovered a better way to organize.

We chose these twelve stories not only to show the range of what is possible with Liberating Structures but also to illustrate how Liberating Leadership emerges in the process. All the protagonists invited everyone to take action or make a contribution. Few decisions were predetermined and formal authority was used sparingly. Rigid old ways were creatively destroyed to make space for innovation. With surprising twists and turns, better-than-expected results materialized.

Here is a summary of the stories and the challenges taken on with Liberating Structures:

Fixing a Broken Child Welfare System—Tim Jaasko-Fisher
How diverse stakeholders, accustomed to adversarial interactions and cynicism about system change, work across functional boundaries to solve chronic problems.

Inclusive High-Stakes Decision Making Made Easy—Craig Yeatman
How inclusive leadership can also be bold and decisive.

Turning a Business Around—Alison Joslyn
How a leader successfully invites everyone in an organization to take more responsibility for turning around a business.

Transforming After-Action Reviews in the Army—Lisa Kimball
How standardized training by experts is used in concert with what can be learned directly from people with field experience.

Inventing Future Health-Care Practice—Chris McCarthy
How hard work, technology, imagination, and a novel form of collaborating bring something really new into being.

Creating More Substance, Connections, and Ideas in the Classroom—Arvind Singhal
How a professor succeeds by transcending "the sage on the stage" pedagogy.

Getting Commitment, Ownership, and Follow-Through—Neil McCarthy

> How to pick up the pace of shared decision making and follow-through among diverse leaders in a multinational business.

Inspiring Enduring Culture Change While Preventing Hospital Infections—Dr. Michael Gardam

> How it is possible to solve a big entangled problem and make enduring cultural changes simultaneously.

Dramatizing Behavior Change to Stop Infections—Sherry Belanger

> How serious and chronic challenges can be successfully addressed with playfulness.

Developing Competencies for Physician Education—Dr. Diane Magrane

> How doctors and researchers can follow and lead simultaneously when success requires everyone to discover together what is working and also make changes together.

Passing Montana Senate Bill 29—Senator Lynda Bourque Moss

> In the unforgiving world of legislating, how it is possible to succeed by building on what is currently working and the aspirations of constituents.

Transcending a Top-Down Command-and-Control Culture—Dr. Jon Velez

> How it is possible for a leader to responsibly let go of control in a way that shifts the culture of an IT organization.

Fixing a Broken Child Welfare System:
Tim Jaasko-Fisher

"Child welfare law is a high-stakes field that can literally mean life or death for a young child," says Tim Jaasko-Fisher, a young lawyer using Liberating Structures to change a broken child welfare system.

 *Tim Jaasko-Fisher is a young lawyer passionate about transforming child welfare law. His dedication to the work comes in part from the empathy he feels for the people trapped in a system that is not working well, either for those administering the system or for its intended beneficiaries.*

The child welfare system is intended to help families and children in abuse and neglect situations. But, Tim says, "resources are often divided into silos despite the fact that virtually everyone working in the field acknowledges that solving the problem requires cross-discipline collaboration." He believes that local solutions are the best bet for fixing the system, and that they will come from the people doing the work. Working out of the University of Washington Law School, Tim relies on Liberating Structures in enabling court systems to unleash cross-functional and interprofessional innovations in serving children and families. One example is a conference session he designed for a group of participants representing all the silos in the system.

Composing a Workshop for Leaders

The people in Tim's workshop embodied all the functions involved in children's welfare work: judges, lawyers, court clerks, social workers. And there were seventy of them. Getting such a large, diverse group together to talk with one another was a rare opportunity, and Tim wanted to make the most of it. His goal for the session was for that roomful of participants to think about their work in a disciplined way. It was an ambitious idea.

Tim recalls, "I had two types of participants: the-everything-is-being-done-TO-me participants and the engaged leaders who were looking for useful methods." One participant summed up the everything-is-being-done-TO-me stance succinctly: "What can you tell me: my court system is a boat that is on fire, under fire, and taking on water? What can you tell me to do?!"

It was clear to Tim that a rational intellectual framework would not be the most effective approach for this group of people. The second group, the engaged leaders, was interested in new approaches and understood that letting go of overcontrol might unleash more positive change. The Liberating Structures Tim chose for the session were intended to engage both groups and spark the system transformation that Tim and others believe is possible.

Tim used **Design StoryBoard** to draw out the overall intention of the session as well as the fine details of each segment. The storyboard included, for example, the method of interaction, a time allocation, a success metric, and illustrations. The design for the one-hour session included **Impromptu Networking**, a form of **Social Network Webbing**, **Agreement-Certainty Matrix**, and **1-2-4-All.**

Notice				
Intention both individual and group is critical — Why are you here?	We can use various mapping tools to "see" our systems.	We must adapt our leadership approach to the type of challenge we face.	Complex problems are social problems and require social technologies	What a couple of phrases of quotes like: How disciplined are you? How pressed?
10 min.	15 min	5 min	10 min	2 min
To meet people where they are at - give them a chance to articulate it themselves	To give people the experience of seeing their social system	To allow people to feel disturbance of leadership challenges	To allow people to feel what it is like to rely on group wisdom to address complex issues.	To give people an opportunity to reflect on how this work impacts their leadership challenge
Speed Networking	Eco Mapping	Complexity line	1-2-4-All	Self reflection

*Tim's **Design StoryBoard** for leaders in the child welfare system. Tim wanted participants to think in a disciplined way, just as he has done with this storyboard. Top-to-bottom headings are Notice (key insight), Time, Intention, Method, and Activity.*

Tim began the session with **Impromptu Networking**, not the expected lecture. He recalls, "This was not a level of interaction participants were used to in our field, particularly to start a conference. It set the tone that participants would do the work in this workshop and visibly raised the energy level in the room." Participants had the opportunity to briefly share with three others what leadership challenge they wished to make progress on that day, what they hoped to get from the workshop, and what insight they brought to the conversation.

Later, Tim walked participants through a **Social Network Webbing**. He believes this method is especially effective in helping isolated and disempowered people to experience the interconnectedness among the various levels and functions in the court system. "Oftentimes, there is not a high level of agreement as to what should be done in a case," he told us, "and the legal portion of the case is seated in a process that is designed to be adversarial by its nature, making collaboration difficult at times."

The mapping process helped the participants visualize a pathway that would lead from their isolated position to a collaborative network of people committed to the same issue. It also helped people see how they could be successful without authority over the entire process.

"A legal process designed to be adversarial makes collaboration difficult."

Later in the session, Tim asked participants to indicate how engaged they had been in the workshop by raising or lowering their hands: a hand down to the knees meant not at all engaged and above the head meant very engaged. Out of seventy participants, not one hand was below shoulder level, and one judicial officer actually stood on his chair to get his hand higher.

In a final segment, Tim asked people to decide if the leadership challenge they identified earlier was simple, complicated, complex, or chaotic. He invited participants to distribute themselves across the room to illustrate the range of challenges. People standing in the front of the room indicated a simple problem; at the back of the room were the people representing chaotic challenges; and the complicated- and complex-problem people arranged themselves in between. This gave everyone a graphic and memorable representation of the distribution of the types of problems the group faced.

Most of the problems were situated in the realm of complicated and complex, and a **1-2-4-All** exercise ignited a conversation about the leadership skills needed for each type of challenge. The group noted that as you moved toward the back of the room—from simple to chaos—the degree of social interaction necessary to address the issue increased. Simple problems could largely be solved with authority and expertise, but complex problems required social interventions, consensus, and dialogue skills. Tim's intention and design for the workshop made it possible for the group to discover this insight for themselves.

Reflections on Design StoryBoard

"Talking about collaboration while listlessly watching PowerPoint presentations will not do!"

Clearly, the constraints of a **Design StoryBoard** drive Tim's creativity. "A storyboard helps me and others see patterns in meeting segments," he says. "Redundancy and boring patterns are revealed. Talking about collaboration while listlessly watching PowerPoint presentations will not do!"

That workshop was just the beginning. Tim's goal for law students and stakeholders in the court system is to take more responsibility for their own learning. Apathy is the enemy, Tim believes. When working with stakeholders on a design, he says, "Open boxes in the storyboard move the process forward without my intervention in a way that engages all those participating." Tim fervently explains: "The answers are not scripted. The gestalt and aesthetic of the interaction is revealed. I ask more of myself and more of the people working in the court system." He says it's as simple as asking, "You tell me: what should go in the box?"

Inclusive High-Stakes Decision Making Made Easy:
Craig Yeatman

Does it pay off for a very well-prepared leader to invite diverse members of a board or management team to shape next steps together on new product launches, investments, and other high-stakes decisions? Not unless the leader starts with a clear purpose and is willing to let go of overcontrol. Then, bold moves can be made very quickly and decisively. Keith's interview with Craig Yeatman shows how.

Craig Yeatman is the managing director of WorldsView™ Consulting and the CEO of WorldsView Holdings, both based in South Africa. He has successfully started up numerous companies and teaches entrepreneurial leadership and organizational development to professionals in the field. His goal is to advance the craft of building sustainable organizations. After hearing that Craig was making big waves back home after a Plexus Institute conference, Keith interviewed him to learn more about his experience with Liberating Structures in business.

Keith: *Was there a moment in which you decided there was no turning back from using Liberating Structures in your practice?*

Craig: I frequently teach a two-day "OD Foundations" program consisting of lectures and presentations. The material is complex and the room is filled with delegates that range from seasoned company executives to young professionals—all of whom are working in OD. So most afternoons are a complete waste of time—so little of the material "lands" in the final sessions.

One day, on the first afternoon, I walked away from the teaching material and picked up my Liberating Structures handbook. I turned two and a half hours of lecture into a few questions on the fly, and used **1-2-4-All** instead of the presentation.

Keith: *So, you replaced a finely vetted "best practices" presentation with an improvised 1-2-4-All microstructure. What happened?*

Craig: The rest of the afternoon flew past. Delegate questions created powerful conversational teaching platforms. The next morning, I took a deep breath and changed the original class into a Liberating Structures design. I combined **Impromptu Networking, Troika Consulting, Conversation**

Café (called Lekgotla in South Africa), and **25/10 Crowd Sourcing** around small snippets of "teaching."

All of us were deeply engaged. And then, almost four months after the workshop, I heard that the group was continuing to process the material, "voluntarily" taking the work forward on their own initiative.

That was my moment. Since then, I have become a proper student of Liberating Structures with action learning as my classroom.

Keith: *So, success with the OD Foundations teaching program got you started. Have you tried Liberating Structures in business settings with difficult or high-stakes decisions to be addressed?*

Craig: I frequently help leaders make decisions about investments, new product launches, and strategy. Because it is very expensive to bring people together, I feel pressure to make the experience intense, creative, and highly productive. For this type of meeting, I am now using Liberating Structures.

For example, in a marketing company meeting I chaired, the executive board members had three hours to present to the independent nonexecs a budget, plan, and merger strategy. I recommended they circulate the presentations in advance and dispense with the on-site presentations altogether. We worked with the assumption that participants would read the packets and grasp key issues.

On the day of the meeting, as you might expect, the nonexecs wanted more information and conventional presentations. I asked that they wait to see if presentations were needed until after we used the Liberating Structure **1-2-4-All**. I asked each individual to write out the story of this business with the merger and without the merger... as well as asked, "What would the revenue, margins, and profitability look like with and without the merger two years into the future?"

Each participant joined in developing elements of the story lines, progressively adding detail and depth via **1-2-4-All**. Execs and nonexecs mixed and shared ideas, and very quickly everyone internalized the story lines. This conversation took only fifteen minutes. Then, all the decisions needed to move forward took only ten minutes. As we moved around the table taking in the votes, each director was smiling, relaxed, and there was general agreement afterward that this was a great way to make a decision such as this.

"I frequently help leaders make decisions about investments, new product launches, and strategy. Because it is very expensive to bring people together, I feel pressure to make the experience intense, creative, and highly productive. For this type of meeting, I am now using Liberating Structures."

The balance of the meeting, Craig told us, was used for the nonexecs to give advice to the executives, in a "Lekgotla" format, an indigenous variation of **Conversation Café.** *Using this Liberating Structure strengthened the bond between the two groups and, Craig believes, set the merger off on the right path.*

Craig: No one asked for a presentation. It was not necessary. As a footnote, the paperwork for the merger was completed within fourteen days, and the staff of the two companies had come together within thirty days. Some four months later, I heard some of the staff talking together and saying that it felt as though they had always been working together—which I like to think has something to do with the gentle way in which the board made their decision, and the spirit that the merging executives took from that board meeting.

Keith: *Clearly, you believe the meeting outcomes were very positive. What was so different about the dynamics of this meeting?*

Craig: Reflecting on my own experience in meetings, I know how quickly I become bored, restless, impatient, and controlling around "time." Very often the topics and linear order of the agenda are not compelling. I tend to be disruptive and impatient when waiting to speak. I cut people off or make a joke, in large part because the agenda is forcing attention on the wrong conversation. My contributions are 20 percent of what they could be if we were only talking about the important challenges.

In this meeting, all of my energy and seemingly most of the energy of the other members was unfettered.

Keith: *What do you think made it possible for you to get positive results and develop shared understanding so quickly?*

Craig: Liberating Structures help people shape the agenda as it unfolds. The issues move themselves into play through each individual's contributions. If the purpose of our agenda item is clear, the conversational focus is self-sorting, emergent, and we move rapidly into the meaty issues. This reduces the pressure on the leader or facilitator to figure it all out—the topics and the order of the agenda—in advance. The creative flow of questions, ideas, and solutions cannot be scripted beforehand.

Keith: *Your expertise in building and sustaining organizations spans twenty-five-plus years. Your success, in part, comes from mastery of facilitation methods. What value do Liberating Structures add to the vast array of change methodologies used in organizations?*

Craig: First, Liberating Structures illuminate the limits of the Big Five conventional microstructures—presentations, managed discussions, status reports, open discussions, and brainstorms—for engaging people.

My favorite sandbox since age twenty-four is getting people together for start-ups. I spent decades getting the right people in the room and focusing attention on a tightly planned agenda. Still, with all my skills and detailed preparation, I started to notice how my best efforts were generating formulaic and unthinking responses. Was my agenda at fault? Did I invite the wrong people?

Discovering Liberating Structures was a slap in the face. The problem was conventional microstructures—not the agenda or the people selected to participate. This was obvious to me *after* it was pointed out. The Big Five conventional approaches cannot deliver. It is very practical to have thirty-three additional structures that are designed for including and engaging everyone.

Keith: *I am curious about you. What made it possible for you to make these "small changes" in your practice as a consultant, facilitator, and entrepreneur?*

Craig: Three things made it possible for me to first play with, and then take more seriously, the idea of the Liberating Structures: my nature; the evangelism and support from Lisa Kimball, Henri Lipmanowicz, and yourself; and the results I have been seeing.

My nature: I have often joked with my wife that there are only two places I like to be when a crowd assembles: either on the podium or in the bar, away from the crowd. I rarely enjoy being spoken at, which has made me a disruptive force when groups gather.

I love speaking, and I love being in conversation about things that matter to me. I was taught "write, don't speak" as a way of managing myself in groups—which inside me felt like trying to contain a whale of energy in a bird-sized body.

When a name was given [Liberating Structures] to ways of being in a group that freed me to engage in a way that I love—without having an unhealthy effect on those around me—I was intrigued. Could there really be thirty-three or more "better ways" of being together in day-to-day organizational life?

Evangelism and support: Lisa Kimball's work provided some motivation and inspiration, and then a tipping point was the effort that has gone into the Liberating Structures website—with the consistent "pattern language"

> "Discovering Liberating Structures was a slap in the face. The problem was conventional microstructures—not the agenda or the people selected to participate. This was obvious to me after it was pointed out. The Big Five conventional approaches cannot deliver."

approach to each Liberating Structure. This gave me confidence to move from patterns I quickly recognized (**1-2-4-All, Conversation Cafe, Appreciative Interview**) to others with which I am less familiar.

Liberating Structures provide massive structures for microencounters, and my whale energy swims easily in that water. It is easy for me to go into Liberating Structures, and so it has been easy for me to bring others with me. I am halfway through the current "set," in that I have used about fifteen Liberating Structures alone or in combination at least once. I am not done yet.

Results: I am not done yet because I see the results, every time I use a Liberating Structure in place of a CS—Controlling Structure, a term I made up to describe conventional microstructures.

Keith: *Would you like to offer advice to other leaders getting started with Liberating Structures?*

Craig: Whenever a group of people gets together, it should be for a purpose. Don't start before you have clarified the purpose of your gathering. Print yourself a Liberating Structures manual that you can carry with you. I love having the "directory" at hand. Plan lightly, drawing your process from good practices in adult learning research and complexity sciences—and then use the simpler Liberating Structures methods to gain confidence. Keith and Henri have thoughtfully set them out in ascending complexity, so you can begin with **Impromptu Networking** or **1-2-4-All** and progress through the set. As soon as possible, combine a couple—and before you know it you will be familiar with the "pattern language" instructions and have the confidence to draw on the full set as your event unfolds.

Craig's experience illustrates how Liberating Structures invite people to shape next steps together, in the moment. We call this phenomenon "simultaneous mutual shaping." It is a very productive "flow state" in which everyone can work at the top of his or her intelligence. Liberating Structures enable a depth of conversation and bold action that cannot be planned in advance but rather emerges out of local interaction among group members.

> "I am not done yet because I see the results, every time I use a Liberating Structure in place of a CS—Controlling Structure, a term I made up to describe conventional microstructures."

Turning a Business Around:
Alison Joslyn

"One year later, we were hitting it out of the park."

The numbers were all going the wrong way, and Alison Joslyn needed to organize a business turnaround—fast. She had a strategy in mind: "We needed to infuse a customer focus into a company that had been very successful with a product focus. Only a few of my executive team members embraced the idea. And I felt that every one of our 250 employees needed to join in." The question was how.

Alison Joslyn was the general manager of a global corporation's Venezuelan subsidiary when she turned to Liberating Structures to turn her unit around. In just one year, the unit went from lagging to leading the industry on key performance metrics.

Alison's unit had tumbled in market position and growth. There had been product-supply challenges, loss of market share, and competitors ascending in customer perceptions. Employees had become discouraged and it showed in their satisfaction scores.

Enter Alison's change initiative, initiated and sustained by a selection of Liberating Structures. "One year later," she says, "all the performance metrics were going in the right direction. We were hitting it out of the park. We became number one in growth in Venezuela. Our internal culture survey score was now ultrahigh."

Engaging everyone in a change initiative was uncharted ground for Alison, a notion not even covered in her management training. In fact, her experience in graduate school made her doubtful of the benefits of broad participation: "Working as a team was an encumbrance. It seemed so hard and frustrating without adding much value. I would rather do it myself. I was rewarded for my work as an individual."

To address the challenge in Venezuela, she started to search for approaches. As luck would have it, the VP of the Latin American region was starting a new experiment. "I got myself invited to the weekend leadership retreat for regional and country leaders," she recalls. "The bottom-up approach to include and unleash everyone was a good fit for our situation. A few months later, we started with an **Open Space** meeting for all 250 employees."

Opening Space + Strong Leadership

Alison's **Open Space** meeting was a dramatic beginning. More than seventy projects to support the turnaround were unleashed, many from frontline employees exercising unexpected leadership. Although Alison and the management team were not comfortable with all the projects, they were thrilled with the unbridled enthusiasm and initiative.

In the meantime, Alison attended a Liberating Structures workshop in Brazil and came back with even more ways to build on the success of the initial **Open Space**. With the seventy project leaders, Alison developed **Min Specs** to constrain and enable self-organization. Still, it was messy. Out of seventy projects, seventeen garnered formal support, and ten of those were able to live within the **Min Specs** over the next six months.

"While excitement was spreading person to person, I took a very firm stance. I very deliberately fanned the flames," Alison told us. "Liberating Structures would not be a one-time thing." She extended the use of Liberating Structures to her own management team meetings, the development of marketing strategies, the big sales convention, and eventually to interactions with customers. "It could have stopped with the successful **Open Space** meeting, but I insisted," she says.

"I very deliberately fanned the flames. Liberating Structures would not be a one-time thing."

Waves of Internal Then External Experiments

Improving performance and integrating Liberating Structures into the business came in waves, with different functions and levels adopting different Liberating Structures at their own pace throughout the organization. First up was the sales convention. One-way PowerPoint presentations and formulaic sales training had dominated the traditional convention. The introduction of lively Liberating Structures approaches sparked fresh enthusiasm and engagement.

Hesitantly at first, marketing and sales directors brought the interactive Liberating Structures methods they had experienced into everyday work. Respected managers in marketing tried Liberating Structures first. One product manager used a **Conversation Café** in an evening meeting with customers, a highly educated professional group. Typically, the meeting would have included a dry PowerPoint lecture, brief Q&A, and dinner. The **Conversation Café** produced true engagement for the first time: BlackBerries never came out, and peer-to-peer and generalist-to-specialist exchanges were collegial and full of learning.

The sales force soon got into the act. Everyone in the sales department was organized top to bottom in a tightly controlled hierarchy and not expected to embrace the new methods quickly. However, after a major meeting using **1-2-4-All**, **User Experience Fishbowl,** and **Conversation Café** for the first time with physician customers, the sales reps started to hear back from influential doctors. The customers loved the new meetings. They wanted more. They wanted to learn Liberating Structures methods to apply in their own work.

"There were stories that competitors were trying to copy our success," Alison told us. "Soon, the sales director and, more importantly, the first-level sales managers were 'all in.' Everyone followed."

"Once the sales director and the first-level sales managers were 'all in,' everyone followed."

Other experiments were unfolding. Alison and the HR director coached others on the management team. In pairs, they used **Design StoryBoard** to sketch out Liberating Structures-inspired agendas to formulate strategy. To build on early successes, the management team wanted a bigger splash. They designed a "Liberating Structures basic training" session for all product managers and sales managers.

The basic training workshop started with a familiar work assignment: design a successful new product launch. No particular process or Liberating Structure was suggested. The autopilot pattern showed itself. Very large groups formed. A few individuals dominated. Quiet people retreated. Relatively weak ideas were put on flip charts. There was very little collaboration among groups.

The second session of the workshop gave participants the same assignment with a twist: design a successful launch for the same new product with using one or more Liberating Structures. The results were like night and day. **1-2-4-All** drew out many more good ideas than the previous approach to the assignment, and **TRIZ** helped make space for unexpected innovative strategies. The participants felt they contributed and were part of the product launch moving forward. In all, they used six Liberating Structures. They had liftoff!

Social Proof Arrived before Business Results

Looking back, Alison recalls, "Spread was happening at all levels." But what did it all mean? "Social proof preceded conventional proof," she says. "I was looking for early indicators: Did many perspectives come out? Are people high-energy? Are groups mixing? Are Blackberries tucked away? Is the top group working as peers? And, are sales reps helping each other?" Alison looked for little things that suggested a bigger turnaround.

Importantly, Alison could also sense changes in the company's relationship with customers. "I sat in the back of the room for our first meeting with sixty general-practice physicians," she says. "They were leaning in and listening intently. The questions were practical, about real concerns. Not the usual 'I am smarter than you' comment. There was freedom to explore and interact at a deeper level."

At first, there were worries that expert presenters would experience a loss of power and prestige: they were not invited to give the traditional lecture. Surprisingly, the specialist-experts also appreciated the freedom to explore the deeper and more practical questions facing nonexperts. Everyone rolled up their sleeves.

"Several months after the meeting," Alison recalls, "one specialist presenter called me over. She told me it had been the most amazing experience. 'At first I felt exposed, then elated,' the presenter said. 'If you do that again, I would love to be included.'"

The takeaway from customers: Alison and the management team had learned that the customer response to Liberating Structures was no different from what they had seen inside their organization. Nine months of internal experience made it possible and relatively comfortable to leap into customer experiments and reach new levels of engagement and commitment.

But wait. There's more. For Alison herself, the experience with Liberating Structures caused a genuine transformation. "Forever, the turnaround changed my way of leading," she told us. "Management is not always about being smarter. I now know that I can drive a business by engaging everyone from the mail guy all the way up. It is practical and powerful to hear every voice."

"There was freedom to explore and interact at a deeper level."

"I now know I can drive a business by engaging everyone from the mail guy all the way up. It is practical and powerful to hear every voice."

Transforming After-Action Reviews in the Army:
Lisa Kimball

The US Army has a longstanding practice of using After-Action Reviews (AAR) to debrief troops returning from combat duty. This story shows how a simple Liberating Structure—the **Users Experience Fishbowl**—replaced a traditional army structure and yielded deep understanding of what deploying troops would be facing in the theater of war.

In a typical AAR, each officer is interviewed individually by multiple organizations over a thirty-day period. The process is closely controlled—detailed, precise, and demanding. The interviewers collate, analyze, and summarize the information. It is then incorporated into briefings provided to the troops entering the war theater, typically via PowerPoint lectures.

In this story of Liberating Structures in action, field officers returning from Afghanistan were going to be interviewed to transfer their specialized knowledge to the people who would replace them. The information thought to be particularly useful to the deploying soldiers was the returning officers' experience in developing trusting relationships with women in Afghan villages. With trusting relationships at the local level, soldiers were able to generate better information to fight the war and possibly dampen the Taliban's efforts to recruit successfully.

*Lisa Kimball, PhD, the former president of the Plexus Institute, a nonprofit organization focused on applying ideas from complexity science to solve social and organizational problems, started using Liberating Structures methods in the mid 1980s, with online networking visionary Frank Burns. She has shown clients in government agencies, corporations, nonprofit organizations, and educational institutions just how simple and powerful Liberating Structures like **Users Experience Fishbowl** can be.*

Transferring On-the-Ground Know-How

Here's how it happened. Lisa had started introducing Liberating Structures in an army leadership program for officers called Starfish Adaptive Leadership.[2] Given the program's focus on action and learning in complex environments, Liberating Structures were included to help officers exploit opportunity and continuously learn in situations where they are in charge but not in control.

An executive from the Army Knowledge Management function who had participated in the Starfish program decided to experiment with **Users Experience Fishbowl** in conducting AARs. Several officers who had returned from the war were asked to simply talk to each other in a fishbowl about their experience of developing trusting relationships with community members, including local women, in Afghan villages. The other participants—both the officers being deployed to the war zone and the members of the knowledge management group responsible for harvesting field intelligence—sat around the outside listening.

The executive-facilitator of the fishbowl told Lisa:

> *Everyone was sitting on the edge of their chairs because they felt they were getting important firsthand, unfiltered information. Every word was important. Moreover, participants got the information plus a sense of how the officers worked together and made sense of confusing signals. The experience AND the information came through.*

For the people who had been interviewers in the traditional AAR process, it was a revelatory experience. They had a chance to see and feel what was conveyed between officers leaving the war zone and those entering it. Some of the questions asked were different and richer than any the interviewers could have imagined. The officers in the fishbowl took the questions very seriously and took notes so that they could be sure to answer all the questions as candidly as possible—if not then, at a later time.

For the officers returning from Afghanistan, the fishbowl was a refreshing and satisfying experience compared to the usual AAR. The traditional AAR interview process was often mind-numbing, producing repetitive answers to questions that had little local flavor. In contrast, the fishbowl conversation evoked many more memories and details. One story sparked another.

Equally important, the returning soldiers were able to make sense of their messy experience together in a way that communicated more detail and nuance to the departing troops. They felt able to share their on-the-ground experience in a way that would truly help their colleagues be safe and effective. The young soldiers who had never deployed were all ears listening to their leaders have a wide-ranging and candid discussion about their concerns. "In the space of a couple hours," the executive facilitating the experiment said, "there was a huge amount of understanding and progress made. The interaction among the participants told more of the story."

"The forthright and heartfelt interaction among the returning soldiers told their story in a way that would truly help those being deployed be safe and effective."

"*They were getting important firsthand, unfiltered information. Every word was important.... The experience AND the information came through.*"

Inventing Future Health-Care Practice:
Chris McCarthy

How do you start inventing the future? How do hard work, hope and history rhyme in a way that something really new comes into being? Members of the Innovation Learning Network (ILN) are turning to Liberating Structures to discover the answers.

ILN network member organizations

Chris McCarthy has a dual role in inventing the future of health care: he is a lead at Kaiser Permanente's Innovation Consultancy, where he serves as an innovation consultant, and also leads the ILN. In both roles, Chris's goal is akin to Dick Fosbury's breaking the Olympic high-jump record by an unimaginable three inches in the 1968 Olympics, where he reinvented high jumping.

The "Fosbury Flop" involved a straight approach, jumping with both feet, and twisting the body 180 degrees looking away from the bar. Before Fosbury's revolutionary invention, all jumpers faced the bar and launched off one foot.

The ILN network was launched in 2006 with the support of the VHA Health Foundation and Kaiser Permanente (KP), the largest health plan in the United States, as a unique way to share methods, transfer ideas, and generate opportunities for interorganizational collaboration. ILN members realized from the outset that they would need fresh approaches to deepen their understanding of patient needs and learn how to break away from current reality. A synergistic mash-up of Design Thinking and Liberating Structures was put into play. Particularly useful Liberating Structures for the task include **Open Space** and **Social Network Webbing.**

Open Space

Every year since the ILN's 2006 inception, the group has used **Open Space** during one of its face-to-face meetings. **Open Space** is especially well suited to the action-orientation and "we fail forward" spirit of innovators, Chris says. "I believe playful curiosity is the best way to attract people into this messy work. **Open Space** gives permission to explore what we know and more importantly what we don't know. Without exploring unfamiliar territory, most innovations fall short."

In **Open Space** sessions, innovators from different organizations have found others who share their curiosity about venturing into unfamiliar territory. Big questions have fueled expansive action-research themes. Some examples:

- *Virtual Worlds: How can we use virtual-world technology to help with inventing new rules?*
  This question cracked open a door to real-world applications: localizing disaster planning with real-time Google weather and traffic data; reducing the spread of infection by incorporating special virtual-reality segments into training sessions; enriching rehab for injured veterans by stimulating movement with Wii technology; and spreading hospital shift-change innovations across the country. Directly and indirectly, ILN members have been urging each other on to discover more.

- *Medication Administration: How can we make the way we administer medications in our hospitals safer and more human-centered?*
  Over the course of just two months, KP, Partners HealthCare, Alegent, and Ascension shared proprietary facts and figures on their current state, practices, improvements, and innovations. All four systems became immediately smarter. KP went on to innovate in the medication-administration process, inventing a system that became known as KP MedRite, and then shared the system back with its ILN partners.

- *CareAnyWhere: How could we enable patients to receive care wherever they are instead of having to travel to hospitals, clinics, or other health-care facilities?*
  This question led to an expansive research and application agenda. Radical inventiveness started to unfold in tangible approaches like hospital-at-home, care at the shopping mall, and home visits, as well as less tangible care methods like e-ICU, Twitter, and Virtual Practice. Eyes opened. Approaches that seemed like science fiction (robo-doc) or retro methods (home visits) started to make practical sense.

"Open Space gives permission to explore what we know and more importantly what we don't know. Without exploring unfamiliar territory, most innovations fall short."

- ***Gamification of Health Care: How could games help people change their behavior in ways that improve health, prevent illness, or help them live more fully with a chronic disease?*** Applications discovered include a virtual-reality game called Snow World, used to treat burn patients who cannot tolerate more pain medication; Nike + iPod "sensor-enabled smart shoes" to help athletes boost their performance and health; and computer games that make it fun for children to learn how to live with diabetes.

The games are designed to be used by individuals, and players also can often be connected to peers or a community with the same challenges. Skeptics walked away inspired by a wide range of serious applications in hand as the game designers had demonstrated how technical, clinical, and social motivations can be combined in powerful ways.

Like other seemingly questionable ILN experiments, exploring games turned out to be both serious and seriously fun. Many of the ILN discoveries are "game changing," and each success rose from humble beginnings. The first Open Space sessions had offered only shadowy hints of what was to come. "When we first started the ILN," says Chris, "we weren't sure what it was, where it was going, or how it would last. Five years later, we know it's the sweet spot of content, technique, and friendship that drives us to return year after year."

"When we first started the ILN, we weren't sure what it was, where it was going, or how it would last. Five years later, we know it's the sweet spot of content, technique, and friendship that drives us to return year after year."

Social Network Webbing

Part of the hidden capability in the ILN is well-developed **Social Network Webbing** via informal networks and relationships. Each member organization has a designated "network weaver," responsible for matching people to people and people to specific projects. This was one result of detailed social network mapping efforts conducted in 2006 and 2007.

Another result is that many members now have local-internal networks to match the global-external ILN. Chris notes, "A year after we started the ILN, we realized that we didn't even know who the internal innovators were at KP, let alone from the outside world." As of this writing, Kaiser Permanente's internal network (dubbed the Garfield Innovation Network, or GIN) has grown to more than four hundred members from five. ILN members also realized that the members with more robust internal innovation networks were making more practical use of the global network.

Reflections on Results

"**Open Space** is one of those amazing ahas of when you realize that simple is truly better," Chris says. "Who would have thought a group of people on the fly could construct their own agenda and self-facilitate? **Open Space** works because so rarely are people who gather at meetings ever given the chance to own it, run it, and decide it. Of course with ownership comes responsibility!"

Open Space and **Social Network Webbing** are the main ways ILN members collectively are inventing the future of health care. A fresh look at fundamental health-care needs, a creative mix of new technologies, and a strong social network are combining to bring the future into focus.

"Open Space works because so rarely are people who gather at meetings ever given the chance to own it, run it, and decide it. Of course with ownership comes responsibility!"

Creating More Substance, Connections, and Ideas in the Classroom
By Arvind Singhal

Arvind Singhal is Samuel Shirley and Edna Holt Marston Professor, Department of Communication, The University of Texas at El Paso. He is also appointed as William J. Clinton Distinguished Fellow, Clinton School of Public Service, University of Arkansas. This article was adapted from "A Liberated Professor Speaks," published at www.liberatingstructures.com.

"The nature of the student feedback I hear has noticeably changed. Qualitatively, it is deeper, more soulful."

Professors who revel in their vocational calling often hear their students say: "Professor, I enjoyed your class. I learned a lot. I thank you, and so on." Such remarks, whether expressed orally, or penned in course evaluations and thank-you notes, warm the heart and buoy the soul. I have been graced and buoyed by such warmth over the past twenty-nine years.

However, in the past eight years or so, the nature of the student feedback I hear has noticeably changed. Qualitatively, it is deeper, more soulful. I increasingly hear: "This class changed my life," "I learned so much about myself in this class," "I am sad that this course is ending for I will miss my classmates," and so on. And, I have even heard students say: "Thank you for teaching me about healthy communities. But thank you also for teaching me how to learn." Such statements more than make a professor's day. They make a student's life!

How do I explain this qualitative shift in student feedback? Perhaps it is because I am getting older, wiser. Perhaps my abilities to connect the classroom with the real world have multiplied appreciably. Perhaps I have learned to better manage classroom conflict. Perhaps I can, at the drop of a hat, pull out a compelling story to illustrate a point. Or, all of the above!

I believe there may be one more explanation. In the past eight years, I have increasingly been exposed to, and have put to practice, some alternative ways to approach and design my classroom interactions: Liberating Structures.

What has the adoption of Liberating Structures done to my classrooms? One of my students (we'll call her GC) wrote the following in her learner reflections:

> *In Dr. Singhal's class we practice Liberating Structures in the way the class is structured and in the way activities are conducted. These*

structures provide an easy-to-learn atmosphere as they are adaptable methods for engagement that make it quick and simple for individuals from all backgrounds to integrate themselves into a discussion. This is exhibited by a simple rearrangement of chairs, removing order and hierarchy in conversation, and to even have space for a few moments to communicate free from course intentions. Through these practices we are working on decentralizing our thinking and actions. Through Liberating Structures we are learning to not adhere to an individual position and to not reject what others have to say.

Acadia Roher, who took my once-a-month Liberating Structures elective seminar at the Clinton School of Public Service, summarized her classroom experience with the following sketch and narrative:

My sketch represents the energy, focus, and expanding humanity that I have witnessed by using Liberating Structures in different settings and groups. I chose bright, vibrant colors to represent the electrifying energy that Liberating Structures seem to create in a room full of people. But the energy is not chaotic, it is instead focused and often creates more substance, connections, and ideas than traditional structures. The purple nucleus represents the focus that Liberating Structures bring, from which the ever-expanding circles of energy and ideas bounce outward.

Acadia's portrayal of Liberating Structures and what they help accomplish

"I chose bright, vibrant colors to represent the electrifying energy that Liberating Structures seem to create in a room full of people."

The Classroom Comes Alive

When I read comments such as GC's and Acadia's, I grin from ear to ear. To hear that Liberating Structures help create more substance, connections, and ideas in a classroom—priceless! Interestingly, Liberating Structures allow for such to happen with no extra resources. The classroom, the teacher, the students, the chalkboard, the laptop, the projector, and the time spent in the classroom remain the same. What changes with Liberating Structures are certain structural conditions that enhance the quality of interactions among participants, leading to very different outcomes.

"What changes with Liberating Structures are certain structural conditions that enhance the quality of interactions among participants, leading to very different outcomes."

Let us give some simple examples.[3] Physically moving the students from a traditional rows-and-columns classroom configuration into a circular seating arrangement changes the nature of the learning environment and the nature of the interactions. The circle structure allows each participant to be equally seen, heard, and acknowledged. There are no backbenchers or frontbenchers. No scope for hiding. The circular setting invites richer participation, allowing those who are present to verbally and nonverbally affirm, support, or question others.

Laughter ripples through a circular classroom far more rapidly and inclusively than in a traditionally structured classroom. I for one have noticed more smiles and nods. Sighs and gasps are also more visible, creating opportunities for deliberation, and spaces for corrective action. As a professor, I experience more winks and nods and quizzical looks and my antennae are constantly processing feedback that is more authentic, accurate, and timely. Such feedback enables one to be nimble, to improvise, to change course, or to maintain it.

Arvind facilitating a Master Class in the Netherlands using a circular seating configuration

I often introduce a "talking stick" when doing small-group work in my classrooms. The talking stick represents a simple structure: whoever holds the stick (can be a pen) will talk, the others will listen. The talking stick has been used by the Navajos for centuries to bestow respect on the one who is talking. After one is finished talking, the stick is usually passed on to the next person. This goes on until all have spoken. In a small-group situation, the talking stick can go around several times so that participants have an opportunity to widen and deepen their own thoughts and to build on the thoughts of the others. No one person dominates and the conversation does not ping-pong (bounce from one to another) as is customary in a traditional classroom brainstorm.

The talking stick, perceptibly, slows the conversation down, making it deeper and richer. [See the **Conversation Café** in Part Four for details.] Once the stick is in circulation, participants often get into a zone, playing off each other—like a jazz improvisation. In ten to fifteen minutes, a small group can have an orderly, respectful, deep, and creative conversation. And multiple small-group conversations can be simultaneously carried out in a classroom, ensuring that all class participants are engaged and participating at the same time.

Simple structures like sitting in a circle, introducing a talking stick, and providing people an equal opportunity to be seen and heard changes the quality of the connections and interactions in a classroom. Imagine if such happens twice or thrice a week over a sixteen-week-long semester course! More diverse inputs lead to a wider and deeper understanding of the issue at hand. Interestingly, within the first week or two, the classroom feels more dynamic, arms begin to uncross, words begin to flow, smiles and laughter rise, and sighs and gasps become more visible and acceptable. Trust rises as relationships deepen over time.

By the third week of classes, even before I enter the classroom, the din of conversational chatter greets me at the door. Multiple conversations are under way, telephone numbers are being exchanged, and most people know the others by their names. After class, participants feel comfortable to hang around. Compassion for others is palpable: someone offers a ride to another, someone puts the chairs back in rows and columns, and someone erases the chalkboard clean. When such happens, and with repeated frequency, I experience immense joy, realizing that the class has begun to act like, feel like, an interconnected whole. I am reinforced, convinced, and affirmed that we, collectively,

"I experience immense joy, realizing that the class has begun to act like, feel like, an interconnected whole."

must be doing something right to build a sense of community, a safe collective space.

"I have often reflected on how the practice of Liberating Structures has enhanced my quality of life as a professor."

My Personal Transformation

I have often reflected on how the practice of Liberating Structures has enhanced my quality of life as a professor. How do I prepare differently? What am I mindful of when in class? Who is the arbiter of knowledge? When do I speak up? When do I let go of the conversation, and so on? There are no clear-cut answers, nor any prescriptions to dole out. But my experiences suggest the following.

The practice of Liberating Structures has helped liberate me from bearing the sole burden of "professing" in a classroom, i.e., being a Sage on Stage, a knower, and a content deliverer.

The practice of Liberating Structures has enabled me to see the vast experiential and intellectual resources participants bring into a classroom, individually and collectively. These resources are usually hidden, lurking, and need a safe environment to find utterance. When such happens, participants learn from peers, a less hierarchical and often more effective mechanism for co-learning than just being at the mercy of the professor.

Operationally, just "letting go" of the thought of "professing" profoundly changes the way my classroom is designed.

I am now deeply mindful about how seats are configured—e.g., in a circle where everyone can be "seen" versus in rows and columns, and how these spatial configurations (geography) affects pedagogy.

I am now deeply mindful about my "positionality" vis-à-vis the participants. Am I seated with the class participants, one participant among many, or am I behind a podium—in control with a PowerPoint clicker? What do such spatial "positionalities" symbolize?

I am constantly thinking about how I can create and frame the structural parameters so that participant conversations are focused and yet are allowed to expand and deepen. I am strategizing about how all participants can be engaged at the same time, whether as individuals who think in silence, or with a partner in a conversational space, or in a small group as a contributing or listening member.

Now, when I prepare to walk into a classroom, I ask not "What is it that I need to do?" but rather "What is it that WE need to do?" I focus on what the participants are "doing" in the classroom for it is the experience of doing that validates that learning has occurred. I have to constantly remind myself to curb my urge of lecturing, or professing an answer when a question is asked, for efficient as it may seem, learning can be quite superficial when people are just passively watching PowerPoint slides, taking copious notes (so they could study for an exam), or listening uncritically to the one behind the podium.

In creating such conditions, the professor in me experiences deep humility. He realizes that no ONE person is (or can be) the arbiter of learning, but rather knowledge is created by the collective in the conversations they have, and the processes they experience.

From Sage on Stage to Chief Enabler

Liberating Structures create the enabling conditions for people to contribute, to ask for help, to develop skills in listening and paraphrasing, and to build trust and safety, while valuing (rather celebrating) diversity and difference.

The design aspects of Liberating Structures go way beyond the frame of "what we need to do in a classroom?" In order for meaningful, collective conversations to occur in a classroom, I am now deeply mindful of what individual class participants need to do prior to coming to class—what texts to read, what lectures/talks to watch in advance, what problems to solve, and what questions or reflections to bring to share with the collective.

As a professor, one asks how class participants might prepare themselves to come into a designated interactional space once/twice/thrice a week at an appointed hour, and benefit from the presence, knowledge, and experience of others, including the professor. This mindfulness also influences the design of what the class participants do, individually or in small groups, in between class sessions to widen and deepen their understanding, to engage in actions and reflections, and such.

My professorial role is now one of a Chief Enabler whose responsibility it is to design and enable a process so that all class participants feel invited, engaged, and allowed to contribute as "whole" people. As an enabler, I bear the responsibility (and challenge) to create the safety and supportive conditions for such invitations, engagements, and contributions to potentially occur. Poetic as it sounds, this process of "enabling" can be difficult and challenging, as the control of the classroom space, time, and content is no longer solely with the professor. The professor exercises some degree of control over the process, and can help provide the frame for structuring conversations, but cannot completely control (or predict) what surfaces from the collective. That means Liberating Structures, necessarily, create the conditions for "surprising" and emergent classroom outcomes—both of a substantive and relational nature. I have seen how, for the most part, these outcomes result in opportunities for deeper, experiential learning for individuals and the collective and deeper friendships and relationships.

With Liberating Structures, a classroom, its participants, and a professor are always a work-in-progress. And that is what learning is all about, no?

Getting Commitment, Ownership, and Follow-Through:
Neil McCarthy

Seattle leadership coach and consultant Neil McCarthy was working with a large multinational business client to shift the patterns of conversation and foster trusting relationships among key leaders. He turned to a couple of Liberating Structures to help the leaders discover for themselves greater clarity of commitment, ownership, and follow-through than anyone thought possible.

Seattle leadership coach and consultant Neil McCarthy uses Liberating Structures to help leaders and their teams discover for themselves how to make the transition to higher levels of performance. "Like volleyball, I focus on being the setter for others to get involved, not on being the one that is always trying to spike the ball by jumping high above your team, solving the problem with individual force and intellectualism," he says "I try to 'let go' so that my clients can practice how to draw out self-discovery and build trust in their teams."

Including More People in Coordinating Global Operations

Neil was working with an engineering group of forty leaders—including a general manager, a business manager, global support based in India, and five functional groups from technical operations—who needed to plan and coordinate activities for the coming fiscal year. Normally, this would happen in a meeting with just eight members of the senior team and be undertaken with relatively low expectations. Past experience with the traditional meeting format suggested that clarity of commitment, ownership, and follow-through would be sketchy. As Neil jested in his conversation with the group leader, "We will collaborate by listening to PowerPoint presentations for hours followed by a frenzy of action planning in the last thirty minutes of the meeting."

This time around, Neil proposed using **What I Need From You (WINFY)** and inviting the entire forty-member leadership team into the conversation. The general manager and Neil had already started working on inclusion with the senior team. "It was not that difficult to shape next steps together with a larger group," said Neil. Neil's trusting relationship and a positive track record with the GM made the use of **WINFY** possible. Both wanted to create a new conversation and spark creative relationships among the leadership team. Both had let go of wanting to know the specific outcomes

"Commitment, ownership, and follow-through will not come from listening to hours of PowerPoint presentations."

in advance. Using a new structure like **WINFY** would make it possible to extend these changes to the larger group.

Shifting the Pattern to a Straight-Up Conversation

Eight separate functional groups drafted two BIG "what I need from you to succeed" requests to be dealt with in a fishbowl conversation. The group leaders brought the requests to the inner circle of the fishbowl, asking each representative of the other seven functions for what they needed. Meticulous notes were jotted down. The larger group looked on in awe. What everyone was seeing for the first time was people making direct, straight-to-the point requests to one another, leader to leader. During the debrief, one participant said, "I have never seen a conversation like this around here. I saw that just about everyone was on the edge of their seat the entire time."

"There had never been a conversation like this. Just about everyone was on the edge of their seat the entire time."

The way the leaders paused between hearing a request and responding to it was remarkable. The quality of listening and capturing the essence of each request was a big change. One participant said, "It was clean. No obfuscation. Straight up. Three unequivocal answers and one brush off—*yes, no, I will try,* and *whatever*—stripped away the unessential."

Another participant said, "Now I know why I never get what I need. The way my leader asked for what our group needs does not translate well among his peers. I am going to have to be very clear about what we ask for and how we ask for it." "Now I know what is important for next year," said another.

As part of the **WINFY** debrief, two different leaders in the group said, "I want to do this in my organization." The general manager decided to use **WINFY** every six months to help his team stay aligned regarding needs.

WINFY helped Neil's clients see the pattern in their usual interactions and then do something about it so they could get on with the work at hand. Business straight up.

Why was **WINFY** so productive? Neil says, "We don't ask directly for what we need. Often, it is a long, drawn-out conversation. We talk about and debate each aspect of the issue so much that the essence of the request gets watered down to the point where it is meaningless and easy to agree just to end the conversation. It is also possible to neglect a request because it is not articulated clearly." What appears to be a ***yes*** becomes a ***whatever*** in practice.

There's one more payoff, says Neil: "As a facilitator, I use **What I Need From You** because it helps me get out of the middle. I am more able to practice nonattachment to a particular outcome or having my own needs respected. My credibility as a consultant is not linked to a predetermined outcome. Rather, my contribution comes with structuring the conversation and working with what surprises unfold."

Inspiring Enduring Culture Change While Preventing Hospital Infections:

Michael Gardam

"What took me by surprise was how a project to prevent the spread of superbugs in hospitals fundamentally changed culture and the way people work," says Dr. Michael Gardam. By the end of the eighteen-month research project he led, people were working more collaboratively, coming forward with new ideas, taking action on their own to start other programs to improve patient care.

Michael Gardam is the medical director for infection prevention and control at the University Health Network in Toronto. In 2009, he put together an eighteen-month research project to prevent the spread of superbugs in hospitals.

Superbugs are virulent or antibiotic-resistant organisms like MRSA, VRE, and clostridium difficile that cause serious infections and are famous for spreading in hospital settings. Despite sustained attempts to break the chain of transmissions, these infections remain one of health care's most serious challenges and transmission rates generally are increasing each year.

Michael's research project to attack the problem involved five hospital sites across Canada. To fund the project, Michael went way out on a limb with the sponsor. He recommended Liberating Structures and another unknown social intervention called Positive Deviance[4] to solve the complex infection-control problem.

It looked like an insurmountable problem at the outset. But just three years later, there was solid proof that Michael's novel approach succeeded. "We have scientific evidence that a social intervention works!" he told us. "Infection rate reductions of 40 to 100 percent across hospital sites get the attention of the medical establishment." The unanticipated bonus was the culture change in the participant hospitals that quickly spread across their systems.

"What took me by surprise was how this project fundamentally changed culture and the way people work."

A Deeper Look into Culture Change with Social Network Analysis and Ethnography

The research team used **Social Network Mapping** to measure how relationships grew over the study period among people in different functions

and units. Before-and-after data revealed that participation in prevention work had increased at all five sites; staff members increased the number and types of hospital staff that they worked with to control infections. Better still, a diverse mix of nonexperts from multiple functions was taking an active role in prevention for the first time. For example, the work of hospital housekeeping staff is critical to protecting patients from superbugs. Yet, before this project, housekeeping had rarely been part of the conversation. Now, housekeepers were being included in the prevention effort.

Clearly, participation was way up, but very little was known about the quality of working relationships that had formed. The researchers were eager to dig into this question more deeply. The research team also wanted to learn if and how *culture* had shifted. In the last months of the project, they conducted **Simple Ethnography** inquiries at each site, focusing on cultural attributes such as visible habits, espoused values, and beliefs (unexamined assumptions). They interviewed people in different functions and levels—from room cleaners to VPs to project coordinators—using an **Appreciative Interview** format. They asked about successful experience in preventing infections and what made the success possible. "Some of the answers moved me," Michael said. "I am not a super-emotional guy … but I was. It is wonderful to think that a research project could have this type of effect on people."

Two stories from the field linger for Michael: "A unit manager told me, 'I used to come to work braced to find out what kind of trouble the nurses had gotten into. I was expected to fix it. Now when I come in, they tell me what they have done to fix anything that came up.'"

In the second story, a unit participating in the superbug project was starting a new cardiac program. Staff members took it on themselves to form a cardiac club. They knew they were the experts on planning a launch on their unit. After the fact, they told the project manager about creating the club.

"The interviews revealed much more than scientific proof," Michael asserts. "Culturally speaking, I think we got beyond a point of no return. We will not be able to put the toothpaste back in the tube."

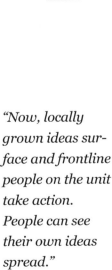

"Now, locally grown ideas surface and frontline people on the unit take action. People can see their own ideas spread."

Michael's reading on some of the significant changes the project produced? "Now, locally grown ideas surface and frontline people on the unit take action. People can see their own ideas spread. That's enticing. After experiencing the freedom and the results that you can achieve, I cannot imagine going back to the old way."

Cultural Attributes, Opposing Yet Comingling

Michael and project coinvestigators are still trying to make sense of the larger cultural shift afoot. Most surprising, the new and old "behaviors" are comingling. One set is not displacing the other. A creative melding is under way.

For example, the interviews revealed that staff more often go to people with local know-how, ask more questions, and use stories to communicate what works. At the same time, dominant patterns persist: paying attention to rank in the hierarchy, "telling not asking," and using hard scientific data to make decisions.

"Most welcome is the enhanced capability to work collaboratively while tapping the up-and-down functional expertise as needed," Michael says. "More frontline staff see their role in the context of a larger system. As a result, managers can step back and responsibly encourage more self-organization while letting go of overcontrol. Nirvana."

"People are more able to work collaboratively while tapping the up-and-down functional expertise as needed. Managers can encourage more self-organization and let go of overcontrol."

Frontiers Ripe for Liberation

"While the results of this study are very promising, this work has affected me in ways that other studies I have been involved with have not," says Michael. "It is hard to recognize that many of the behaviors that are unintentionally drilled into you in medicine, such as 'I talk, you listen,' are contributing to problems rather than helping to bring about solutions. This work has changed the way I work and interact with others—I am far, far more likely to answer a question with a question. I'm sure it irritates some people to no end, but I am interested in their opinion and approach to the problem. Why should I think that I should be the one with all the answers just because I'm a doctor?"

"This work has changed the way I work and interact with others."

This project demonstrated that expecting fundamental change to emerge from the bottom up was a sound and practical idea. The results were so persuasive that the project even made it into the popular media.[5] What's more, even before the project's end, study participants had started to apply Liberating Structures and Positive Deviance to new challenges, in and out of hospital settings. **Improv Prototyping, Discovery & Action Dialogue,** and **TRIZ** were widely employed in the study hospitals.

"I don't believe that many things are impossible. Like surfing a big wave, if you don't try to control everything, it's a great ride."

Without much direct help from Michael and the research team, diverse projects have blossomed in nursing homes, clinics, and NGOs across Canada.

Looking forward, Michael muses, "I find I am more attracted to complex problems—the impossible stuff. In part because I don't believe that many things are impossible. Like surfing a big wave, if you don't try to control everything, it's a great ride."

Dramatizing Behavior Change to Stop Infections:
Sherry Belanger

Sherry Belanger knew better than anyone that the behaviors that spread superbugs are resistant to change. She also knew that prevention ideas coming from outside rarely work. "Anything imposed on my staff—new policies, laminated posters, or free coffee coupons—will not work well," Sherry says. "If it does not come from them, follow-through will suffer." So she found a novel way to reduce infections in her unit: **Improv Prototyping**. "Improv is really fun, visual, and powerful," Sherry says. "No one can watch it and not be influenced!"

 *Sherry Belanger is a nurse who serves as a patient-care coordinator on 4-East at Kelowna General Hospital (KGH) in British Columbia, Canada. She also is the energetic project manager of a core group working to stop the transmission of superbugs (antibiotic-resistant organisms such as MRSA, VRE, and C-difficile) that cause stubborn infections. In addition to using **Improv Prototyping** to motivate prevention within her unit and across hospital departments, the group employed **Social Network Webbing** to coordinate action and attract cross-functional participation.*

Within three weeks of returning from the kickoff meeting for the national **Improv Prototyping** project in Toronto, Sherry and her team had staged Improv scenes in one of the hospital units and with the senior leadership team.[6] Their debut with the top leaders was an especially big hit, Sherry recalls: "We wanted to get leaders talking about superbug prevention." The playful approach Sherry's team took unleashed serious attention, energy, and momentum among the managers beyond expectations.

From that early success, Sherry's team members were ready, literally and figuratively, to act their way into promoting safer practice. The team visited units and groups across the hospital and often used **Discovery & Action Dialogues** to learn about challenges specific to each unit, which they then used to generate "the material" for **Improv Prototyping**. For example, on a drug rehab unit, staff wanted to help patients with infections safely visit the communal kitchen. The team's dialogues yielded the plotline for a scene dubbed "Mr. Munchie" to highlight the issue and promote careful use of the kitchen facilities.

Another pair of Improv skits the team developed was called "Speaking Truth to Power" and came from its work with a group of second-year nursing

> *"Anything imposed on my staff will not work well. If it does not come from them, follow-through will suffer."*

students. The aim was to help student nurses remind others about safe practice, particularly when the person being reminded holds a more powerful position.

Sherry recalls the scenes: "We asked for volunteers and two students stepped up to do the acting. Along with a member of our core group, they acted out two scenes. Scene 1: A student nurse is in an isolation room with a patient when a physician enters without isolation gear on, carrying the patient chart. The physician is very overbearing and brushes off the student. Scene 2: A replay of the scene with the student nurse inviting the physician to step aside, away from the patient, and helping the physician get into the isolation gown." A lively group debrief followed the two scenes.

Three weeks later, a group of second-year students that had experienced the skits was doing part of their clinical rotation on Sherry's unit. A physiotherapist stopped Sherry in the hall and let her know how impressed she was that one of the students had stopped a physician who was entering an isolation room without the proper gear. Just like the Improv scene, the doctor was rushing into the room, carrying the patient chart, without donning a gown or gloves.

"I went to find the student," Sherry told us, "to let her know she was doing a fantastic job. Her name is Marisa."

"I might not have stopped him if I hadn't seen the Improv. I realized that it is everyone's responsibility to speak up to stop the transmission of superbugs."

When Sherry spoke with her, Marisa said, "I didn't even have to think about what I was going to say—it just came out. I might not have stopped him if I hadn't seen the Improv. I realized that it is everyone's responsibility to speak up to stop the transmission of superbugs."

The physician did not comply with her attempt to stop him from going into the room unprotected, but Marisa was not intimidated. "When it comes to safety," she told Sherry, "there should be no hierarchy. We should all do our part to protect ourselves and our patients. We shouldn't be less important because we are students."

The story spread through the hospital like wildfire.

Marisa in front of an isolation precautions room

Capturing everyone's imagination is central to making progress with superbug prevention. To succeed, everyone, from doctors to student nurses to room cleaners, has to change his or her habits and routines. Marisa inspired many others to "speak truth to power." Just as important, Marisa developed the real-life confidence to do the right thing to stop the transmission of superbugs.

Developing Competencies for Physician Education:
Diane Magrane

How to enable medical-school faculty to follow the lead of their students and nonphysician colleagues in undertaking a complex research project? When success requires that everyone on the research team discover what is working and together make changes, doctors have to follow and lead simultaneously. Here's how Liberating Structures helped to guide a multidisciplinary study of how medical students can better attend to the spiritual needs of patients.

Diane Magrane, MD, is the director of the International Center for Executive Leadership in Academics at Drexel University College of Medicine, where she works with physician leaders who are so smart and so successful, they sometimes have difficulty learning new behaviors. So she often turns to Liberating Structures to engage fellow academic leaders and lays each one out like a teacher's lesson plan. "Education cuts through the politics and the educator then becomes an inside advocate for new ideas," says Diane.

Diane Magrane was asked to facilitate a national conference to develop uncommon competencies and learning objectives for medical-student education. She agreed to the project on the condition that the group approach the task collaboratively, with an open mind for new insights from exploring how physicians might better attend to the spiritual needs of patients.

The people selected to work on the project were exceptionally diverse: the teams of participants represented eight different medical schools and included professors, palliative-care specialists, pastoral-care professionals, and a handful of students. So Diane chose a variety of Liberating Structures for the competency-development process, beginning with **Discovery & Action Dialogues (DAD)** weeks before the conference. She explains:

25/10

> *I had previously guided different groups through a process of designed competencies for medical-student training. We always used creative methods and interdisciplinary small-group discussions. As the facilitator, I ended up doing a lot of cataloguing and using my formal authority to move the project forward. Too often, participants advocated and jockeyed to protect their discipline. The process required a powerful mediator.*

I wanted this project to be different!

Diane introduced the **DADs** first with the project organizers and then with each team in a telephone conference. Each group conducted three or more **DADs** in academic and clinical settings and then contributed reports of their findings as source materials for the summit (see box).

Action Research with Discovery & Action Dialogue

In preparation for our conference, you are responsible for facilitating and collecting data from three **DADs**. A variety of settings is recommended: with medical students only; with a preselected mix of students, residents, RNs, MDs, and patients; with a mixed group on a hospital unit; and in an extreme setting in which attending to spiritual needs is MORE difficult (e.g., ICU).

Here are the dialogue questions:

1. How do you know when the spiritual needs of patients are being neglected?
2. How do YOU attend to your own spiritual needs and the spiritual needs of patients?
3. What prevents you from doing this or taking these actions all the time?
4. Is there a person or a unit/group that seems to be particularly successful at attending to spiritual needs? How do they do it?
5. Do you have any ideas?
6. What steps would start to bring these ideas to life? Any volunteers?
7. Who else needs to be involved?

"Participants learned how to suspend their assumptions and discover how much they could discover by using their natural curiosity."

"It was fascinating watching them learn how to suspend their assumptions about how spirituality shows up in clinical care and watching them discover how much they could discover by using their natural curiosity," Diane says.

The premeeting work took them to a different place than they would have been without those explorations. By using **DADs**, they discovered a much deeper and richer perspective on how spiritual needs were tended to under a wide range of situations and extreme conditions.

A surprise came when an unusual group of suspects emerged, Diane told us. *Medical students were a major source of insight. Whereas many of the clinicians felt encumbered by the crunch of time in clinical encounters, grousing that they did not have time to tend to spiritual needs in addition to the medical needs of patients, students on clinical rotations observed physicians doing just that—sharing difficult diagnoses with patients in a manner that respected spiritual needs. They could tell us how busy doctors were able to compassionately attend to spiritual needs while completing the rest of their technical duties.*

The work was extremely collaborative and open—and continued to produce unforeseen insights. For example, in the course of analyzing the **DADs** conversations, one unexpected competency the participants identified was tending not only to the spiritual needs of patients but also to those of practitioners and students.

What's more, Diane says, "they surprised themselves by integrating spirituality into their work at the conference." A striking example occurred in the final moments of the gathering:

*"In the closing circle, when we read out loud the top ten ideas from **25/10 Crowd Sourcing**, a deep silence followed. I recall discomfort until one of the members asked, "Can we read the others?" We proceeded to read and acknowledge every single idea. A deep respect for each individual had emerged. A community of belonging had formed."*

"A deep respect for each individual emerged. A community of belonging formed."

By the end of the conference, participants had developed medical-school competencies as well as methods of assessment and evaluation in six areas:

Knowledge: Acquire the foundational knowledge necessary in integrating spirituality in the care of patients.

Patient Care: Integrate spirituality into daily clinical practice.

Communication: Communicate with patients, family, and healthcare team about spiritual issues.

Compassionate Presence: Establish a compassionate presence with patients, family, and colleagues.

Professional Development: Incorporate spirituality into professional development.

Health Systems: Apply knowledge of health-care systems to advocate for spirituality in patient care.

Using more **DADs**, participants had identified the behaviors that would enable effective practice of each of the competencies. The behaviors, in turn, helped to generate evaluation of teaching and learning methods.

Reflecting on Learning and Leadership

"This is not a rule-driven process but something that emerges. Leaders see themselves in a new way."

Diane's goal is to help leaders feel confident in messy situations, believing more in themselves when the path forward is challenging. She is keenly aware that she does not solve problems for people. Rather, she helps them discover their own solutions: "I am there to catch them if they fall back."

Diane genuinely believes that if we dig deeply enough, we all can find more courage to lead, and teach. "I push people and myself to cognitive, spiritual, and emotional deepening," she says. "This is not a rule-driven process familiar to academics but rather something that emerges. Leaders see themselves in a new way. Emergence is not in their vocabulary."

In the case of Diane's competency-development conference, Liberating Structures helped to construct a research project that included many voices not often heard. The structure made it possible to integrate insights from unusual suspects (e.g., students, clergy) and on-the-ground experience in extreme settings. The group experienced powerful learning and generated very practical results for medical-student education.

Passing Montana Senate Bill 29:
Senator Lynda Bourque Moss

A legislative session seems an unlikely setting for giving away power to gain widespread support. That didn't stop senator Lynda Bourque Moss, who had inherited a very complicated bill to address driving under the influence of alcohol in her state. She chalks up her success in getting SB 29 passed to her use of Liberating Structures.

Montana state senator Lynda Bourque Moss is an artist with a master of fine arts degree. She brings an intuitive sensibility to her work in the legislature and in heading up a regional foundation. The community is her "palette." She believes that Liberating Structures give more shape and depth to how we relate, and she attributes the passage of SB 29 to the way Liberating Structures enabled including and engaging traditionally opposing voices in the DUI conversation.

It is exceptionally difficult to pass a bill that mandates new behavior, much less a bill that ignites the passions of industry and advocacy groups. Key constituent groups see the challenge from different perspectives, typically opposing ones. "Mandatory bills are seen as negative and can be killed by invoking 'too much government,'" Linda told us. "Plus, the liquor industry is very powerful. They can make or break legislation like this."

To get the process going on Montana Senate Bill 29: Responsible Alcohol Sales and Service Act, Lynda engaged the whole spectrum of concerned citizens and special-interest groups. She convened conversations with MADD (Mothers Against Drunk Driving), the gambling association, the taverns association, the restaurant association, convenience store owners, the Montana Highway Patrol, and the Department of Revenue, which oversees taxing and distribution of alcohol in Montana. Two Liberating Structures helped guide Lynda along the way to passage: **Appreciative Interviews** and **Min Specs**.

Lynda started with **Appreciative Interviews**. "Most legislation is grounded in existing law," she told us. "You amend by adding or deleting. For SB 29, nothing in the law was used as reference. Rather, I asked 'What do we need to do?' and 'What works now?'"

This line of questioning sparked engagement and unleashed a set of fresh perspectives.

Let It Happen, Don't Make It Happen

Each constituent group knew the DUI challenge inside out. Novel ideas on *what worked* to prevent alcohol-related tragedies came from their unique perspectives. The organizations selling alcohol were held liable for accidents. The people serving and selling alcohol lost needed jobs. MADD parents lost children and family members. State agencies picked up the pieces. Lynda tapped the experience and imagination of everyone at the table. She recalls, "Unlikely parties came together: all the amendments came from them, not me. I was more a facilitator than a law-MAKER."

The stories from the **Appreciative Interviews** also revealed **Min Specs** to Lynda: the must dos and must not dos for everyone to share responsibility for preventing DUIs.

First, she learned that training for servers and sellers must be mandatory, as should be personal fines and the threat of license revocation for the employer. This would reduce liability premiums and give the legislation teeth. Second, the requirements for servers must be reasonable, respectful, and flexible. For example, part-time workers needed their training certificates to be transferable as they changed jobs. Third, servers and sellers needed to learn how to truly say "no." Clearly, the core behaviors and social skills needed to do their job were not trivial, nor widely practiced.

In the last hour before the final vote, a threat popped up. All the work done to craft the bill could have been lost. Surprisingly, a group of Senate staffers who had not been directly involved in the process stepped forward with support. Why? Lynda suspects it had everything to do with the very inclusive approach used to create SB 29. This legislation was something new, unmistakably a product of all the constituents' voices.

"Unlikely parties came together. I was more a facilitator than a law-MAKER."

"The very inclusive approach used to create SB 29 made it unmistakably a product of all the constituents' voices."

Transcending a Top-Down, Command-and-Control Culture: Jon Velez

"When I became chief information officer, IT was known as the place you went to be told, 'You can't have that,'" Jonathan Velez told us. "Employees in the department were valued for doing what they were told and saying, 'Yes, sir.' There is a cultural legacy of top-down, command and control."

Jonathan Velez, MD, is chief information officer of Memorial Health System in Colorado Springs. He has joined with system CEO Larry McEvoy to shift the culture toward more interdependency and shared accountability everywhere in the organization.

Jon started working shoulder to shoulder with Memorial Health System CEO Larry McEvoy to transform the culture and create a more collaborative relationship-centered organization. Both Jon and Larry are MDs, trained as emergency-medicine physicians, so they appreciate the importance of trust, coordination, and autonomy among team members to accomplish goals quickly.

They also appreciate that the dominant command-and-control culture is a dragon with two heads. Hospitals are filled with experts who embrace control. It's not only the IT experts but also the busy nurses and doctors who can overuse command-and-control behaviors. For many of the challenges these groups handle, including and unleashing others is unnecessary. Whether it's solving certain technical IT problems or providing "simple" acute medical care, customers and patients don't need to be trusted partners to succeed.

Immersion Workshop to Turn Novices into Expert Contributors

Nonetheless, Jon and Larry have big ideas. Their strategy is to shift patterns in internal operations (for example, in information technology and finance) as well as to support a patient-centered Bedside Trust Initiative. With the goal of unleashing innovation novices to become expert contributors, everyone from top to bottom in the Memorial Health System IT department was invited to a Liberating Structures Immersion Workshop.

One hundred thirty members of the IT department (plus forty of their internal customers from the finance and clinical departments) spent three days

"To turn innovation novices into expert contributors, everyone was invited to a Liberating Structures Immersion Workshop."

"Staff meetings are now like magic because people contribute in ways they did not anticipate."

together, applying Liberating Structures methods to the challenges they care about most.

That workshop sparked a wide range of improvements, from advancing clinical transformation projects, through innovations like the Bedside Trust Initiative and physician partnerships, to redesigning the IT request process, to radically shifting how everyday meetings are conducted. "Staff meetings are now fun," Jon says. "It feels like magic because people contribute in ways they did not anticipate."

Jon and other users have incorporated their favorite Liberating Structures into their daily work. Jon regularly uses **1-2-4-All**, **Min Specs**, and **What, So What, Now What?** He reports, "Staff members moved from the assumption that 'my idea is not that important' to seeing that not only did 'my idea' add value but also others are thinking along the same lines. Once everyone believes their contribution matters, the team gets much smarter about solving complex challenges."

Mountains Beyond Mountains

Similar progress has been made in patches across the organization. However, it feels like there are mountains beyond mountains yet to climb. The legacy culture runs very deep: the unwanted dependent tendencies to wait for someone else to take responsibility, game the system, and blame managers for what is wrong linger. Jon and Larry want more interdependency and shared accountability everywhere in the department.

Even though Jon is doing his best to help employees to let go of overcontrol and practice more self-organization, old behaviors pop up. "The other day, two employees referred to themselves as 'peons,'" Jon told us. "I cringed." Clearly, some employees seem unable to believe that this cultural transformation is anything more than talk. "On the one hand, employees want to make more decisions. On the other hand, when invited to create an IT decision-making council—made up of nonmanagement employees and with the responsibility of making some important decisions—the response has been less than enthusiastic."

Not deterred, Jon keeps the focus on culture and behaviors. For example, a federal Medicare inspection turned into a big success. The visit had revealed a long list of tasks and fixes with a deadline to comply with confidentiality and safety regulations. The work was done in record time with few flaws. Jon asked the staff, "Why? How can we build on this success?"

Jon had his own answers in mind. Precisely four. He convened the team to deal with the question using **1-2-4-All**. Quickly, the answers expanded from four to eight. "Four of the key factors were not on my list," Jon told us. "I was thrilled, although that doesn't mean I liked everything I heard."

In the process, Jon and the team discovered a surprising paradox: their success in the Medicare inspection hinged on tapping elements of the old command-and-control culture. "They said it felt like we met in the war room," Jon shared. "The general laid out strategy and tactics to get all the tasks done. The chain of command helped us move quickly and accurately." A surprising paradox indeed.

The revelation left Jon wondering, "Does the organization need a break from working on interdependency, or do I need to push harder? It seems counterintuitive, but I am contemplating telling them to just do it. A **Wicked Question** indeed. Liberate yourselves now!"

"A Wicked Question emerged: how to invite and insist on liberation throughout the department?"

Paradox: Leaders Stepping Up While Stepping Back

Jon is transforming along with the IT department. Individually and collectively, they are shaping a way forward. His original idea about transformation is not as simple as stopping command and control and starting liberated self-organization. Rather, he is working with two opposing tendencies: control and letting go. Depending on the situation, comingling approaches can create robust and productive results.

"In some places, the culture seems to be stuck in a dependent rut," Jon muses. "You can tell a team about a better way to work together and even get agreement. What you don't always get is movement. In other words, I might need to dictate, 'Come on, we're moving out of the rut!' to get a team unstuck."

These paradoxical tendencies make it hard to know when to step up and when to step back. On the other hand, Jon can see clearly that members of his group are learning a new pattern for themselves. Now they have access to more than a single command-and-control structure to achieve results. A new culture that includes and transcends the old is coming into existence.

"Like a newborn colt, a new culture that transcends and includes the old is wobbling its way into existence."

PART FOUR
The Field Guide to Liberating Structures

Part Four contains your ready-to-use repertoire of thirty-three Liberating Structures.

For each structure here, we provide a step-by-step outline of what to do to put it into practice immediately plus a brief description of what to expect as a result, tips on successful use, and ideas for designing variations. Also included are examples of how managers, frontline workers, and facilitators have used each structure in different types of organizations and communities as well as information on sources and some suggestions for getting additional information or supporting materials.

"I can't understand why people are frightened of new ideas. I'm frightened of the old ones."
John Cage

How To Navigate The Field Guide

The information on all thirty-three Liberating Structures is displayed in the same format. Under its name in the main heading, there is a tagline that expresses its essential characteristic and an estimate of the approximate minimum time required to use the structure in a group setting.

We then describe each structure in a standard format that includes the following entries:

WHAT IS MADE POSSIBLE: A brief explanation of what you can accomplish

FIVE STRUCTURAL ELEMENTS—MIN SPECS: What to do and how to do it, step by step:

1. Structuring the invitation
2. How space is organized and materials needed
3. How participation is distributed
4. How groups are configured
5. Sequence of steps and time allocation

WHY? PURPOSES: Primary reasons for using this Liberating Structure

TIPS AND TRAPS: Useful advice for ensuring the best possible outcomes

RIFFS AND VARIATIONS: Alternatives or embellishments for you to try and ideas for designing others

EXAMPLES: A few actual applications to inspire you to find opportunities that exist in your context

ATTRIBUTION: Sources of inspiration or invention

COLLATERAL MATERIAL: Useful presentation materials and templates plus illustrations of Liberating Structures in action. Additional materials are available on the website: www.liberatingstructures.com

Before—and after—you use any Liberating Structure, we recommend that you read through its entire description. Obviously, it is necessary to read all the way through the step-by-step explanation of what to do before attempting to use a structure for the first time. It also never hurts to do a dry run, mentally or with a pilot group. After each experience using a Liberating Structure, take the time to reread the description and to reflect on what happened; it will greatly accelerate your learning, deepen your understanding, and spark ideas for creative variations and combinations (use **What, So What, Now What?**). Finally, recall that Part Two: Getting Started and Beyond is full of ideas and advice on how to put Liberating Structures to work in various settings, from a one-time meeting to large-scale organizational change initiatives.

However you decide to begin, remember that this Field Guide is not meant to be an instruction manual. The descriptions are brief synopses of essential points to remember: the minimum instructions you need to start using any of the Liberating Structures. For many of the structures, there are volumes of additional materials available on our own and others' websites and in books and articles. To dig deeper, start with the references here in Tips and Traps and Attributions and, at the end of the book, in the Learning Resources.

Finally, this Field Guide is a map, not the territory. The territory will be discovered through your lived experience with Liberating Structures. The map is simply designed to help you with designing a wide range of activities. The **Design Storyboards** Liberating Structure and Part Two: Getting Started and Beyond are good points of departure for your exploration. You may also find it useful to have Liberating Structures Design Cards handy for composing; see *http://liberatingstructures.com/cards*

Playfully Serious Icons

Every icon in the Field Guide was designed to illustrate the particular essence of each Liberating Structure. The fabulous artist Lesley Jacobs worked with us to create images that are playful but have a serious purpose: to become over time a form of visual shorthand that jogs the memory of users and signals what is coming without the need for explanation. The icons also provide you with symbols that you can use to simplify your planning and designing activities. Their deliberately playful style is intended to attract your attention and incite you to use them. Finally, the icons are a reminder that playfulness is positive energy that promotes participation in the lively search for answers that is unleashed by Liberating Structures.

One Liberating Structure can transform a meeting, a classroom, or a conversation. Using many of them together, on a regular basis, can transform an organization, a community, or a life.

Menu Of 33 Liberating Structures V 2.2

This menu represents version 2.2 of a growing collection of Liberating Structures. We recommend that you start with the simpler Liberating Structures in the left-hand column (e.g., **1-2-4-All**), build your experience, and then move to the more intricate ones in the next two columns. Some of the simpler Liberating Structures are used as building blocks for others. However, should some tagline in column three inspire you, all the information you need to start experimenting can be found here in the Field Guide.

Impromptu Networking
Focusing on People, Purpose & the Power of Loose Connections

 TRIZ
Designing a Perfectly Adverse System to Make Space for Innovation

 What, So What, Now What? W³
Reflecting on Your Progress and Making Adjustments-As-You-Go

 Conversation Café
Making Sense of and Forming Consensual Hunches about Challenges

 Appreciative Interviews
Discovering & Building On the Roots Causes of Success

 1-2-4-All
Conversing in Cycles: Self-Reflection, Pairs, & Small Groups

9 Whys
Becoming Clear About Purpose

15% Solutions
Noticing the Influence & Discretion You Have Now

Ecocycle
Engaging Groups in Growing and Sifting Their Portfolio of Activities

 Shift & Share
Spreading Good Ideas from the Grass Roots Up & the Fringe In

25-To-10 Crowd Sourcing
Vetting Powerful Ideas and Igniting Action

 Min Specs
Unleashing Innovation by Specifying Only "Must-do's" & "Must-not-do's"

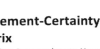 **Wise Crowds**
Tapping the "Wisdom of Crowds"

 **Wicked Questions**
Framing a Paradoxical Challenge That Engages Everyone's Imagination

 Purpose-To-Practice
Designing for Shared Ownership, Adaptability, and Resilience

 Improv Prototyping
Developing Inventive Solutions to Chronic Challenges

Agreement-Certainty Matrix
Matching Approaches to Your Different Types of Challenges

 What I Need From You
Surfacing Needs and Working Across Silos

 Heard, Seen, Respected
Practicing Deeper Listening and Empathy

 Social Network Webbing
Drawing Out Informal Connections & Adaptability

Design StoryBoards
Detailing Design Elements for Meetings & Innovation Efforts

 Open Space
Liberating Inherent Action & Leadership In Large Groups

 Discovery & Action Dialogue (DAD)
Discovering Solutions To Big Challenges In Plain Sight

 Integrated~Autonomy
Moving from *Either-Or* to *Both-And* Creative Solutions

 Generative Relationships
Understanding Patterns in Relationships that Create Surprising Value

 Critical Uncertainties
Preparing and Practicing Strategy-Making for Surprising-Yet-Plausible Futures

 User Experience Fishbowl
Sharing Insights Gained from Field Experience with a Larger Community

 Drawing Together
Drawing Out Insight that Precedes Logical Understanding

 Panarchy
Spreading Your Innovation or Good Idea At Many Levels Simultaneously

Troika Consulting
Guiding Your Next Steps with Colleagues

Celebrity Interview
Exploring Big Challenges with an Expert or Leader

Helping Heuristics
Practicing Progressive Methods for Helping Others and Asking for Help

Simple Ethnography
Making Field Observations of User Experience

1-2-4-All

Engage Everyone Simultaneously in Generating Questions, Ideas, and Suggestions (12 min.)

What is made possible? You can immediately include everyone regardless of how large the group is. You can generate better ideas and more of them faster than ever before. You can tap the know-how and imagination that is distributed widely in places not known in advance. Open, generative conversation unfolds. Ideas and solutions are sifted in rapid fashion. Most importantly, participants own the ideas, so follow-up and implementation is simplified. No buy-in strategies needed! Simple and elegant!

FIVE STRUCTURAL ELEMENTS—MIN SPECS

1. Structuring Invitation

- Ask a question in response to the presentation of an issue, or about a problem to resolve or a proposal put forward (e.g., What opportunities do YOU see for making progress on this challenge? How would you handle this situation? What ideas or actions do you recommend?)

2. How Space Is Arranged and Materials Needed

- Unlimited number of groups
- Space for participants to work face-to-face in pairs and foursomes
- Chairs and tables optional
- Paper for participants to record observations and insights

3. How Participation Is Distributed

- Everyone in the group is included (often not the facilitator)
- Everyone has an equal opportunity to contribute

4. How Groups Are Configured

- Start alone, then in pairs, then foursomes, and finally as a whole group

5. Sequence of Steps and Time Allocation

- Silent self-reflection by individuals on a shared challenge, framed as a question (e.g., What opportunities do YOU see for making progress on this challenge? How would you handle this situation? What ideas or actions do you recommend?) 1 min.

- Generate ideas in pairs, building on ideas from self-reflection. 2 min.
- Share and develop ideas from your pair in foursomes (notice similarities and differences). 4 min.
- Ask, "What is one idea that stood out in your conversation?" Each group shares one important idea with all (repeat cycle as needed). 5 min.

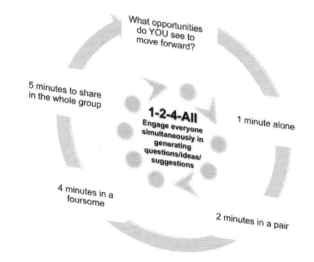

WHY? PURPOSES

- Engage every individual in searching for answers
- Avoid overhelping and the overcontrol-dependency vicious cycle
- Create safe spaces for expression, diminish power differentials
- Express "silent" conversations and expand diversity of inputs
- Enrich quality of observations and insights before expression
- Build naturally toward consensus or shared understanding

TIPS AND TRAPS

- Firmly facilitate quiet self-reflection before paired conversations
- Ask everyone to jot down their ideas during the silent reflection
- Use bells for announcing transitions
- Stick to precise timing, do another round if needed
- In a large group during "All," limit the number of shared ideas to three or four
- In a large group, use a facilitator or harvester to record output not shared

- Invite each group to share one insight but not to repeat insights already shared
- Separate and protect generation of ideas from the whole group discussion
- Defer judgment; make ideas visual; go wild!
- When you hit a plateau, jump to another form of expression (e.g., Improv, sketching, stories)
- Maintain the rule of one conversation at a time in the whole group
- Do a second round if you did not go deep enough!

RIFFS AND VARIATIONS

- Graphically record insights as they emerge from groups
- Use Post-it notes in Rounds 2 and 3
- Link ideas that emerge to Design Storyboards, Improv Prototyping, Ecocycle Planning
- Go from groups of 4 to groups of 8 with consensus in mind. Colleague Liz Rykert calls this Octopus!

*Above: **1-2-4-All** generates lively engagement in Puerto Rico*

EXAMPLES

- Use after a speech or presentation, when it is important to get rich feedback (questions, comments, and ideas), instead of asking the audience, "Any questions?"

- A group of managers used two rounds of 1-2-4-All to redesign their less-than-stimulating weekly meeting.
- For a spontaneous conversation that starts after the topic of a meeting has been announced
- For a group that has been convened to address a problem or an innovation opportunity
- For unlocking a discussion that has become dysfunctional or stuck
- In place of a leader "telling" people what to think and do (often unintentionally)
- For a group that tends to be excessively influenced by its leader
- Read Craig Yeatman's story in Part Three: Stories from the Field about using **1-2-4-All** to help manage a merger decision, "Inclusive High-Stakes Decision Making Made Easy."

ATTRIBUTION

Liberating Structure developed by Henri Lipmanowicz and Keith McCandless

Above: multiple pairs "parallel processing" a shared challenge in Seattle

Impromptu Networking

Rapidly Share Challenges and Expectations, Build New Connections (20 min.)

What is made possible? You can tap a deep well of curiosity and talent by helping a group focus attention on problems they want to solve. A productive pattern of engagement is established if used at the beginning of a working session. Loose yet powerful connections are formed in 20 minutes by asking engaging questions. Everyone contributes to shaping the work, noticing patterns together, and discovering local solutions.

FIVE STRUCTURAL ELEMENTS—MIN SPECS

1. Structuring Invitation

- Ask, "What big challenge do you bring to this gathering? What do you hope to get from and give this group or community?"

2. How Space Is Arranged and Materials Needed

- Open space without obstructions so participants can stand in pairs and mill about to find partners

3. How Participation Is Distributed

- Everybody at once with the same amount of time (no limit on group size)
- Everyone has an equal opportunity to contribute

4. How Groups Are Configured

- Pairs
- Invite people to find strangers or colleagues in groups/functions different from their own

5. Sequence of Steps and Time Allocation

- In each round, 2 minutes per person to answer the questions. 4-5 min. per round
- Three rounds

WHY? PURPOSES

- Initiate participation immediately for everyone provided the questions are engaging

- Attract deeper engagement around challenges
- Invite stories to deepen as they are repeated
- Help shy people warm up
- Affirm individual contributions to solutions
- Emphasize the power of loose and new connections
- Suggest that little things can make a big difference

TIPS AND TRAPS

- Use one challenge question and one give-and-take question
- Ask questions that invite participants to shape the direction of their work together
- Use Impromptu Networking before you begin meetings and conferences
- Use bells (e.g., tingsha) to help you shift participants from first, to second, to third rounds
- Ask questions that are open-ended but not too broad
- Invite serious play
- Have three rounds, not one or two
- If you choose to share output, do it carefully and preserve confidentiality

RIFFS AND VARIATIONS

- Play with different questions: What problem are you trying to solve? What challenge lingers from our last meeting? What hunch are you trying to confirm?
- Taking a group outside a meeting room increases the fun factor
- Link to **Social Network Webbing**
- Invite participants to make a simple plan to follow up via **15% Solutions**
- Make it slower or faster depending on your schedule

*Above: Al fresco **Impromptu Networking** in Colorado*

EXAMPLES

- For sparking deeper connections on the first day of class, college professors have asked their students, "Why did you choose to attend this class? What do you want to learn from and offer to members of this class?"
- For jump-starting a cross-functional, interdisciplinary learning session, Tim Jaasko-Fisher used **Impromptu Networking** with judges, lawyers, clerks, and social workers. See "Fixing a Broken Child Welfare System" in Part Three: Stories from the Field.
- For connecting far-flung innovators and disparate prototypes among members of the Innovation Learning Network. See "Inventing Future Health-Care Practice" in Part Three: Stories from the Field.

ATTRIBUTION

Liberating Structure developed by Henri Lipmanowicz and Keith McCandless. Inspired by June Holley, network weaver.

Nine Whys

Make the Purpose of Your Work Together Clear (20 min.)

What is made possible? With breathtaking simplicity, you can rapidly clarify for individuals and a group what is essentially important in their work. You can quickly reveal when a compelling purpose is missing in a gathering and avoid moving forward without clarity. When a group discovers an unambiguous shared purpose, more freedom and more responsibility are unleashed. You have laid the foundation for spreading and scaling innovations with fidelity.

"If you want to build a ship, don't drum up people to collect wood and don't assign them tasks and work, but rather teach them to long for the endless immensity of the sea." Antoine de Saint-Exupery

FIVE STRUCTURAL ELEMENTS—MIN SPECS

1. Structuring Invitation

- Ask, "What do you do when working on _____ (the subject matter or challenge at hand)? Please make a short list of activities." Then ask, "Why is that important to you?" Keep asking, "Why? Why? Why?" up to nine times or until participants can go no deeper because they have reached the fundamental purpose for this work.

2. How Space Is Arranged and Materials Needed

- Unlimited number of groups
- Chairs for people to sit comfortably face-to-face; no tables or equipment needed.

3. How Participation Is Distributed

- Everyone has an equal opportunity to participate and contribute

4. How Groups Are Configured

- First pairs, then groups of four, then the whole group (**2-4-All**)

5. Sequence of Steps and Time Allocation

- Each person in a pair is interviewed by his or her partner for 5 minutes. Starting with "What do you do when working on _____?" the interviewer gently seeks a deeper answer by repeating the query: "Why is that important to you?" Switch roles after 5 minutes. 10 min.
- Each pair shares the experience and insights with another pair in a foursome. 5 min.

- Invite the whole group to reflect by asking, "How do our purposes influence the next steps we take?" 5 min.

WHY? PURPOSES

- Discover what is truly important for the group members
- Lay the groundwork for the design that will be employed
- Ignite organizational momentum through the stories that emerge
- Provide a basis for progress evaluation
- Generate criteria for deciding who will be included

 Powerful Purpose
A powerful purpose attracts participation and has two essential attributes.

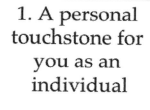

| 1. A personal touchstone for you as an individual | 2. Fundamental justification for the existence of your work to the larger community |

TIPS AND TRAPS

- Create a safe and welcoming space; avoid judgments
- Keep going! Dig deep with compassion. Vary the ways of asking "why?" For example, ask, "If last night, while you slept, your dream came true, what would be different?"
- Make sure the question asked is, "Why is it important to YOU?" (meaning not THE amorphous organization or system but you personally)
- Share the variety of responses and reflect on differences among group members. What common purpose emerges?
- If someone gets stuck ask, "Does a story come to mind?"
- Maintain confidentiality when very personal stories are shared

- Make clarifying purpose with **Nine Whys** a routine practice in your group

RIFFS AND VARIATIONS

- Ask the small groups whether "a fundamental justification for committing time and money to the work" emerged in the conversation. A clear personal purpose plus a community justification can quickly fuel the spread of an initiative. Work toward a single sentence that powerfully justifies the group's work to others: "We exist to...!"
- In a business context, ask, "Why would people spend their money with you? Why would leaders want you to operate your business in their country?"
- Add 10 *how* questions after you have clarity around why (it becomes MUCH easier).
- A good purpose is never closed. Make it dynamically incomplete by inviting everyone to make contributions and mutually shape understanding of the deepest need for your work.
- Record answers on Post-it notes, number them, and stick on a flip chart. You can arrange the answers in a triangle: broad answers on the top and detailed answers on the bottom. Compare and debrief.
- Ask, "Why is that important to your community?" "Why? Why? Why?..."
- Use the chat function during a webinar to start formulating a purpose statement: participants reflect on the Nine Whys questions, sharing their ideas in the chat box.
- Link to **Purpose-To-Practice; Generative Relationships; Wise Crowds; What, So What, Now What?** and many other Liberating Structures.

EXAMPLES

- For crafting a compelling shared purpose to launch a collaborative research organization. The Quality Commons, a health-service research network composed of representatives from seven health systems across the United States, used **Nine Whys** as one step in the **Purpose-To-Practice** Liberating Structure.
- For the beginning of any coaching session, including **Troika Consulting** or **Wise Crowds**.

- For clarifying the purpose behind the launch of a new product.
- For anchoring each element of a **Design Storyboard** by asking, "Why is this activity or element important to you? What does it add to the flow of exchanges among participants?"
- For you as an individual to clarify your personal purpose

ATTRIBUTION

Liberating Structure developed by Henri Lipmanowicz and Keith McCandless. Inspired by Geoff Bellman, author and consultant.

COLLATERAL MATERIALS

Below: presentation materials we use to introduce Nine Whys

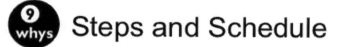

Steps and Schedule

1. Ask your partner, "When working on _____ [the challenge at hand], what do you do?" Make a short activities list. **1 minute**
2. Ask "why" questions until you make a discovery about your partner's bedrock purpose. **5 minutes**
   - Why is it important to you?
   - First answer, "_____...." Hmmm, why is that important to you?
   - Second answer, "_____...." OK, if your dream came true last night, what would be different today?
   - Keep asking, "Why... why... why...."
   - Record a brief statement
3. Switch roles. Repeat steps 1-3.
4. Move to a group of four or six, discussing similarities and differences. Use discretion in sharing your partner's purpose. **5 minutes**
5. In the whole group, share exciting discoveries. Make note if a group Purpose materializes! **4 minutes**

Wicked Questions

Articulate the Paradoxical Challenges That a Group Must Confront to Succeed (25 min.)

"How wonderful that we have met with a paradox. Now we have some hope of making progress." Niels Bohr

What is made possible? You can spark innovative action while diminishing "yes, but…" and "either-or" thinking. **Wicked Questions** engage everyone in sharper strategic thinking by revealing entangled challenges and possibilities that are not intuitively obvious. They bring to light paradoxical-yet-complementary forces that are constantly influencing behaviors and that are particularly important during change efforts. **Wicked Questions** make it possible to expose safely the tension between espoused strategies and on-the-ground circumstances and to discover the valuable strategies that lie deeply hidden in paradoxical waters.

FIVE STRUCTURAL ELEMENTS—MIN SPECS

1. Structuring Invitation
- Ask, "What opposing-yet-complementary strategies do we need to pursue simultaneously in order to be successful?"

2. How Space Is Arranged and Materials Needed
- Groups of 4 to 6 chairs with or without small round tables
- Paper for recording

3. How Participation Is Distributed
- Everyone involved in the work or topic is included
- Everyone has an equal opportunity to contribute

4. How Groups Are Configured
- Individually
- Small groups (6 people or smaller)
- Whole group

5. Sequence of Steps and Time Allocation
- Introduce the concept of **Wicked Questions** and paradox. Illustrate with a couple of examples of **Wicked Questions**. Give the following template, "How is it that we are … and we are … simultaneously?" as the sentence to complete by inserting the two opposite strategies that are at play. 5 min.

- First alone then in small groups, each participant generates pairs of opposites or paradoxes at play in his or her work using the **Wicked Question** format. 5 min.
- Each group selects its most impactful and wicked Wicked Question. All selected Wicked Questions are shared with the whole group. 5 min.
- Whole group picks out the most powerful ones and further refines the Wicked Questions. 10 min.

WHY? PURPOSES

- Describe the messy reality of the situation while engaging collective imagination
- Develop innovative strategies to move forward
- Avoid wild or "bipolar" swings in policy and action
- Evaluate decisions: Are we advancing one side or the other or attending to both?
- Ignite creative tension, promoting more freedom and accountability as the discovery process unfolds

TIPS AND TRAPS

- Make sure that participants express both sides of the paradox in an appreciative form: "How is it that we are _____ and we are _____ simultaneously?" and not in opposition of each other
- Use a variety of examples to make the paradoxical attributes accessible
- Work in quick cycles, failing forward as you make the questions perfectly wicked
- Avoid nasty questions that appoint blame or are unbalanced on one side. Here is an example of a nasty question: "How can we focus on our customers when we are forced to spend more and more time on the headquarters' bureaucracy?"
- Avoid data questions that can be answered with more analysis
- Invite participants to include others in making their questions more wicked
- Draw on field experience; ask, "When have you noticed these two things to be true at the same time?"
- There are no quick fixes to Wicked Questions and you may need to return to the challenge periodically with additional rounds of Wicked Questions

Wicked Questions engage everyone in sharper strategic thinking by revealing entangled challenges and possibilities that are not intuitively obvious.

- Often a handful of people are very skilled at generating Wicked Questions: let them shine and inspire the rest of the group!

RIFFS AND VARIATIONS

- Use **Wicked Questions** to evaluate and launch **Improv Prototyping, Ecocycle**, and **25/10 Crowd Sourcing**
- When you have a strong Wicked Question, don't stop there! Follow with **15% Solutions** and **1-2-4-All** to generate and sift ideas. Making progress on any one Wicked Question can shift what is possible.
- Learn more from Brenda Zimmerman in *Edgeware* and www.change-ability.ca/Change-Ability.html

EXAMPLES

- For parenting advice: "How is it that you are raising your children to be very loyal/attached to the family and very independent individuals simultaneously?"
- For helping leaders discover how to include everyone in stopping infections: "As infection-control leaders, how is that you have stepped up and stepped back to help a unit take more ownership of prevention practices?"
- For managing large global operations: "How is that we are always and never the same... an organization with a singular global identity and we are uniquely adapted to each local setting? How is it that we are integrated and autonomous?"
- For a functional department, such as HR, finance, legal, etc., to bring to light the Wicked Questions that capture the essence of the function in the context of the department's organization
- For surfacing personal Wicked Questions, for instance, with respect to one's relationship to one other person or in connection to a personal challenge. For instance, "How is it that I am simultaneously dedicated to my work and being fully present for my family?"

*Above: Developing **Wicked Questions** in Madrid*

ATTRIBUTION

Liberating Structure developed by Henri Lipmanowicz and Keith McCandless. Inspired by professors Brenda Zimmerman (see *Edgeware*) and Scott Kelso (see *The Complementary Nature*).

Appreciative Interviews (AI)

Discovering and Building on the Root Causes of Success (60 min.)

What is made possible? In less than one hour, a group of any size can generate the list of conditions that are essential for its success. You can liberate spontaneous momentum and insights for positive change from within the organization as "hidden" success stories are revealed. Positive movement is sparked by the search for what works now and by uncovering the root causes that make success possible. Groups are energized while sharing their success stories instead of the usual depressing talk about problems. Stories from the field offer social proof of local solutions, promising prototypes, and spread innovations while providing data for recognizing success patterns. You can overcome the tendency of organizations to underinvest in social supports that generate success while overemphasizing financial support, time, and technical assistance.

FIVE STRUCTURAL ELEMENTS—MIN SPECS

1. Structuring Invitation

- Ask, "Please tell a story about a time when you worked on a challenge with others and you are proud of what you accomplished. What is the story and what made the success possible? Pair up preferably with someone you don't know well."

2. How Space Is Arranged and Materials Needed

- Unlimited number of groups
- Chairs for people to sit in pairs face-to-face; no tables needed.
- Paper for participants to take notes
- Flip chart to record the stories and assets/conditions

3. How Participation Is Distributed

- Everyone is included
- Everyone has equal time and opportunity to contribute

4. How Groups Are Configured

- First pairs, then groups of 4.
- Encourage groups to be diverse

5. Sequence of Steps and Time Allocation

- Describe the sequence of steps and specify a theme or what kind of story participants are expected to tell. 3 min.
- In pairs, participants take turns conducting an interview and telling a success story, paying attention to what made the success possible. 7–10 min. each; 15–20 min. total.
- In groups of 4, each person retells the story of his or her pair partner. Ask participants to listen for patterns in conditions/assets supporting success and to make note of them. 15 min. for groups of 4.
- Collect insights and patterns for the whole group to see on a flip chart. Summarize if needed. 10-15 min.
- Ask, "How are we investing in the assets and conditions that foster success?" and "What opportunities do you see to do more?" Use **1-2-4-All** to discuss the questions. 10 min.

WHY? PURPOSES

- Generate constructive energy by starting on a positive note.
- Capture and spread tacit knowledge about successful field experience.
- Reveal the path for achieving success for an entire group simultaneously
- By expecting positive behaviors, you can bring them forth (Pygmalion effect)
- Spark peer-to-peer learning, mutual respect, and community building.
- Give permission to explore complex or messy challenges
- Create a new exciting group narrative, e.g., "how we are making order out of chaos!"
- Repeating interviews in rapid cycles may point to *positively deviant* local innovations

TIPS AND TRAPS

- Flip malaise and negative themes to "When is it that we have succeeded, even in a modest way?"
- Start with, "Tell me a story about a time when...."
- Ask people to give a title to their partner's story
- Invite additional paired interviews before building up to patterns

- Invite participants to notice when they form a judgment (about what is right or wrong) or an idea about how they can help, then to "let it go"
- Make the stories and patterns visible to everyone
- Learn more from Appreciative Inquiry practitioners at http://appreciativeinquiry.case.edu/

RIFFS AND VARIATIONS

- Graphically record story titles and conditions/assets on a large wall tapestry
- Write up and publicize a few of the most inspiring stories
- Draw out stories that help participants make a leap of understanding from a small example of behavior change to a broad change in values or a shift in resource allocation (or both!). Give participants an example.
- Track how the stories start to fill in and bring life to the group's vision
- Groups of eight instead of four are an option
- Follow with **Min Specs,** exploring the must dos and must not dos required for future success

Below: an **Appreciative Interview** under way in Peru

EXAMPLES

- For bringing customer focus to life with "stories when you had a creative and positive interaction with a customer"

- For revising college courses with "stories when a course or learning experience had a profound influence on your life"
- For repairing a relationship between a patient and a doctor with "stories when you were able to accept openly responsibility for making a medical error"
- For building trust and morale in an NGO with "stories when you experienced here in the office the esprit de corps of work in the field. What made that possible?"
- For looking beyond the launch of a transformation initiative with "stories of first successes in the field that can guide our strategy for the next two years"

ATTRIBUTION

Liberating Structure developed by Henri Lipmanowicz and Keith McCandless. Inspired by and adapted from professor David Cooperrider, Case Western Reserve University, and consultant Dr. Tony Suchman.

COLLATERAL MATERIALS

 Interviewing Tips

- Sit face-to-face and knee-to-knee for the interview
- Ask about the context
  - When, Where, Who, How
- DO NOT share your own experience
- Collect details of the journey:
  - Status quo, barriers, action, surprises, reversals, discoveries
- Try to find a moment that sums up the drama and the deeper meaning
- If inspired, offer your storyteller an engaging title for their story
- Listen carefully so you can retell the highlights

*Above: **Appreciative Interview** wall tapestry illustrating the assets and conditions that support success in the stories*

TRIZ

Stop Counterproductive Activities and Behaviors to Make Space for Innovation (35 min.)

What is made possible? You can clear space for innovation by helping a group let go of what it knows (but rarely admits) limits its success and by inviting creative destruction. **TRIZ** makes it possible to challenge sacred cows safely and encourages heretical thinking. The question *"What must we **stop doing** to make progress on our deepest purpose?"* induces seriously fun yet very courageous conversations. Since laughter often erupts, issues that are otherwise taboo get a chance to be aired and confronted. With creative destruction come opportunities for renewal as local action and innovation rush in to fill the vacuum. Whoosh!

"Every act of creation is first an act of destruction." Pablo Picasso

FIVE STRUCTURAL ELEMENTS—MIN SPECS

1. Structuring Invitation

- In this three-step process, ask: 1. "Make a list of all you can do to make sure that you achieve the worst result imaginable with respect to your top strategy or objective."

  2. "Go down this list item by item and ask yourselves, 'Is there anything that we are currently doing that in any way, shape, or form resembles this item?' Be brutally honest to make a second list of all your counterproductive activities/programs/procedures." 3. "Go through the items on your second list and decide what first steps will help you stop what you know creates undesirable results?"

2. How Space Is Arranged and Materials Needed

- Unlimited number of small groups of 4 to 7 chairs, with or without small tables
- Paper for participants to record

3. How Participation Is Distributed

- Everybody involved in the work is included
- Everyone has an equal opportunity to contribute

4. How Groups Are Configured

- Groups with 4 to 7 participants
- Established teams or mixed groups

5. Sequence of Steps and Time Allocation

- After introduction, three segments, 10 minutes for each segment
- Introduce the idea of **TRIZ** and identify an unwanted result. If needed, have the groups brainstorm and pick the most unwanted result. 5 min.
- Each group uses **1-2-4-All** to make a first list of all it can do to make sure that it achieves this most unwanted result. 10 min.
- Each group uses **1-2-4-All** to make a second list of all that it is currently doing that resembles items on their first list. 10 min.
- Each group uses **1-2-4-All** to determine for each item on its second list what first steps will help it stop this unwanted activity/program/procedure. 10 min.

WHY? PURPOSES

- Make it possible to speak the unspeakable and get skeletons out of the closet
- Make space for innovation
- Lay the ground for creative destruction by doing the hard work in a fun way
- **TRIZ** may be used before or in place of visioning sessions
- Build trust by acting all together to remove barriers

TIPS AND TRAPS

- Enter into **TRIZ** with a spirit of serious fun
- Don't accept ideas for doing something new or additional: be sure suggestions are about stopping activities or behaviors, not about starting new things. It is worth the wait.
- Begin with a VERY unwanted result, quickly confirm your suggestion with the group
- Check in with groups that are laughing hard or look confused
- Take time for groups to identify similarities to what they are doing now and explore how this is harmful
- Include the people that will be involved in stopping the activities that come out and ask, "Who else needs to be included?"
- Make real decisions about what will be stopped (number your decisions 1,2,3...) in the form of "I will stop" and "we will stop."

RIFFS AND VARIATIONS

- Go deeper with a second or third round to refine or deepen understanding of unwanted results.
- Link these results (creative destruction) to a broad review of activities via **Ecocycle Planning.**
- Share action steps: then go deeper and string together with **Troika Consulting, Wise Crowds,** or **Open Space.**

EXAMPLES

- For reducing harm to patients experiencing safety lapses (e.g., wrong-side surgery, patient falls, medication errors, iatrogenic infections) with cross-functional groups: "How can we make sure we always operate on the wrong side?"
- For helping institutional leaders notice how it is they inadvertently exclude diverse voices: "How can we devise policies and practices that only work for a select few?"
- For IT professionals: "How can we make sure we build an IT system that no one will want to use?"
- For leadership groups: "How can we make sure we keep doing the same things with the same people while asking for different results?"

ATTRIBUTION

Liberating Structure developed by Henri Lipmanowicz and Keith McCandless. Inspired by the eponymous Russian engineering approach.

COLLATERAL MATERIAL

*Below: presentation materials for introducing **TRIZ***

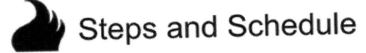

Steps and Schedule

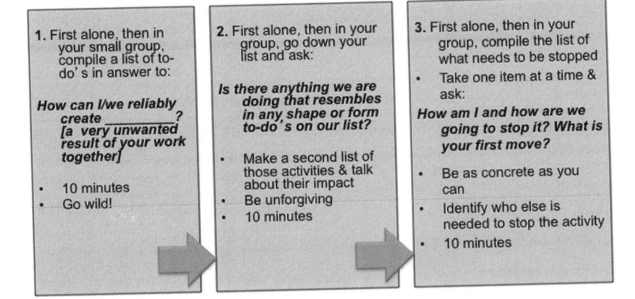

1. First alone, then in your small group, compile a list of to-do's in answer to:

***How can I/we reliably create _____?
[a very unwanted result of your work together]***

- 10 minutes
- Go wild!

2. First alone, then in your group, go down your list and ask:

Is there anything we are doing that resembles in any shape or form to-do's on our list?

- Make a second list of those activities & talk about their impact
- Be unforgiving
- 10 minutes

3. First alone, then in your group, compile the list of what needs to be stopped

- Take one item at a time & ask:

How am I and how are we going to stop it? What is your first move?

- Be as concrete as you can
- Identify who else is needed to stop the activity
- 10 minutes

15% Solutions

Discover and Focus on What Each Person Has the Freedom and Resources to Do Now (20 min.)

What is made possible? You can reveal the actions, however small, that everyone can do immediately. At a minimum, these will create momentum, and that may make a BIG difference. **15% Solutions** show that there is no reason to wait around, feel powerless, or fearful. They help people pick it up a level. They get individuals and the group to focus on what is within their discretion instead of what they cannot change. With a very simple question, you can flip the conversation to what can be done and find solutions to big problems that are often distributed widely in places not known in advance. Shifting a few grains of sand may trigger a landslide and change the whole landscape.

"You cannot cross the sea merely by standing and staring at the water." R. Tagore

FIVE STRUCTURAL ELEMENTS—MIN SPECS

1. Structuring Invitation

- In connection with their personal challenge or their group's challenge, ask, "What is your 15 percent? Where do you have discretion and freedom to act? What can you do without more resources or authority?"

2. How Space Is Arranged and Materials Needed

- Unlimited number of groups.
- Chairs for people to sit in groups of 2-4; no tables required.

3. How Participation Is Distributed

- Everyone is included
- Everyone has an equal opportunity to contribute

4. How Groups Are Configured

- First alone
- Then in pairs or small groups

5. Sequence of Steps and Time Allocation

- First alone, each person generates his or her own list of 15% Solutions. 5 min.
- Individuals share their ideas with a small group (2 to 4 members). 3 min. per person and one person at a time

- Group members provide a consultation to one another (asking clarifying questions and offering advice). 5 to 7 min. per person and one person at a time

WHY? PURPOSES

- Move away from blockage, negativism, and powerlessness
- Have people discover their individual and collective power
- Reveal bottom-up solutions
- Share actionable ideas and help one another
- Build trust
- Remember unused capacity and resources (15 percent is always there for the taking)
- Reduce waste
- Close the knowing-doing gap

TIPS AND TRAPS

- Check each item to assure that it is within the discretion of the individual
- Be ready for BIG things to emerge via the butterfly effect
- Reinventing the wheel is OK
- Each 15% Solution adds to understanding of what is possible
- Clear, common purpose and boundaries will generate coherence among many 15% Solutions
- Make it a routine to ask for 15% Solutions in meetings (15% Solutions are otherwise commonly unnoticed and overlooked)
- While introducing the idea, tell a story about a small change made by an individual that sparked a big result
- Learn more from professor Gareth Morgan, who has popularized the concept at www.imaginiz.com/index.html under the tab Provocative Ideas

RIFFS AND VARIATIONS

- Natural fit with **Troika Consulting, Wise Crowds, Open Space, Helping Heuristics,** and **Integrated~Autonomy**
- Returning to a group, you can ask, "What have you done with your 15 percent lately?"

EXAMPLES

- For any problem-solving or planning activity in which you want individuals to take initiative
- For inclusion in the conveners report in **Open Space** sessions
- For any challenge that requires many people to change for success to emerge
- For generating small "chunks" of success that can be combined into a simple prototype that is easy and cheap to test (low-fidelity prototype)

ATTRIBUTION

Liberating Structure developed by Henri Lipmanowicz and Keith McCandless. Inspired by professor Gareth Morgan.

COLLATERAL MATERIAL

*Below: presentation materials for introducing **15% Solutions***

15% **Insights**

- Always there for the asking (and taking)
- Most unused or unnoticed source of influence
- BIG things may emerge via the Butterfly effect
- Reinventing the wheel is OK
- Each 15% Solution will add to your understanding of what is possible
- Clear, common purpose and boundaries generate coherence among many small solutions

Troika Consulting

Get Practical and Imaginative Help from Colleagues Immediately (30 min.)

What is made possible? You can help people gain insight on issues they face and unleash local wisdom for addressing them. In quick round-robin "consultations," individuals ask for help and get advice immediately from two others. Peer-to-peer coaching helps with discovering everyday solutions, revealing patterns, and refining prototypes. This is a simple and effective way to extend coaching support for individuals beyond formal reporting relationships. **Troika Consulting** is always there for the asking for any individual who wishes to get help from colleagues or friends.

"To listen is very hard, because it asks of us so much interior stability that we no longer need to prove ourselves by speeches, arguments, statements or declarations. True listeners no longer have an inner need to make their presence known. They are free to receive, welcome, to accept." Henri Nouwen

FIVE STRUCTURAL ELEMENTS—MIN SPECS

1. Structuring Invitation

- Invite the group to explore the questions "What is your challenge?" and "What kind of help do you need?"

2. How Space Is Arranged and Materials Needed

- Any number of small groups of 3 chairs, knee-to-knee seating preferred. No table!

3. How Participation Is Distributed

- In each round, one participant is the "client," the others "consultants"
- Everyone has an equal opportunity to receive and give coaching

4. How Groups Are Configured

- Groups of 3
- People with diverse backgrounds and perspectives are most helpful

5. Sequence of Steps and Time Allocation

- Invite participants to reflect on the consulting question (the challenge and the help needed) they plan to ask when they are the clients. 1 min.
- Groups have first client share his or her question. 1-2 min.
- Consultants ask the client clarifying questions. 1-2 min.

- Client turns around with his or her back facing the consultants
- Together, the consultants generate ideas, suggestions, coaching advice. 4-5 min.
- Client turns around and shares what was most valuable about the experience. 1-2 min.
- Groups switch to next person and repeat steps.

WHY? PURPOSES

- Refine skills in asking for help
- Learn to formulate problems and challenges clearly
- Refine listening and consulting skills
- Develop ability to work across disciplines and functional silos
- Build trust within a group through mutual support
- Build capacity to self-organize
- Create conditions for unimagined solutions to emerge

TIPS AND TRAPS

- Invite participants to form groups with mixed roles/functions
- Suggest that participants critique themselves when they fall into traps (e.g., like jumping to conclusions)
- Have the participants try to notice the pattern of support offered. The ideal is to respectfully provoke by telling the client "what you see that you think they do not see"
- Tell participants to take risks while maintaining empathy
- If the first round yields coaching that is not good enough, do a second round
- Beware that two rounds of 10 minutes per client is more effective than one round of 20 minutes per client.
- Keep the spaces safe: if you share anything, do it judiciously
- Questions that spark self-understanding or self-correction may be more powerful than advice about what to do
- Tell clients to try and stay focused on self-reflection by asking, "What is happening here? How am I experiencing what is happening?"
- Make **Troika Consulting** routine in meetings and conferences

RIFFS AND VARIATIONS

- Meld with **15% Solutions**: each client shares a 15% Solution, asking for coaching
- Inviting the client to turn around and sit facing away from his or her consultants once the question has been shared and clarified deepens curiosity, listening, empathy, and risk taking for all. The alternative of not turning around is an option.
- Restrict the coaching to generating only questions to clarify the challenge: no advice giving (aka Q-Storming)
- String together with **Helping Heuristics; Heard, Seen, Respected; Nine Whys**

EXAMPLES

- For the beginning or end of staff meetings
- After a presentation, for giving participants time to formulate and sift next steps
- For students to help one another and to promote peer-to-peer learning
- In the midst of conferences and large-group meetings
- As a self-initiated practice within a group

ATTRIBUTION

Liberating Structure developed by Henri Lipmanowicz and Keith McCandless.

COLLATERAL MATERIAL

*Below: presentation materials for introducing **Troika Consulting***

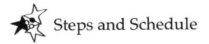 Steps and Schedule

1. Form groups of three
2. 7-10 minutes per person
3. Spend 1-2 minutes sharing your action ideas (including 15% Solutions)
4. Spend 5-7 minutes receiving feedback and advice from your consultants
5. For 1-2 minutes, thank your consultants
6. Switch to the next person…

What, So What, Now What? (W³)

Together, Look Back on Progress to Date and Decide What Adjustments Are Needed (45 min.)

What is made possible? You can help groups reflect on a shared experience in a way that builds understanding and spurs coordinated action while avoiding unproductive conflict. It is possible for every voice to be heard while simultaneously sifting for insights and shaping new direction. Progressing in stages makes this practical—from collecting facts about *What Happened* to making sense of these facts with *So What* and finally to what actions logically follow with *Now What*. The shared progression eliminates most of the misunderstandings that otherwise fuel disagreements about what to do. Voila!

FIVE STRUCTURAL ELEMENTS—MIN SPECS

1. Structuring Invitation

- After a shared experience, ask, "WHAT? What happened? What did you notice, what facts or observations stood out?" Then, after all the salient observations have been collected, ask, "SO WHAT? Why is that important? What patterns or conclusions are emerging? What hypotheses can you make?" Then, after the sense making is over, ask, "NOW WHAT? What actions make sense?"

2. How Space Is Arranged and Materials Needed

- Unlimited number of groups
- Chairs for people to sit in small groups of 5-7; small tables are optional
- Paper to make lists
- Flip chart may be needed with a large group to collect answers

3. How Participation Is Distributed

- Everyone is included
- Everyone has an equal opportunity to contribute at each table
- Small groups are more likely to give a voice to everyone if one person facilitates and keeps everybody working on one stage/question at a time.

4. How Groups Are Configured
- Individuals
- Groups of 5-7
- Whole group
- Groups can be established teams or mixed groups

5. Sequence of Steps and Time Allocation
- If needed, describe the sequence of steps and show the Ladder of Inference. If the group is 10–12 people or smaller, conduct the debrief with the whole group. Otherwise, break the group into small groups.
- First stage: WHAT? Individuals work 1 min. alone on "What happened? What did you notice, what facts or observations stood out?" then 2–7 min. in small group. 3–8 min. total.
- Salient facts from small groups are shared with the whole group and collected. 2–3 min.
- If needed, remind participants about what is included in the So What? question.
- Second stage: SO WHAT? People work 1 min alone on "Why is that important? What patterns or conclusions are emerging? What hypotheses can I/we make?" then 2–7 min. in small group. 3–8 min. total.
- Salient patterns, hypotheses, and conclusions from small groups are shared with the whole group and collected. 2–5 min.
- Third stage: NOW WHAT? Participants work 1 min. alone on "Now what? What actions make sense?" then 2–7 min. in small group. 3–8 min. total.
- Actions are shared with the whole group, discussed, and collected. Additional insights are invited. 2–10 min.

WHY? PURPOSES
- Build shared understanding of how people develop different perspectives, ideas, and rationales for actions and decisions
- Make sure that learning is generated from shared experiences: no feedback = no learning
- Avoid repeating the same mistakes or dysfunctions over and over
- Avoid arguments about actions based on lack of clarity about facts or their interpretation

- Eliminate the tendency to jump prematurely to action, leaving people behind
- Get all the data and observations out on the table first thing for everyone to start on the same page
- Honor the history and the novelty of what is unfolding
- Build trust and reduce fear by learning together at each step of a shared experience
- Make sense of complex challenges in a way that unleashes action
- Experience how questions are more powerful than answers because they invite active exploration

TIPS AND TRAPS

- Practice, practice, practice ... then **What, So What, Now What?** will feel like breathing
- Check with small groups to clarify appropriate answers to each question (some groups get confused about what fits in each category) and share examples of answers with the whole group if needed
- When sharing in the whole group, collect one important answer at a time from different small groups. Avoid long repetitive lists from a single group. Seek out unique answers that are full of meaning for the group's participants.
- Intervene quickly and clearly when someone jumps up the Ladder of Inference
- Don't jump over the So What? stage too quickly: it can be challenging for people to link observations directly to patterns, meanings, or conclusions. This is the most difficult of the three questions. Use the Ladder of Inference as a reminder of what steps are included in So What?
- Appreciate candid feedback and recognize it
- Build in time for the debrief—don't trivialize it, don't rush it
- Make it the norm to debrief with W^3, however quickly, at the end of everything

RIFFS AND VARIATIONS

- Insert a "What If? question, "What can we/should we try, test, or explore?" between So What? and Now What? to develop ideas for research or experiments.

- For the What? question, spend time sifting items that arise into three categories: facts with evidence, shared observations, and opinions
- For the So What? Question, sift items into patterns, conclusions, hypotheses/educated guesses, beliefs
- Invite a small group of volunteers to debrief in front of the whole room. People with strong reactions and diverse roles should be invited to join in.

EXAMPLES

- For drawing out the history and meaning of the events prior to your gathering, start a meeting with **W³**
- For debriefing any meeting topic that generates complex or controversial responses
- For groups with people who have strong opinions or individuals who dominate the conversation
- For groups with people who have difficulty listening to others with different backgrounds
- For use in place of a leader "telling" people what to think, what conclusions to draw, or what actions to take (often unintentionally)
- As a standard discipline at the end of all meetings
- Right after a shocking event

ATTRIBUTION

Liberating Structure developed by Henri Lipmanowicz and Keith McCandless. Chris Argyris introduced the "Ladder of Inference" in *Reasoning, Learning, and Action: Individual and Organizational* (San Francisco: Jossey-Bass, 1982). Peter Senge popularized it in *The Fifth Discipline: The Art and Practice of the Learning Organization* (New York: Doubleday, 1990).

COLLATERAL MATERIAL

Below: Presentation materials for introducing **What, So What, Now What?**

Ladder of Inference

Emphasizes the value of a step-by-step progression in debriefing or after-action conversations. The value of staying LOW on the ladder is visually reinforced. Misunderstandings and arguments can be avoided.

Actions	I take based on beliefs
Beliefs	I adopt about the world
Conclusions	I draw from assumptions
Assumptions	I make based on meanings
Meanings	I add (cultural & personal)
Data	I select from observations

3. Now What?

2. So What?

1. What?

Observable data and experiences

Discovery & Action Dialogue (DAD)

Discover, Invent, and Unleash Local Solutions to Chronic Problems (25–70 min.)

"Live the questions now and perhaps without knowing it you will live along someday into the answers." Rainier Maria Rilke

What is made possible? DADs make it easy for a group or community to discover practices and behaviors that enable some individuals (without access to special resources and facing the same constraints) to find better solutions than their peers to common problems. These are called positive deviant (PD) behaviors and practices. **DADs** make it possible for people in the group, unit, or community to discover **by themselves** these PD practices. **DADs** also create favorable conditions for stimulating participants' creativity in spaces where they can feel safe to invent new and more effective practices. Resistance to change evaporates as participants are unleashed to choose freely which practices they will adopt or try and which problems they will tackle. **DADs** make it possible to achieve frontline ownership of solutions.

FIVE STRUCTURAL ELEMENTS—MIN SPECS

1. Structuring Invitation

- Invite people to uncover tacit or latent solutions to a shared challenge that are hidden among people in their working group, unit, or community. Ask anybody interested in solving the problem to join a small group and participate in a **DAD.** In the group, ask seven progressive questions:

  1. How do you know when problem X is present?
  2. How do you contribute effectively to solving problem X?
  3. What prevents you from doing this or taking these actions all the time?
  4. Do you know anybody who is able to frequently solve problem X and overcome barriers? What behaviors or practices made their success possible?
  5. Do you have any ideas?
  6. What needs to be done to make it happen? Any volunteers?
  7. Who else needs to be involved?

2. How Space Is Arranged and Materials Needed

- **DADs** take place in a local setting or unit

- Groups may be standing or sitting around a table
- Paper, flip chart, or software/projection equipment needed to record insights and actions

3. How Participation Is Distributed
- Facilitator introduces the questions
- Everyone who is around is invited to join and be included
- Everyone in the group has an equal opportunity to contribute

4. How Groups Are Configured
- Facilitator works with a partner to serve as a recorder
- Group size can be 5–15 people
- Diversity in roles and experience is an important asset

5. Sequence of Steps and Time Allocation
- State the purpose of the initiative being discussed and the DAD and invite brief round-robin introductions. 5 min.
- Ask the 7 questions one by one in the order given in the Invitation. Address them to the whole group and give everyone the opportunity to speak to each question. Make sure your recorder captures insights and action ideas as they emerge—big ones may emerge when you least expect it. 15–60 min.
- Ask your recorder to recap insights, action ideas, and who else needs to be included. 5 min.

Above: button from a Canadian infection-control project that employed DADs extensively

WHY? PURPOSES

- Engage frontline people in finding solutions to thorny challenges
- Discover tacit and latent behaviors and practices that are positively deviant from the norm
- Spark the emergence of new solutions
- Inspire rather than compel behaviors that solve complex problems
- Generate changes that are sustained because they are discovered and invented by the people doing the work, rather than imported and imposed
- Solve local problems locally and spread momentum across units
- Build relationships between people in diverse functions and levels that otherwise don't work together to solve problems

TIPS AND TRAPS

- Question #2 often consists of two parts: how the problem affects the individual personally and how it affects others. For instance, "What do you do to protect yourself from infections and what do you do to prevent infection transmissions?" or "What do you do to keep your students engaged and what do you to keep yourself energized and enthusiastic?"
- Hold the **DADs** where the participants work to minimize obstacles for participation
- Make impromptu invitations for people to join in as you enter the area
- Create an informal "climate," starting with introductions and an anecdote if appropriate
- Maintain eye contact and sit with the group (not higher or away from the group)
- Be sure you talk much less than participants, encouraging everyone to share stories and "sift" for action opportunities
- Draw out stories that help participants make a leap of understanding from a small example of behavior change to a broad change in values or a shift in resource allocation (or both!). Ask questions that invite participants to be as descriptive as possible. Read "Dramatizing Behavior Change to Stop Infections" in Part Three: Stories from the Field

- Notice when you form judgments in your head about what is right or wrong, then count to ten and "let it go" before you say anything (you may need to ask for the help of your recorder or a facilitator colleague)
- Avoid statements like "that's a good idea" and leave space for participants to make their own assessments
- Demonstrate genuine curiosity in everyone's contributions without answering the questions yourself: study at the feet of the people who do the work
- Do not give or take assignments!
- Don't judge yourself too harshly: it takes practice to develop a high level of skill with this approach to facilitation. Be sure to ask your recorder for direct feedback.

RIFFS AND VARIATIONS

- Use **TRIZ**-like questions instead of the first three, namely: (1) What can you do to make sure that problem X becomes much worse? (2) Is there anything you are doing that in any way, shape, or form looks like any of the practices you just listed? (3) What is preventing you from stopping these practices?
- Use insights and barriers that surface to develop scripts for **Improv Prototyping** scenes and organize Improv sessions
- Use the same sequence and type of questions to guide one-on-one conversations
- With virtual groups, use the chat function to share answers to each question, then select powerful stories/behaviors/actions to be vocalized with the whole group

EXAMPLES

- For reducing harm to patients experiencing safety lapses (e.g., wrong-side surgery, patient falls, medication errors, iatrogenic infections) with cross-functional groups
- For use as an ethnographic data-collection tool within a multisite research project
- For eliminating practices that keep professionals from helping clients change unproductive behaviors

- For a series of local dialogues to help community members discover solutions to a chronic problem (e.g., disruptive children in a classroom, a cycle of violence that is not solved only by punishing offenders)
- For researching and unleashing action to build professional competencies (e.g., in medical schools and social-service agencies). See "Developing Competencies for Physician Education" in Part Three: Stories from the Field.
- For use in a one-on-one conversation to find approaches to a tough challenge

ATTRIBUTION

Liberating Structure developed by Henri Lipmanowicz and Keith McCandless together with a group of coaches working to eliminate MRSA transmissions in hospitals: Sharon Benjamin, Kevin Buck, Lisa Kimball, Curt Lindberg, Jon Lloyd, Mark Munger, Jerry Sternin, Monique Sternin, and Margaret Toth. Inspired by Jerry and Monique Sternin's work in Positive Deviance.

COLLATERAL MATERIAL

Below: presentation materials to introduce DAD

Core Questions & Their Purpose

How do you know when ____ *the problem* is present?	~ Affirm the participant's existing knowledge of the problem ~ Provide opportunities to get questions on the table
How do YOU contribute effectively to ____ *solving the problem?*	~ Focus on personal practices, NOT on what other people don't do ~ Amplify/confirm the participant's knowledge of effective practices
What prevents you from doing this or taking these actions all the time?	~ Identify real barriers and constraints to the effective behavior ~ *What prevents you?* identifies barriers rather than *Why don't you?* which sounds judgmental
Is there anyone you know who is able to frequently ____ *solve the problem, overcoming barriers?* How?	~ Establish that getting around barriers is possible ~ Identify the existing-but-uncommon successful strategies ~ Spark curiosity and inventiveness
Do you have any ideas?	~ Identify the supports that make the desired behavior more likely ~ Provide an opportunity for participants to generate and share new ideas for enabling the desired behavior
What needs to be done to make it happen? Any volunteers?	~ Identify action steps, target dates & feedback loops for metrics ~ Invite volunteers for each action step (capture ideas that don't yet have an identified action plan or volunteer in your "butterfly" net.
Who else needs to be involved?	~ Widen the circle of people involved in discovering and inventing solutions, drawing in *unusual suspects*

Tips for Facilitating

Do not:

- Answer questions that have not been asked directly to you
- Miss opportunities to "catch butterflies" – record actions to be taken by participants (NOT YOU) as they pop up
- Come away with a to-do list for yourself
- *Decide about me without me...* instead invite "them" into the next dialogue
- Respond positively or negatively to contributions, instead the group sift through their own assessments (e.g., ask, "How do others think or feel about this suggestion?"

Do:

- Start with the purpose, *We are here to stop/start _____!*
- "Give" questions back to the group, wait at least 20 seconds for a response (looking at your shoes can help!)
- Encourage quiet people to talk
- Flip cynical assertions by asking, "If I understand you correctly, no one has ever done this successfully or well!"
- Work through all the questions without worrying about the order: the dialogue WILL be non-linear
- Maintain humility, you "sit at the feet" of people with solutions

25/10 Crowd Sourcing

Rapidly Generate and Sift a Group's Most Powerful Actionable Ideas (30 min.)

What is made possible? You can help a large crowd generate and sort their bold ideas for action in 30 minutes or less! With **25/10 Crowd Sourcing**, you can spread innovations "out and up" as everyone notices the patterns in what emerges. Though it is fun, fast, and casual, it is a serious and valid way to generate an uncensored set of bold ideas and then to tap the wisdom of the whole group to identify the top ten. Surprises are frequent!

"Reality is only a consensual hunch." Lily Tomlin

FIVE STRUCTURAL ELEMENTS—MIN SPECS

1. Structuring Invitation

- Invite participants to think big and bold and discover the most attractive of their ideas together by asking, "If you were ten times bolder, what big idea would you recommend? What first step would you take to get started?"

2. How Space Is Arranged and Materials Needed

- Open space without chairs or tables
- Participants will be standing and milling about
- Index cards, one for each participant

3. How Participation Is Distributed

- Everyone is included and participates at the same time
- Everyone has an equal opportunity to contribute

4. How Groups Are Configured

- Individually to generate bold idea and first step and write on index card
- Everyone standing to pass cards around
- Pairs to exchange thoughts
- Individually to score the card participants have in their hand
- Whole group for sharing highest final scores and ideas

5. Sequence of Steps and Time Allocation

- Explain the process. First, every participant writes on an index card his or her bold idea and first step. Then people mill around and cards are passed from person to person to quickly review. When the bell rings, people stop passing cards and pair up to exchange thoughts on the cards in their hands. Then participants individually rate the idea/step on their card with a score of 1 to 5 (1 for low and 5 for high) and write it on the back of the card. When the bell rings, cards are passed around a second time until the bell rings and the scoring cycle repeats. This is done for a total of five scoring rounds. At the end of cycle five, participants add the five scores on the back of the last card they are holding. Finally, the ideas with the top ten scores are identified and shared with the whole group. 3 min.

- Demonstrate one exchange-and-scoring interaction using a sample index card to clarify what is expected during the milling, namely no reading aloud of the cards, only passing the cards from person to person so that each person has one and only one card in hand. The process can be confusing for some people. 2 min.

- Invite each participant to write a big idea and first step on his or her card. 5 min.

- Conduct five 3-minute exchange-and-scoring rounds with time for milling (and laughing) in between. 15 min.

- Ask participants to add the 5 scores on the back of the card they are holding

- Find the best-scoring ideas with the whole group by conducting a countdown. Ask, "Who has a 25?" Invite each participant, if any, holding a card scored 25 to read out the idea and action step. Continue with "Who has a 24?," "Who has a 23".... Stop when the top ten ideas have been identified and shared. 5 min.

- End by asking, "What caught your attention about 25/10?" 2 min.

WHY? PURPOSES

- Develop a group's ability to quickly tap their own sources of wisdom
- Obtain results that are more likely to endure because they were generated transparently from within and without imported advice
- Spark synergy among diverse views while building coherence
- Encourage novice innovators to think boldly and come up with practical first steps
- Create an environment in which good ideas can bubble up

TIPS AND TRAPS

- Some of the scoring may be erratic. If a participant at the end of round five has a card with more or less than five scores, ask the participant to calculate the average of the scores and multiply this average by 5.
- Invite the group to choose one big idea and first-action step and revise it so that it is expressed even more clearly and compellingly
- Suggest a seriously fun but clear rating scale, for example: 1 = not your cup of tea to 5 = sends me over the moon. The crowd needs to understand and agree with the rating system if it is to be used for decisions.
- As you start and demonstrate one exchange-and-scoring interaction, take your time and ask for feedback, particularly if it is a large group.
- To make it hard to peek at scoring from earlier rounds, cover the back of the card with a Post-it note
- Post all the cards on a wall or on tapestry paper, with the highest-scoring cards on the top

Below: workshop participant in Italy posting the top-performing bold ideas

RIFFS AND VARIATIONS

- Move to developing action plans or to **Open Space** with your Top 10
- Do a second round **of 25/10 Crowd Sourcing** that includes others not in the present group (aka Cloud Sourcing!)
- Include **25/10 Crowd Sourcing** at the beginning and end of a meeting
- Array your Top 10 in an **Agreement-Certainty Matrix**
- Instead of asking for bold ideas, ask, "If you could unmake one decision that is holding you back, what would it be? What is your first step to unmake it?"
- Instead of bold ideas, ask, "What courageous conversation are you not having? What first step could spark your courage?"
- Instead of bold ideas, ask, "What do you hope can happen in the future? What practical first step can you take now to tip the balance in this direction?"

EXAMPLES

- For prioritizing ideas and galvanizing the community after an **Open Space** Technology or "Unconference" (participant-driven) meeting
- For illuminating bold ideas at the start of a conference or task-force meeting
- For wrapping up an important meeting
- For a closing circle to share ideas and reinforce bonds among group members. See "Developing Competencies for Physician Education" in Part Three: Stories from the Field.

ATTRIBUTION

Liberating Structure developed by Henri Lipmanowicz and Keith McCandless. Inspired by improvisationalists, including Keith Johnstone.

Shift & Share

Spread Good Ideas and Make Informal Connections with Innovators (90 min.)

What is made possible? You can quickly and effectively share several innovations or useful programs that may lie hidden within a group, organization, or community. **Shift & Share** gets rid of long large-group presentations and replaces them with several concise descriptions made simultaneously to multiple small groups. A few individuals set up "stations" where they share in ten minutes the essence of their innovations that may be of value to others. As small groups move from one innovator's station to another, their size makes it easy for people to connect with the innovator. They can quickly learn where and how new ideas are being used and how they might be adapted to their own situations. Innovators learn from the repetition, and groups can easily spot opportunities for creative mash-ups of ideas.

FIVE STRUCTURAL ELEMENTS—MIN SPECS

1. Structuring Invitation

- Invite participants to visit several innovators who will share something new or innovative they are doing and that may be of value to them

2. How Space Is Arranged and Materials Needed

- A large space where 5 to 8 stations can be set up far enough from each other to minimize interference with one another
- A suitable number of chairs to accommodate the small groups at each station
- Space for a display as needed by presenters

3. How Participation Is Distributed

- A few members of the group, the presenters, share their work
- Everyone else in the small groups has an equal opportunity to participate and contribute

4. How Groups Are Configured

- Presenters set up their individual stations
- The whole group is split into the same number of small groups as there are presenters, for instance, 7 small groups if there are 7 presenters

- Groups stay together while they rotate through all the innovation stations

5. Sequence of Steps and Time Allocation

- Describe the process: explain that small groups will move from station to station for a 10-minute presentation and brief questions and feedback period. If it wasn't done in advance, identify the 3 to 7 presenters for the innovation stations (can be people who volunteer in the moment). Form the same number of small groups as there are presenters. 5 min.
- Each small group goes to a different station, where presenters conduct their sessions (repeated up to 7 times). 10 min. per station/session
- Participants ask questions or provide feedback. 2 min. per station/session
- Small groups move to the next station. 1 min. per move
- Repeat until groups have visited all stations.
- Total time for visiting 6 stations is approximately 90 minutes.

WHY? PURPOSES

- Quickly share ideas and innovations
- Enable people to recognize that they are innovating or have the potential to innovate
- Build trust and a community of practice among members
- Reveal how the formal technological hierarchy can obscure the hidden contributions of frontline innovators
- Quickly give participants a sense of the innovation landscape
- Explore and expose bottom-up and fringe-in innovations
- Spark friendly competition, mash-ups, and collaboration

Below: a group gathered for an eight-minute Shift & Share presentation in Seattle

TIPS AND TRAPS

- Pick presenters by digging deep into the informal social networks (presentation skills and charisma are less important than content for this approach)
- Keep tightly to the schedule: use a loud sound or tingsha bells to signal the shift from one station to the next
- When possible prepare the presenters: 10 minutes is much shorter than they are used to!
- Invite presenters to tell stories that help the audience make the leap from understanding a small example of behavior change to seeing a broad change in values or a shift in resource allocation, or both
- Invite presenters to supplement their presentations with examples and objects that participants can see and touch
- Encourage presenters to entertain and engage the imagination of the audience
- Trust that people will follow up to get more depth if they are interested

RIFFS AND VARIATIONS

- Invite the roving groups to use **What, So What, Now What?** to debrief what they experienced
- Like a PechaKucha Night presentation, add snacks and drinks at each station
- Shorten the presentation time to 8 minutes
- Do not establish set groups; instead mash up with **Open Space** (individuals use their two feet to go where they are most curious about and where they are learning something)
- If you do a second round, leave a few stations open for impromptu presenters
- Use with virtual groups by creating a series of chat rooms. The groups then select a handful of sessions they want to attend
- String together with **Improv Prototyping** to generate variations on ideas presented

EXAMPLES

- For orienting new members of a research consortium to the depth and breadth of innovations within the whole community
- For introducing technology applications at a conference, mixing presenters from within the field with commercial vendors
- For highlighting the programs and people from two "sides" of a newly merged organization

ATTRIBUTION

Liberating Structure developed by Henri Lipmanowicz and Keith McCandless. Inspired by Chris McCarthy and the Innovation Learning Network.

*Below: presentation materials we use to introduce **Shift & Share***

Steps and Schedule

Preparation	Start Round I
• Invite individuals to share 8-10 minute presentations of prototypes or innovations • Divide the community into 7 learning groups. Count off: 1,2,3,4,5,6,7 • Assign each presenter a letter (A, B, C, D as needed) for a station in the room • Each presenter repeats their presentation to each group	• Presenters have 8-10 minutes with each group. This includes any questions and comments... so "cut to the chase." • Ding. Time to shift. • Group 1, go to Station B. Group 2, go to Station C... Group 7, go to Station A. • And so on for 7 rounds.

Wise Crowds

Tap the Wisdom of the Whole Group in Rapid Cycles (15 min. per person)

What is made possible? Wise Crowds make it possible to instantly engage a small or large group of people in helping one another. You can set up a **Wise Crowds** consultation with one small group of four or five people or with many small groups simultaneously or, during a larger gathering, with a group as big as one hundred or more people. Individuals, referred to as "clients," can ask for help and get it in a short time from all the other group members. Each individual consultation taps the expertise and inventiveness of everyone in the group simultaneously. Individuals gain more clarity and increase their capacity for self-correction and self-understanding. **Wise Crowds** develop people's ability to ask for help. They deepen inquiry and consulting skills. Supportive relationships form very quickly. During a **Wise Crowds** session, the series of individual consultations makes the learning cumulative as each participant benefits not only from being a client but also from being a consultant several times in a row. **Wise Crowds** consultations make it easy to achieve transparency. Together, a group can outperform the expert!

"Every journey has a secret destination of which the traveler is not aware." Martin Buber

FIVE STRUCTURAL ELEMENTS—MIN SPECS FOR A SMALL WISE CROWDS

1. Structuring Invitation

- Ask each participant when his or her turn comes to be the "client" to briefly describe his or her challenge and ask others for help.
- Ask the other participants to act as a group of "consultants" whose task it is to help the "client" clarify his or her challenge and to offer advice or recommendations.

2. How Space Is Arranged and Materials Needed

- Groups of 4 or 5 chairs arranged around small tables or in circles without tables
- Paper for participants to take notes

3. How Participation Is Distributed

- Everyone is included
- Everyone has an equal amount of time to ask for and get help
- Everyone has an equal opportunity to offer help

4. How Groups Are Configured

- Groups of 4 to 5 people
- Mixed groups across functions, levels, and disciplines are ideal
- The person asking for help, the "client," turns his or her back on the consultants after the consultation question has been clarified.

5. Sequence of Steps and Time Allocation

Each person requesting a consult (the client) gets fifteen minutes broken down as follows:

- The client presents the challenge and request for help. 2 min.
- The consultants ask the client clarifying questions. 3 min.
- The client turns his or her back to the consultants and gets ready to take notes
- The consultants ask questions and offer advice, and recommendations, working as a team, while the client has his or her back turned. 8 min.
- The client provides feedback to the consultants: what was useful and what he or she takes away. 2 min.

WHY? PURPOSES

- Generate results that are enduring because each individual and the group produced them together without "outside expertise"
- Refine skills in giving, receiving, and asking for help
- Tap the intelligence of a whole group without time-consuming up and sideways presentations
- Liberate the wisdom and creativity that exists across disciplines and functional silos
- Replace boring briefings and updates with an effective and useful alternative
- Actively build trust through mutual support and peer connections
- Practice listening without defending

TIPS AND TRAPS

- Invite a very diverse crowd to help (not only the experts and leaders)
- Invite participants to critique themselves when they fall into traps (e.g., jumping to action before clarifying the purpose or the problem). See **Helping Heuristics** for a complete list of unwanted patterns when helping or asking for help.
- Remind participants to try to stay focused on the client's direct experience by asking, "What is happening here? How are you experiencing what is happening?"
- Advise the consultants to take risks while maintaining empathy
- Avoid having some participants choosing not to be clients: everybody has at least one challenge!
- If the first round is weak, try a second round
- Invite participants not to shy away from presenting complex challenges without easy answers

RIFFS AND VARIATIONS

- Restrict the consulting to asking only honest, open questions, focusing on helping the client gain personal clarity. In other words, forbid recommendations and advice (thinly veiled as a question) or any speeches whatsoever! This is also called Q-Storming and is similar to a Quaker Clearness Committee.
- Can be used with groups of up to 7 people but not more.
- The "large format" of **Wise Crowds** makes it possible for one person to ask a whole room for help. See the detailed description of the five structural elements/min specs below.
- Use **Wise Crowds** with virtual groups by using the chat function to share answers from a small number of consultants, then opening the chat line and whiteboard to the whole group for additional feedback
- Link to and string with **Helping Heuristics** plus **Heard, Seen, Respected (HSR), Nine Whys, Troika Consulting, What I**

Need From You, and **Appreciative Interviews**. These Liberating Structures offer a variety of productive choices for helping.

Below: self-administered aid to deepen listening during Wise Crowds

Wise Crowds For Large Groups
(1 hr.)

FIVE STRUCTURAL ELEMENTS—MIN SPECS FOR LARGE GROUPS

1. Structuring Invitation
- Ask the participant who is the "client" to describe his or her challenge, the status of any work in progress, and the advice or help he or she is looking for
- Ask the other participants to act as a group of "consulting teams" whose task it is to help the "client" clarify his or her challenge and to offer advice or recommendations.

2. How Space Is Arranged and Materials Needed
- One chair for the client in the front of the room
- Screen and projector only if absolutely indispensable
- Three chairs for the primary consultants in the front of the room
- Groups of 5–8 chairs arranged around small tables, or in circles without tables, for all the satellite consulting teams
- Paper for participants to take notes
- Index cards at each table to write recommendations
- Microphones for the client and primary consultants

3. How Participation Is Distributed
- The client has a specific amount of time to present and ask for help
- The primary consulting team has a fixed amount of time to offer help
- Everyone else on each consulting team has an equal opportunity to contribute help during the balance of the time, which is also fixed

4. How Groups Are Configured
- Individual client
- One group of 2 to 3 primary consultants
- Any number of satellite groups of 5 to 7 people as consulting teams
- Mixed groups across functions, levels, and disciplines are ideal

5. Sequence of Steps and Time Allocation
Each person requesting a consult (the client) gets one hour broken down as follows:

- The client presents his or her consulting question and selects the 2-4 individuals who will form the primary consulting team. The primary consultants move and occupy their chairs in the front of the room. 2 min.
- The client presents the challenge and request for help. 10 min.
- The primary consultants pose clarifying questions to the client, using microphones so that all participants can hear them. 10 min.
- The client turns his or her back to the primary consultants and gets ready to take notes.
- The primary consultants jointly form advice and recommendations, working as a team while the client has his or her back turned. Microphones are used so that all others in the room can follow their discussion. 7 min.
- Every satellite consulting team separately critiques the work of the primary consulting team and generates its own recommendations for the client. 10 min.
- While the satellite teams work, the client turns around and uses this ten-minute period to discuss with the primary consulting team.
- Do one round to gather the critiques from the satellite teams first and then a second round to gather their recommendations. Gather only one comment or recommendation per team, with no repeats. It may be useful to ask the satellite teams to write their recommendations for the client on 3-by-5-inch index cards. 10 min.
- The client provides feedback to the consultants: what was useful and what he or she takes away. 2 min.
- Invite a full-group conversation reflecting on the process, so what, and now what. 5 min.
- NOTE: The timing for each step can be adjusted depending on the complexity of the problem and the size of the group, but it is essential to stick strictly to the schedule and not let discussions drag beyond the time set. It is always better to have a second round instead.

EXAMPLES

- For multisite research/learning groups to support and learn from each other
- For professionals in a national fellowship program to share progress and get help with the action learning projects

- To replace progress presentations and reviews
- For managers trying to solve problems associated with a merger
- For foundation grantees trying to scale up their socio-tech innovations
- For getting advice on improving a relationship with one other person
- For salespeople (distributed over a large geography) getting help with developing and keeping new customers

ATTRIBUTION

Liberating Structure developed by Henri Lipmanowicz and Keith McCandless. Inspired by Quaker Clearness Committees.

Conversation Café

Engage Everyone in Making Sense of Profound Challenges (35 to 60 min.)

What is made possible? You can include and engage any number of people in making sense of confusing or shocking events and laying the ground for new strategies to emerge. The format of the **Conversation Café** helps people have calm and profound conversations in which there is less debating and arguing, and more listening. Sitting in a circle with a simple set of agreements and a talking object, small groups will engage in rounds of dialogue with little or no unproductive conflict. As the meaning of their challenge pops into focus, a consensual hunch is formed that will release their capacity for new action.

FIVE STRUCTURAL ELEMENTS—MIN SPECS

1. Structuring Invitation
- Invite all the participants to gather in small groups to listen to one another's thoughts and reflect together on a shared challenge while respecting six dialogue agreements.

2. How Space Is Arranged and Materials Needed
- Unlimited number of 5 to 7 chairs around small tables
- Talking object (e.g., talking stick, stone, or art object)
- Markers and one or two pieces of flip-chart paper per table optional

3. How Participation Is Distributed
- Everyone is included
- Everyone has an equal opportunity to contribute

4. How Groups Are Configured
- Mixed, diverse groups of 5–7 participants

5. Sequence of Steps and Time Allocation
- State the theme of the conversation, usually in the form of a question
- Explain there will be four rounds of conversation at every table, two first rounds using a talking object, the third one as open conversation, and a final round with the talking object. Give the duration of each round.
- Distribute the talking objects

- Read the six **Conversation Café** agreements. See text in Collateral Material below.
- Ask for someone at each table to volunteer as the host. The host is a full participant whose role is to gently intervene only when a participant visibly fails to observe one of the six agreements, most frequently talking on and on
- First round with the talking object: each person shares what he or she is thinking, feeling, or doing about the theme or topic. 1 min. per person
- Second round with the talking object: each person shares thoughts and feelings after having listened to everybody at the table. 1 min. per person
- Third round: open conversation (option to use talking object). 20–40 min.
- Fourth round with the talking object: each member shares "take-aways." 5–10 min.

WHY? PURPOSES

- Make sense of a complex, difficult, or painful situation and lay the ground for being able to move on
- Generate new ideas and momentum for innovation
- Build shared understanding of how people develop different perspectives and ideas
- Avoid arguments based on lack of understanding
- Build trust and reduce fear with an opportunity for catharsis
- Help participants appreciate that conversation involves talking and listening

TIPS AND TRAPS

- Always use the talking object: they make the difference
- Have the host or participants reread the six agreements before starting the first round
- Do not assign tasks: there should be no intention that the dialogue will directly lead to action
- Host the dialogue like a dinner party, encouraging everyone to contribute while keeping the conversation open-ended and spontaneous
- Use **Wicked Questions** to deepen conversation

- If there is a problem, ask, "Are we following our agreements?"
- Encourage people to speak their mind
- Encourage quiet people to talk
- Select talking objects that may have symbolic meaning for participants
- Encourage participants to draw or record insights on the flip-chart "tablecloth"
- Learn more from Vicki Robin and friends, who created the Conversation Café for use in communities @ www.conversationcafe.org

RIFFS AND VARIATIONS

- All participants but one at each table can move to different tables every 20 minutes World-Café style (see www.worldcafe.com for more information).
- Link to Graphic Recording. Place flip-chart paper on each table to collect insights from each group. Encourage drawing and playful exploration.
- To move into action, string together with **W³ (What, So What, Now What?), 15% Solutions, Design StoryBoards, User Experience Fishbowl,** or **Open Space**.

Below: a talking object invites deeper listening in Paris

EXAMPLES

- For making sense of and start recovering from a major setback or shock in the market or operating environment (e.g., first used in US communities after 9/11)
- For exploring a new topic or trend that is not well understood
- For handling a topic where there will be strong feelings expressed
- For reflecting after a major change: What does it mean? What assumptions can we make? What conclusions make sense? What can we now believe?

ATTRIBUTION

Liberating Structure developed by Henri Lipmanowicz and Keith McCandless. Inspired by and adapted from Vicki Robin and Susan Partnow, codevelopers of Conversation Cafés.

COLLATERAL MATERIAL

Below: presentation materials we use to introduce Conversation Café

Agreements and Steps

Agreements	Steps
• Suspend judgment as best you can • Respect one another • Seek to understand rather than persuade • Invite and honor diverse opinions • Speak what has personal heart and meaning • Go for honesty & depth without going on & on & on	1. Use talking-object in rounds 1, 2 & 4 2. 1st and 2nd rounds speaking without interruption. Option to pass. People without the talking object are invited *to listen.* 3. 3rd round of lively conversation 4. 4th round to share "take-aways" 5. Gather insights as the whole group re-assembles

Peruvian folk-art finger puppet serving as talking object

Min Specs

Specify Only the Absolute "MUST DOs" and "MUST NOT DOs" for Achieving a Purpose (35 to 50 min.)

What is made possible? By specifying only the minimum number of simple rules, the **Min Specs** that must ABSOLUTELY be respected, you can unleash a group to innovate freely. Respecting the **Min Specs** will ensure that innovations will be both purposeful and responsible. Like the Ten Commandments, Min Specs are enabling constraints: they detail only must dos and must not dos. You will eliminate the clutter of nonessential rules, the Max Specs that get in the way of innovation. Often two to five **Min Specs** are sufficient to boost performance by adding more freedom AND more responsibility to the group's understanding of what it must do to make progress. Out of their experience in the field, participants shape and adapt **Min Specs** together, working as one. Following the rules makes it possible for the group to go wild!

FIVE STRUCTURAL ELEMENTS—MIN SPECS

1. Structuring Invitation

- In the context of a challenging activity or a new initiative, invite the participants to first generate the entire list of all the do's and don'ts that they should pay attention to in order to achieve a successful outcome. This is the list of maximum specifications (Max Specs).
- After the list of Max Specs has been developed, ask the participants to reduce it to the absolute minimum needed to achieve their purpose. Invite them to sift through the list one item at a time and eliminate every rule that gets a positive answer to the question, "If we broke or ignored this rule, could we still achieve our purpose?"

2. How Space Is Arranged and Materials Needed

- Groups of 4 to 7 chairs around small tables
- Paper to record Max and Min Specs

3. How Participation Is Distributed

- Everyone involved in the activity or program can participate
- Everyone has an equal opportunity to contribute

4. How Groups Are Configured

- Start individually then small groups of 4 to 7
- Whole group for sharing

5. Sequence of Steps and Time Allocation

- Generate the list of all must-do and must-not-do activities (Max Specs), at first alone for one minute then consolidate and expand in the small group for five minutes. Make list as complete as possible in a short time. 6 min.
- Each small group tests each spec on its Max Spec list against the purpose statement. If the spec can be violated and the purpose still achieved, the spec is dropped from the list. 15 min.
- Do a second round if needed. 15 min.
- Compare across small groups and consolidate to the shortest list. 15 min.

WHY? PURPOSES

- Evaluate and decide what is absolutely essential for success
- Open space for new possibilities
- Reduce frontline frustration and free people from micromanagement
- Focus or redirect resources and energies where it matters
- Help guide scaling up and spreading innovations with fidelity

TIPS AND TRAPS

- Start with a complete list of dos
- Include as many players/stakeholders as possible
- Be ruthless in dropping dos: don't allow max specs to creep in
- Do extra rounds as needed
- Make the **Min Specs** official! Live by them (no "yes but")
- Give more weight to direct experience in the field rather than conceptual knowledge
- Keep the **Min Specs** alive by adapting them based on field experiences and Simple Ethnography observations
- If groups are having difficulty, you may need to circle back to clarify purpose and make sure that it is down to what is truly important.
- Learn more in Brenda Zimmerman's *Edgeware* or at www.plexusinstitute.com/edgeware/archive/think/

RIFFS AND VARIATIONS

- Do a second round of purpose testing with the question, "If you followed all the **Min Specs** except this one, would you achieve your purpose?" If yes, you can drop that spec from the list.
- Instead of developing **Min Specs** for the present, ask people to speculate on what Min Specs should shape action in the future. Use them to inform the present.
- Do Min Specs with virtual groups by using the chat function to share answers to each "can you violate this specification and achieve your purpose?" question. When your **Min Specs** list is getting shorter and tighter, open the voice conversation to all.
- **Simple Ethnography** or **Nine Whys** may reveal implicit or tacit Min Specs (dig deeper!)

Below: Min Specs guide a self-organizing pattern in Brazil

EXAMPLES

- Senator Lynda Bourque Moss used Min Specs to identify the must dos and must not dos for all the stakeholders to share responsibility for preventing the habit of driving while intoxicated and support new state legislation. Read Lynda's story, "Passing Montana Senate Bill 29" in Part Three: Stories from the Field.

- After a company-wide **Open Space** meeting, Alison Joslyn developed a set of **Min Specs** with the new project leaders of a corporate turn-around. See "Turning A Business Around" in Part Three.
- Include **Min Specs** with any assignment given or received.

ATTRIBUTION

Liberating Structure developed by Henri Lipmanowicz and Keith McCandless. Inspired by professor Kathleen Eisenhardt and author Paul Plsek (see Zimmerman, Lindberg, and Plsek *Edgeware*).

COLLATERAL MATERIAL

Below: presentation materials we use to introduce Min Specs

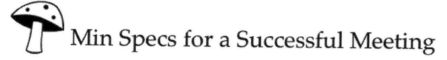

Min Specs for a Successful Meeting

List of requirements to have **A Successful Meeting**	Can you violate this requirement and still achieve your purpose? If "yes," cross it off your list.
1. Announce a time and location	Min Spec
2. Recruit an expert speaker	NOT a Min Spec
3. Prepare a detailed agenda	NOT a Min Spec
4. Project PowerPoint slides	NOT a Min Spec
5. Articulate a compelling purpose	Min Spec

Improv Prototyping

Develop Effective Solutions to Chronic Challenges While Having Serious Fun (20 min. per round)

What is made possible? You can engage a group to learn and improve rapidly from tapping three levels of knowledge simultaneously: (1) explicit knowledge shared by participants; (2) tacit knowledge discovered through observing each other's performance; and (3) latent knowledge, i.e., new ideas that emerge and are jointly developed. This powerful combination can be the source of transformative experiences and, at the same time, it is seriously fun. Participants identify and act out solutions to chronic or daunting problems. A diverse mix of people is invited to dramatize simple elements that work to solve a problem. Innovations represented in the Improv sketches are assembled incrementally from pieces or chunks that can be used separately or together. It is a playful way to get very serious work done!

Sources of Knowledge for Innovation

Explicit	Tacit	Latent/Emerging
ASK What people tell you they do when you ask		
	OBSERVE What behaviors you see when you watch people in action	
		CREATE EXPERIENCE What you jointly develop when you experiment together

Telling

++

+++++

Sources of Knowledge & Innovation, adapted from Alan Duncan, MD (Mayo Clinic), designed for VHA Health Foundation (2006).

FIVE STRUCTURAL ELEMENTS—MIN SPECS

1. Structuring Invitation

- Invite participants to identify a frustrating chronic challenge in their work, then to playfully experiment, invent, and discover better ways to address the challenge by acting out the situation and possible solutions.

2. How Space Is Arranged and Materials Needed

- An open space or stage at the front or in the middle of a room
- If needed, props for the scene or scenes to be offered
- Small clusters of chairs to accommodate all participants

3. How Participation Is Distributed

- Everyone is included either as players or observers
- A few volunteers to be "players"
- Everyone else acts as observers and evaluators, then cocreative players

4. How Groups Are Configured

- One small group of players on "the stage"
- All others, the observers, in small groups in front or around the stage

5. Sequence of Steps and Time Allocation

- Explain what will be done and describe the sequence of steps. 2 min.
- Set the stage by describing the scenario that will be acted out and the various roles. 3 min.
- Players on stage enact the scene. 3–5 min.
- Each small observer group debriefs with **1-2-4-All** to identify successful and unsuccessful "chunks" from the scene that they just observed. 5 min.
- Each observer group then pieces together the successful chunks into a new prototype and volunteers from within the group act out the new prototype for their own group only. 5 min.
- Participants from one of the observer groups who judge that they have an improved prototype volunteer to come on stage and enact their version in front of the whole group. 3–5 minutes.
- Continue with as many rounds as necessary to arrive at one or more prototypes that are good enough to put into practice.

WHY? PURPOSES

- Enable people to act their way into new thinking: **Improv Prototyping** is a rehearsal for real life
- Break a task that seems daunting into smaller pieces
- Engage and focus everyone's imagination on solving messy challenges
- Break through frozen or resistant behaviors
- Create an engaging and fun alternative to dry or unproductive training
- Work across functional and disciplinary barriers
- Help people learn from peers that have behaviors that solve the problem

TIPS AND TRAPS

- Be as inclusive as possible: invite everyone in different roles to join in
- Draw meaningful themes and dramatic lines for each scene from **Discovery & Action Dialogues** and **Simple Ethnography**
- Consider creating three supporting roles depending on the complexity of the scenario: stage manager, creative director, and facilitator.
- Replay scenes that do not capture the imagination or generate new ideas
- Invite people to let go of assumptions and biases by putting themselves in the shoes of others, e.g., doctor plays nurse and nurse plays doctor, student plays professor
- Invite creative director to gently redirect the players as needed

RIFFS AND VARIATIONS

- With the goal of discovering better (and worse) actions, invite the audience to replay the scene in small groups. Start with separate small groups staging their own impromptu Improvs, then invite face-off competitions judged by an "applause-o-meter"
- Link to and string with **Design StoryBoards, Shift & Share**, and **User Experience Fishbowl** to help spread the innovations (specify *what is* and *what could be*)

EXAMPLES

- Hospital trainers have substituted **Improv Prototyping** for conventional courses

- For sales reps to invent new ways to interact with their customers
- For managers to make their interactions with people who report to them more productive
- For health-care providers to practice end-of-life and palliative-care conversations with patients and family members
- For teachers to discover effective responses to disruptive classroom behaviors
- For training young nurses to stand their ground on safety issues (see "Dramatizing Behavior Change to Stop Infections" in Part Three: Stories from the Field).

ATTRIBUTION

Liberating Structure developed by Henri Lipmanowicz and Keith McCandless. Inspired by Antonas Mockus (former mayor of Bogota) and Improv artists.

COLLATERAL MATERIAL

*Below: presentation materials we use to introduce **Improv Prototyping***

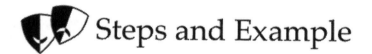

Steps and Example

Four steps:

1. Set the stage by selecting a place, players, and a single line to be delivered
2. A Creative Director should start and stop the action, replaying the scene (with a twist) as needed
3. Give the players improv coaching support as needed (e.g., one conversation at a time)
4. After each scene, a facilitator should invite reflection on what happened (and what did not happen) via 1-2-4-All.

Setting the Stage with Hand Washing Safety

- You notice a colleague that is not practicing safely. *You are feeling brave today.* ;-) You decide to help your colleague notice their behavior is putting patients at risk. The behavior you are witnessing is a chronic problem. You have tried everything and have decided, *I will try something new.*
- Two players: a nurse and a doctor in an isolation precautions patient room.
- Line: "I did not notice that you washed your hands."

Helping Heuristics

Practice Progressive Methods for Helping Others, Receiving Help and Asking for Help (15 min.)

"You cannot help a man permanently by doing for them something they could and should do for themselves."
Abraham Lincoln

What is made possible? Participants can gain insight into their own pattern of interaction and habits. **Helping Heuristics** make it possible for them to experience how they can choose to change how they work with others by using a progression of practical methods. Heuristics are shortcuts that help people identify what is important when entering a new situation. They help them develop deeper insight into their own interaction patterns and make smarter decisions quickly. A series of short exchanges reveals heuristics or simple rules of thumb for productive helping. Try them out!

FIVE STRUCTURAL ELEMENTS—MIN SPECS

1. Structuring Invitation
- Invite participants to view all human interactions as offers that are either accepted or blocked (e.g., Improv artists are trained to accept all offers)
- Ask them to act, react, or observe four patterns of interaction
- Invite them to reflect on their patterns as well as to consider shifting how they ask, offer, and receive help

2. How Space Is Arranged and Materials Needed
- Any number of participants, standing
- No tables in the way of people standing face-to-face!

3. How Participation Is Distributed
- Everyone has an equal opportunity to learn and to contribute
- Participants switch into one of three possible roles as the activity progresses

4. How Groups Are Configured
- Groups of 3: two participants interacting face-to-face in the roles of client and coach plus one observer
- Whole group for the debrief

5. Sequence of Steps and Time Allocation

- Explain that there will be four rounds of 1–2-minute improvised inter-actions. Groups choose one member to be a "client," another a "coach," with the third acting as "observer." Roles can stay the same or change from round to round. The fourth round will be followed by 5 minutes of debrief. 2 min.
- During every round the person in the role of client shares a challenge he or she is passionate about. While the observer pays close attention, the coach responds in a sequence of patterns that is different for each round as follows.
- During the first round, the response pattern is "Quiet Presence": the coach accepts all offers with compassionate listening (see the Liberating Structure **Heard, Seen, Respected (HSR)**). 2 min.
- During the second round, the response pattern is "Guided Discovery": the coach accepts all offers, guiding inquiry for mutual discoveries (see the Liberating Structure **Appreciative Interview**). 2 min.
- During the third round, the response pattern is "Loving Provocation": the coach interjects advice, accepting and blocking as needed when the coach sees something that the client does not see (see the Liberating Structure **Troika Consulting**). 2 min.
- During the fourth round, the response pattern is "Process Mindfulness": the coach and client accept all offers from each other, working at the top of their intelligence while noticing how novel possibilities are am-plified. 2 min.
- Debrief the impact of all four helping patterns as experienced by cli-ents, coaches, and observers. 5 min.
- Based on the debrief, repeat all rounds or only some for all participants to practice various response patterns.

WHY? PURPOSES

- Reduce/eliminate common errors and traps when people are giving or asking for help
- Change unwanted *giving help* patterns that include: premature solu-tions; unneeded advice; adding pressure to force use of advice; moving to next steps too quickly; trying too hard not to overhelp

- Change unwanted *asking for help* patterns that include: mistrusting; not sharing real problem; accepting help without ownership; looking for validation, not help; resenting not getting enough

TIPS AND TRAPS

- Encourage people to change roles in each round
- Develop trust, inquire humbly, create climate of mutual discovery
- Focus on patterns that will help *the client* finding his or her own solutions (self-discovery in a group)
- Do not ignore status differences, the setting, body language, demeanor, subtle signals
- The first cycle of four rounds can be used as preparation for deeper work on any single pattern
- After initial cycle, let trios choose the patterns they want to focus on in their group

RIFFS AND VARIATIONS

- Invite participants to create their own profile, self-identifying their default patterns and opportunities for growth
- Incorporate the helping progression into other Liberating Structures that focus on give-and-take: **Troika Consulting, Wise Crowds, What I Need From You, Improv Prototyping, Simple Ethnography**
- Start with "fun" patterns: neutral (zero response) and blocking by ignoring or interrupting

EXAMPLES

- Used when **Wise Crowds** or **What I Need From You** does not achieve a group's intended purpose—for example, when participants have fallen into one of the unwanted *asking for* or *giving help* patterns
- For nurses, coaches, teachers, or anyone else in the helping professions to renew and learn new relational skills
- For any group working to improve interprofessional coordination

- For Liberating Structures facilitators to dig deeper into underlying patterns that cut across many Liberating Structures
- For expanding options when frustrated with trying to help another person

ATTRIBUTION

Liberating Structure developed by Henri Lipmanowicz and Keith McCandless. Inspired by author/professor Edgar Schein (see *Helping* in Learning Resources).

COLLATERAL MATERIAL

*Below: presentation materials we use to introduce **Helping Heuristics***

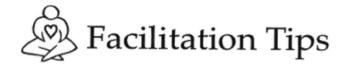 Facilitation Tips

Four Patterns	Key Goals
1. Quiet Presence	• *Establish trust, reduce status differences, listen with empathy*
2. Guided Discovery	• *Guide inquiry in search of mutual discoveries*
3. Loving Provocation	• *Interject your advice & suggestions to make progress*
4. Process Mindfulness	• *Deepen awareness of helping and relational dynamics*

User Experience Fishbowl

Share Know-How Gained from Experience with a Larger Community (35 to 70 min.)

What is made possible? A subset of people with direct field experience can quickly foster understanding, spark creativity, and facilitate adoption of new practices among members of a larger community. Fishbowl sessions have a small inside circle of people surrounded by a larger outside circle of participants. The inside group is formed with people who made concrete progress on a challenge of interest to those in the outside circle. The fishbowl design makes it easy for people in the inside circle to illuminate what they have done by sharing experiences while in conversation with each other. The informality breaks down the barriers with direct communication between the two groups of people and facilitates questions and answers flowing back and forth. This creates the best conditions for people to learn from each other by discovering answers to their concerns themselves within the context of their working groups. You can stop imposing someone else's practices!

FIVE STRUCTURAL ELEMENTS—MIN SPECS

1. Structuring Invitation
- Ask those in the fishbowl to describe their experience—the good, the bad, and the ugly—informally, concretely, and openly. Invite them to do it in conversation with each other as if the audience wasn't there and they were sharing stories around a watering hole or stuck in a van on the way to the airport. Firmly, ask them to avoid presenting to the audience.
- Invite the people outside the fishbowl to listen, observe nonverbal exchanges, and formulate questions within their small groups.

2. How Space Is Arranged and Materials Needed
- Three to 7 chairs in a circle in the middle of a room
- Microphones for inner circle if whole group is larger than 30 to 40
- If possible, a low stage or bar stools make it possible for people in the outer circle to better see the interactions
- As many chairs as needed in an outer circle around the inner circle, in clumps of 3 to 4 chairs

- In large groups, have additional microphones ready for outside circle questions

3. How Participation Is Distributed
- Everyone in the inner circle has an equal opportunity to contribute
- Everyone in the outer circle has an equal opportunity to ask questions

4. How Groups Are Configured
- One inner circle group of 3–7 people
- One outer circle in multiple small satellite groups of 3–4 people
- **1-2-4-All** configuration for the debrief

5. Sequence of Steps and Time Allocation
- Explain the fishbowl configuration and steps. 2 min.
- Inner circle conversation goes on until it ends on its own. 10 to 25 min.
- Satellite groups in outer circle formulate observations and questions. 4 min.
- Questions submitted to the inner circle are answered, and back-and-forth interaction between inner and outer circles goes on as needed until all the questions are answered. 10 to 25 min.
- Debrief using **W³ (What? So What? Now What?)** and ask, "What seems possible now?" 10 to 15 min.

WHY? PURPOSES
- Get down-to-earth field experience and all the questions and answers about new endeavors out on the table for everyone to understand at the same time
- Create conditions for new ideas to emerge
- Make space for every participant's imagination and experience to show up
- Build skills in listening, storytelling, pattern-finding, questioning, and observing
- Celebrate early adopters and innovators who have gained field experience (often failing forward and vetting the prototype)

TIPS AND TRAPS
- For inner circle, pick only people with direct personal experience (without regard to rank)

- Pick people for the fishbowl (inner circle) who are representative of the distinct roles and functions that require coordination for success
- Encourage inner-circle people to share concrete, very descriptive examples rather than opinions
- Advise inner-circle people to imagine being in a car or a bar sharing stories and having a conversation
- Encourage everyone to share both successes and failures, "the good, the bad, the ugly"
- Enforce the "no speeches" and "talk to each other, not to the outer circle" rules!
- Have fun and encourage animated storytelling

RIFFS AND VARIATIONS

- Leave an open chair or two in the inner circle for someone unexpected to jump in
- With virtual groups, people in the outside circle use the chat function to share questions "to all" or in "pairs" as the conversation unfolds among "the fishes of the inner circle."
- Mash-up or string together **User Experience Fishbowl** with **Improv Prototyping, 25/10 Crowd Sourcing, Ecocycle Planning, Simple Ethnography, Shift & Share**

EXAMPLES

- For transferring on-the-ground knowledge from officers returning from Afghanistan to those replacing them (see "Transforming After-Action Reviews in the Army" in Part Three: Stories from the Field).
- During a Liberating Structures workshop, a few experienced practitioners share stories to deepen the understanding of new users about how to get started and how to get practical results
- During a doctors' meeting, an inner circle of specialists discussed a challenging case in the middle of a group of primary-care physicians, sparking a discussion of the case from specialist and primary-care perspectives
- A pilot group of salespeople shared with the rest of the sales force their experience with a new handheld reporting device. The **User**

Experience Fishbowl helped everybody become comfortable that they knew all they needed to know to adopt the innovation.

- For a public-sector organization trying to expand beyond "hidden" pockets of uplifting service
- Members of an executive management team conducted their meeting in a fishbowl surrounded by all their managers.

ATTRIBUTION

Liberating Structure developed by Henri Lipmanowicz and Keith McCandless and inspired by immersing ourselves in many different kinds of fishbowls over the years.

COLLATERAL MATERIAL

*Below: presentation materials we use to introduce **Users Experience Fishbowl***

User's Experience Fishbowl
Specialists and general practice physicians in Italy are sharing experience about complicated cases.

Heard, Seen, Respected (HSR)

Practice Deeper Listening and Empathy with Colleagues (35 min.)

What is made possible? You can foster the empathetic capacity of participants to "walk in the shoes" of others. Many situations do not have immediate answers or clear resolutions. Recognizing these situations and responding with empathy can improve the "cultural climate" and build trust among group members. **HSR** helps individuals learn to respond in ways that do not overpromise or overcontrol. It helps members of a group notice unwanted patterns and work together on shifting to more productive interactions. Participants experience the practice of more compassion and the benefits it engenders.

FIVE STRUCTURAL ELEMENTS—MIN SPECS

1. Structuring Invitation
- Invite participants to tell a story to a partner about a time when they felt that they were not heard, seen, or respected.
- Ask the listeners to avoid any interruptions other than asking questions like "What else?" or "What happened next?"

2. How Space Is Arranged and Materials Needed
- Chairs facing each other, a few inches between knees
- No tables

3. How Participation Is Distributed
- Everyone has an equal amount of time, in turn, to participate in each role, as a storyteller and a listener

4. How Groups Are Configured
- In pairs for the storytelling
- Then foursomes for reflecting on what happened

5. Sequence of Steps and Time Allocation
- Introduce the purpose of **HSR**: to practice listening without trying to fix anything or make any judgments. 3 min.
- One at a time, each person has 7 minutes to share a story about NOT being heard, seen, or respected. 15 min.

- Partners share with one another the experiences of listening and story-telling: "What did it feel like to tell my story; what did it feel like to listen to your story?" 5 min.
- In a foursome, participants share reflections using 1-2-4, asking, "What patterns are revealed in the stories? What importance do you assign to the pattern?" 5 min.
- As a whole group, participants reflect on the questions, "How could **HSR** be used to address challenges revealed by the patterns? What other Liberating Structures could be used?" 5 min.

WHY? PURPOSES

- Reveal how common it is for people to experience not being heard, seen, or respected
- Reveal how common it is for people to behave in a way that makes other people feel they are not being heard, seen, or respected
- Improve listening, tuning, and empathy among group members
- Notice how much can be accomplished simply by listening
- Rely on each other more when facing confusing or new situations
- Offer catharsis and healing after strains in relationships
- Help managers discern when listening is more effective than trying to solve a problem

TIPS AND TRAPS (FOR INTRODUCING HSR)

- Say, "Your partner may be ready before you. The first story that pops into mind is often the best."
- Make it safe by saying, "You may not want to pick the most painful story that comes to mind."
- Make it safe by saying, "Protect carefully the privacy of the storyteller. Ask what parts, if any, you can share with others."
- Suggest, "When you are the listener, notice when you form a judgment (about what is right or wrong) or when you get an idea about how you can help, then *let it go*."

RIFFS AND VARIATIONS

- If you are feeling brave, replace the word "respected" with "loved" (i.e., the *agape* form of love—seeking the highest good in others without motive for personal gain.)

- String **HSR** together with other Liberating Structures that help to mend relationships: **Troika Consulting, Helping Heuristics, Generative Relationships STAR, Appreciative Interviews, Conversation Café**

EXAMPLES

- For regular meetings to improve the quality of listening and tuning in to each other
- For transition periods when questions about the future are unanswerable (e.g., post-merger integration, market disruptions, social upheaval) and empathetic listening is what is needed
- When individuals or groups have suffered a loss and need a forum to share their grief or despair
- To improve one-on-one reporting relationships up and down in an organization

ATTRIBUTION

Liberating Structure developed by Henri Lipmanowicz and Keith McCandless. Inspired by Seeds of Compassion practitioners and consultant Mark Jones.

COLLATERAL MATERIAL

*Below: presentation materials we use to introduce **HSR***

 HSR Steps

1. With a partner, tell a story about a time when you were NOT heard, seen or respected. 7 minutes for each story.

2. When listening, **don't try to fix anything**. Only ask questions if needed (e.g., *what else, go on, tell me more*)

3. Switch roles, repeat steps 1 & 2

4. In groups of 4 to 8, use What, So What, Now What? to reflect on the experience

Drawing Together

Reveal Insights and Paths Forward Through Nonverbal Expression (40 min.)

What is made possible? You can help people access hidden knowledge such as feelings, attitudes, and patterns that are difficult to express with words. When people are tired, their brains are full, and they have reached the limits of logical thinking, you can help them evoke ideas that lie outside logical, step-by-step understanding of what is possible. Stories about individual or group transformations can be told with five easy-to-draw symbols that have universal meanings. The playful spirit of drawing together signals that more is possible and many new answers are expected. **Drawing Together** cuts through the culture of overreliance on what people say and write that constrains the emergence of novelty. It also provides a new avenue of expression for some people whose ideas would otherwise not surface.

"A vivid imagination compels the whole body to obey." Aristotle

FIVE STRUCTURAL ELEMENTS—MIN SPECS

1. Structuring Invitation
- Invite participants to tell a story about a challenge they face, or a common challenge, using only five symbols and no words

2. How Space Is Arranged and Materials Needed
- An open wall with tapestry paper or easels with blank pages in flip charts
- Water-based markers; soft pastels if you are feeling colorful

3. How Participation Is Distributed
- Everyone is included since the five symbols are easy for everyone to draw
- All participants make their individual drawings simultaneously

4. How Groups Are Configured
- Individually to practice the drawing of the symbols
- Individually to make first and second drafts of their drawings
- Small groups of 1–4 others to interpret the drawings
- Whole group for debrief (using **1-2-4-All** for large groups)

5. Sequence of Steps and Time Allocation

- Introduce the idea of drawing together by drawing and describing the meaning of each symbol. 5 min.

  - Circle = wholeness;
  - Rectangle = support;
  - Triangle = goal;
  - Spiral = change;
  - Star person [equidistant cross] = relationship

- Invite participants to practice drawing the five symbols: circle, rectangle, triangle, spiral, star person. 5 min.
- Invite participants to combine the symbols to create the first draft of a story, working individually and without words, about "the journey" of working on a challenge or an innovation. 10 min.
- Invite participants to create a second draft, in which they refine their story by dramatizing the size, placement, and color of the symbols. 10 min.
- Ask participants to invite another individual or their small group to interpret their drawings. Remind them that the person who has done the drawing does not speak. 5 min.
- Ask the whole group, "Together, what do the drawings reveal?" Use **1-2-4-All** with larger groups. 5 min.

*Below: visual stories created in 40-minute **Drawing Together** sessions*

 Stories Without Words
Examples from **Drawing Together** in Peru, Belgium and Canada.

WHY? PURPOSES

- Reveal insight or understanding not accessible with verbal or linear methods
- Tap all the sources of knowledge for innovation (explicit, tacit, latent/emergent)
- Signal that a quest or journey in search of new discoveries is under way
- Develop and deepen shared understanding of a vision or complex dynamics
- Create closer connections among group members

TIPS AND TRAPS

- Remind participants that the drawing is not the object by saying, "Refined drawing skills are not required—get over your need for perfection! Childlike drawing looks playful and captures the imagination of others!"
- Don't help too much with drawing skills
- Help participants accept whatever emerges in the drawings (there are often surprises)
- Draw or present an example of a story that helps others make a leap of understanding
- Record the participants drawing with cameras and video recorders
- Return to the drawings when you reconvene as a group
- Remember that drawing can be powerfully therapeutic; be prepared for emotional responses

RIFFS AND VARIATIONS

- One person can visually map conversations during a meeting (add words if you must)
- Start small: use a single sheet of 8½ " by 11" paper to get started
- Computer tablets can be used instead of paper for participants to learn how to tell a story with the five symbols on their tablets
- Use the Hero's Journey as a template for the stories
- Use as a template a progression from status quo, through call to novelty, discovery, validation, early adoption, and spread

EXAMPLES

- For a refreshing change of pace in a long meeting when a creative burst is needed
- When there are strong differences in perspective and the group is in a rut
- For visual facilitation of a meeting or conference, where drawings are created as the conversation unfolds
- For revealing obscure or hidden relationships when working on a complex project (e.g., one doctoral student had a eureka moment via **Drawing Together**)
- For helping a vision statement come to life (particularly for visually oriented people)
- For individual work, to visualize tacit or latent approaches to a challenge

ATTRIBUTION

Liberating Structure developed by Henri Lipmanowicz and Keith McCandless. Inspired by David Sibbet (The Grove, www.thegrove.com) and Angeles Arrien (see *Signs of Life*).

Design StoryBoards—Basic

Define Step-by-Step Elements for Bringing Meetings to Productive Endpoints (25–70 min.)

What is made possible? The most common causes of dysfunctional meetings can be eliminated: unclear purpose or lack of a common one, time wasters, restrictive participation, absent voices, groupthink, and frustrated participants. The process of designing a storyboard draws out a purpose that becomes clearer as it is matched with congruent microstructures. It reveals who needs to be included for successful implementation. Storyboards invite design participants to carefully define all the micro-organizing elements needed to achieve their purpose: a structuring invitation, space, materials, participation, group configurations, and facilitation and time allocations. Storyboards prevent people from starting and running meetings without an explicit design. Good designs yield better-than-expected results by uncovering tacit and latent sources of innovation.

 ## Launching an Initiative
Multiple disciplines and functional groups are involved. Note that facilitation is shared.

Agenda Item	Goal	LS Micro-Structure	Why this LS?	Steps / Timing	Facilitator / Participants
Welcome	Form working group, get acquainted	Impromptu Networking	Demonstrates respect for each person & discipline included	3 rounds in pairs, 5 minutes each	Carlos, all
Preparing to Launch Project	Make space for innovation	TRIZ, 1-2-4-All	Some of our successful practices have become overly mature (rigid) over time	3 steps, 10 minutes each	Jenny, groups of 4 then whole group
Attracting Broad Participation	Define and sharpen purpose	Nine Whys	We want to attract broad participation, innovating in many settings without formal controls	One rounds of 1-2-4, 30 minutes total	Katie, then groups of four
Action Planning	Identify action, get started now	25-To-10 Crowdsourcing	We have a *do-er* culture that benefits from self-discovery in a group	25 minutes for 5 rounds + action group formation	Carlos, all

FIVE STRUCTURAL ELEMENTS—MIN SPECS

1. Structuring Invitation
- Invite a design team (a representative subset of the group) to create a detailed plan, including visual cues, for how participants will interact to achieve their purpose

2. How Space Is Arranged and Materials Needed
- An open wall with tapestry paper or flip-chart pages
- 2-by-4-inch Post-its and/or Liberating Structures Playing Cards
- A blank storyboard (see Collateral Material)

3. How Participation Is Distributed
- Everyone involved in the design and planning of the meeting has an equal opportunity to contribute

4. How Groups Are Configured
- **1-2-All** or 1-All in rapid cycles for each step below

5. Sequence of Steps and Time Allocation
- Clarify the purpose of your work together (use **Nine Whys** if needed). 2 to 5 min.
- Describe the standard approach or microstructure you would normally use for this session (including who is normally present) and assess how it succeeds and fails in achieving the stated purpose. 5 to 10 min.
- Reexamine and strengthen the purpose statement if needed. 2 to 5 min.
- Reexamine and decide who needs to participate or be involved. 2 to 5 min.
- Brainstorm alternative microstructures (both conventional and Liberating Structures) that could achieve the purpose. Determine whether the purpose can be achieved in one step. If not, what must be the purpose of the first step? Continue with first step only. 5 to 10 min.
- Determine which microstructures are best suited to achieving the purpose; choose one plus a backup. 2 to 10 min.
- Decide who will be invited and who will facilitate the meeting. Enter all your decisions in the blank storyboard. 2 to 10 min.
- Determine the questions and process you will use to evaluate your design (e.g., Did the design achieve desired outcomes? Did the group

work together in a productive way? Does something new seem possible now? Use **What, So What, Now What?**) 2 to 5 min.

- If multiple steps are needed, confer with the design team and arrange a meeting to work on an **Advanced Design StoryBoard** (see description below). 5 to 10 min.

WHY? PURPOSES

- Evoke a purpose that is clear for all
- Make the work in meetings productive and enjoyable for all
- Give everyone a chance to make contributions
- Foster synergy among participants
- Help everyone find his or her role by making the design process visible
- Reveal the weaknesses of the current practice and step up from it
- Tap all the sources of knowledge for innovation (explicit, tacit, latent/ emergent)

TIPS AND TRAPS

- Encourage and seriously play with fast iterations; repeat and deepen your design
- At a minimum, work in pairs (a second set of eyes and ears really helps) or small groups
- Use icons and sketches to quickly develop shared understanding and actionable ideas
- Always include a design debrief (**What, So What, Now What?**)
- Don't skimp on the time necessary to generate a good design. A good design will reduce wasted meeting time by much more than it took to create it. A bad design will generate frustration.

RIFFS AND VARIATIONS

- Use the same approach to map ethnographic observations of a current practice
- Use a pie chart to illuminate and balance the goals and flow of your design

EXAMPLES

- For management meetings of all stripes
- Project reviews
- Classroom sessions
- Brainstorming sessions
- One-on-one meetings
- Planning a learning session for a conference. See "Fixing a Broken Child Welfare System" in Part Three: Stories from the Field.

ATTRIBUTION

Liberating Structure developed by Henri Lipmanowicz and Keith McCandless.

Design StoryBoards—Advanced

Define Step-by-Step Elements for Bringing Transformation and Innovation Initiatives to Productive Endpoints (18 hours to days/weeks)

What is made possible? You can avoid many of the traps that turn transformation initiatives and innovation projects into failures: the lack of a clear and common purpose, overall and for every stage of the initiative; inadequate engagement and participation; voices that are essential but not included; frustrated participants and nonparticipants; resistance to change; groupthink; nightmarish implementation for a disproportionally small impact. A comprehensive design is a series of basic designs (see **Design StoryBoards— Basic** above) linked together over a period of time. The design unfolds iteratively over days, weeks, months, or sometimes years depending on the scale of the project. Small cycles of design operate within larger cycles, scaling up and out as the initiative proceeds. You can easily include more people and more diversity in the design group for larger-scale projects. You can reflect the twists and turns in a transformation or innovation effort by a careful *and* ad hoc selection of participants (including unusual suspects since they are often the source of novel approaches).

FIVE STRUCTURAL ELEMENTS—MIN SPECS

1. Structuring Invitation

- Invite an initial design team to create a detailed plan, including visual cues, for how participants will interact to achieve their purpose

2. How Space Is Arranged and Materials Needed

- An open wall with tapestry paper or flip-chart pages
- 2-by-4-inch Post-its and/or Liberating Structures Playing Cards
- A blank storyboard template (see Collateral Materials)

3. How Participation Is Distributed

- Everyone on the design team involved in the design and planning of the project has an equal opportunity to contribute

4. How Groups Are Configured

- **1-2-All** or 1-All in rapid cycles for each step below

5. Sequence of Steps and Time Allocation

- Determine the composition of a design team that includes all relevant stakeholders and assemble the team (the composition can be adjusted ad hoc over time as the work progresses). 1 to 3 hrs.
- Design team clarifies the overall purpose of the initiative (use **Nine Whys** or a more elaborate microstructure as needed). 1 to 6 hrs.
- Describe in detail what happens when people use the current product, service, or approach that you wish to transform/improve. You may need to use a method like the Liberating Structure called **Simple Ethnography** to gather data for an accurate description of this current user experience. 6 hrs. to days or weeks.
- Based on the users' experience, assess how the current product, service, or approach succeeds and fails in achieving the stated purpose. 3 hrs. to days.
- Reexamine and strengthen the purpose statement if needed. 1 to 6 hrs.
- Reexamine and decide who needs to participate in the core design group and who needs to participate on the periphery to help with vetting or field testing. 1 to 3 hrs.
- Brainstorm and outline alternative microstructures (both conventional and Liberating Structures) that help achieve the purpose. 3 hrs. to days.
- Break up your outline into steps or chunks that can be designed and function independently (don't try to put together a comprehensive design from the start). 1 to 6 hrs.
- Determine a design for one step, selecting microstructures that are suited to achieving the purpose; choose one plus a backup. Repeat and continue with each step. 1 to 6 hrs.
- Decide whether any testing or vetting of your design is feasible or desirable. Consider testing in waves and in different configurations. 1 to 6 hrs.
- Implement the first step in a simulated or field setting. Continue testing in more extreme conditions.
- Evaluate the first and then the subsequent steps of your design. Determine the questions and process you will use to evaluate your overall design (e.g.: Did the design achieve desired outcomes? Did the group work together and coordinate tasks in a productive way? Does

something new seem possible now? Use **What, So What, Now What?**).
- Repeat design cycle and refine the design for the next step, and so on...

WHY? PURPOSES

- Make a significant and enduring advance by breaking away from current reality
- Provide enough time for new behaviors to take shape and spread, expanding what others believe is possible to accomplish
- See additional Purposes under **Design StoryBoards–Basic** above.

TIPS AND TRAPS

- Resist the urge for action and do not skimp on time spent designing the storyboard then assessing and adjusting it
- Establish a core design team and keep the door open to others that want to join in
- Don't forget to include users!
- Share the design widely
- Remember that a design makes it possible to improvise as you go: if one element of your design is not achieving its purpose, go to your backup (or a backup of your backup)
- Shoot for the moon with your feet firmly on the ground (i.e., anchored in user's experience research)
- Use icons and sketches to quickly develop shared understanding

RIFFS AND VARIATIONS

- In place of focus groups with users, invite the users to participate in designing a storyboard to improve their experience with a product or service
- Find an illustrator or cartoonist to dramatize your work

EXAMPLES

- For redesigning the exchange of information and responsibilities at shift change

- For transforming from a product-centric to a customer-focused market strategy
- For reforming how academic training prepares students for practice in the field
- Read "Turning a Business Around" in Part Three: Stories from the Field. Alison Joslyn's management team used Design StoryBoard to formulate strategy discussions and launch Liberating Structures "basic training" for product managers and sales reps.
- See examples in Chapter 7, "From Strings to Storyboards"

ATTRIBUTION

Liberating Structure developed by Henri Lipmanowicz and Keith McCandless.

Celebrity Interview

Reconnect the Experience of Leaders and Experts with People Closest to the Challenge at Hand (35 to 60 min.)

What is made possible? You can enable a large group of people to connect with a leader or an expert (the celebrity) as a person and grasp the nuances of how that person is approaching a challenge. With a well-designed interview, you can turn what would otherwise be a passive, often boring presentation into a personal narrative that is entertaining, imparts valuable knowledge, and reveals the full range of rational, emotional, and ethical/moral dynamics at play. You can often turn the interview into an invitation to action, drawing out all the elements needed to spark the participant group's imagination and encourage cohesive action.

FIVE STRUCTURAL ELEMENTS—MIN SPECS

1. Structuring Invitation
- Invite the celebrity to let go of his or her formal presentation or speech and answer the *harder* questions on everyone's mind in a casual "talk show" format
- Invite group members to listen, see the person behind the celebrity, and write down questions with colleagues

2. How Space Is Arranged and Materials Needed
- Interviewer and celebrity in the front of the room where everyone can see and hear the interaction (lapel microphones, bar stools, or living-room furniture recommended)
- Unlimited number of people in a space where they can sit to view the interview and later form small groups (theater-style seating is OK)
- 3-by-5-inch cards to collect questions generated via **1-2-4**

3. How Participation Is Distributed
- Part one, interview: everyone has an equal opportunity to listen
- Part two, questions: everyone has an equal opportunity to engage with one another to formulate questions

How Groups Are Configured
- Whole group for interview
- Individuals, pairs, small groups for **1-2-4** to generate questions

Sequence of Steps and Time Allocation
- Interviewer welcomes and introduces the celebrity and topic to be discussed. 3 min.
- Interviewer asks questions that the audience would be expected to ask (both humor and gravity are appropriate). 15–30 min.
- Invite participants to generate additional questions in a 1-2-4 conversation and then on 3-by-5-inch cards. 5–10 min.
- Interviewer sifts the cards, looking for patterns and asking additional questions to the celebrity. 5–10 min.
- Interviewer makes closing comments, thanks the celebrity. 1 min.

WHY? PURPOSES

- Create or boost a connection between an expert or leader and an audience
- Give substance and depth to a topic
- Avoid boring lectures and PowerPoint presentations
- Engage every individual in generating questions for further exploration
- Shed light on the person behind the position or expertise
- Bring big concepts to life with stories that come out in the interview

TIPS AND TRAPS

- A good sequence of starting questions is: What first inspired you in this work? What challenges you in this work? What keeps you going in this work? What do you hope can happen for us in this work?
- Give the questions to the celebrity in advance
- If possible, send background materials to participants in advance
- Do not allow the introduction to become a minilecture
- Interview questions should not be trivial or easy to answer
- Interviewer must ask repeatedly for stories and concrete details that illustrate concepts
- Interviewer may ask the celebrity, "*Why* is _____ important to YOU (not the larger organization or system)?"

RIFFS AND VARIATIONS

- Have fun with riffs from the talk-show genre: channel Oprah, Stephen Colbert, or your favorite celebrity interviewer
- The interviewer can conduct research in advance of the session, asking participants, "What do you want to know but would not dare to ask? What is the most important thing you want to know about this person or the work ahead?"
- Use a storytelling template to structure your interview (e.g., the Hero's Journey).
- For strategy sessions, dig deeper into challenges by asking: What is happening around us that demands creative adaptation? What happens if we do nothing? Given our purpose, what seems possible now? If our current strategies were obliterated last night, what parts would you bring back today?
- Use with virtual groups. Conduct the voice/video interview while inviting all other participants to develop questions and comments in pairs or groups. Share the top questions via the chat function to "all" when the interview is complete.
- String together with **User Experience Fishbowl, Open Space, DAD,** and **What I Need From You**

EXAMPLES

- For a leader or leaders to help launch a new initiative
- To welcome and get to know a new leader coming into the organization
- To personalize and deepen the contributions of an expert
- For debriefing the experience of a few participants in an important event
- As an alternative to a case-study presentation: the interviewer helps to revive the story and the local context underneath the analysis

ATTRIBUTION

Liberating Structure developed by Henri Lipmanowicz and Keith McCandless. Inspired by seriously playful improvisers in Venezuela.

Social Network Webbing

Map Informal Connections and Decide How to Strengthen the Network to Achieve a Purpose (1 hr.)

What is made possible? Social Network Webbing quickly illuminates for a whole group what resources are hidden within their existing network of relationships and what steps to take for tapping those resources. It also makes it easy to identify opportunities for building stronger connections as well as new ones. The inclusive approach makes the network visible and understandable to everybody in the group simultaneously. It encourages individuals to take the initiative for building a stronger network rather than receiving directions through top-down assignments. Informal or loose connections—even your friends' friends' friend—are tapped in a way that can have a powerful influence on progress without detailed planning and big investments.

FIVE STRUCTURAL ELEMENTS—MIN SPECS

1. Structuring Invitation
- Invite the members of a core working group with a shared purpose to create a map of their network and to decide how to expand and strengthen it
- Ask them to name the people they are currently working with and those they would like to include in the future (i.e., people with influence or expertise they need to achieve their purpose)
- Invite them to "weave" connections in the network web to advance their purpose

2. How Space Is Arranged and Materials Needed
- A long open wall with a tapestry paper or multiple flip-chart pages
- 2-by-2-inch Post-it notes in at least 8 colors
- Bold-tip black pens (e.g., Sharpies)

3. How Participation Is Distributed
- Everyone involved in the core working or planning group is included
- Everyone has an equal opportunity to contribute

4. How Groups Are Configured
- **1-2-4-All** to generate the names of all the key groups

- Everyone together to generate the names of people in the network and construct the map

5. Sequence of Steps and Time Allocation

- Create a legend of all the key groups in the network and assign a Post-it color or symbol for each. 5 min.
- Every core group member prints clearly his or her name on a Post-it. Put the Post-its in a group in the center of the wall. 5 min.
- Ask all core group members, "What people do you know that are active in this work?" Tell them to create a Post-it with each of their names. Ask them to arrange the Post-its based on each person's degrees of separation from each design group member. 10 min.
- Ask all core group members, "Who else would you like to include in this work?" Invite them to brainstorm and create Post-its for the other people they would like to include. Ask them to build the map of Post-its as a web with a core and periphery structure (mimicking the actual and desired spread of participation). They may need to add new legend categories and colors. 10 min.
- Tell the core group to step back and ask, "Who knows whom? Who has influence and expertise? Who can block progress? Who can boost progress?" Ask them to illustrate the answers with connecting lines. 15 min.
- Ask the group to devise strategies to: 1) invite, attract, and "weave" new people into their work; 2) work around blockages; and 3) boost progress. 10 min.

WHY? PURPOSES

- Tap the informal connections that have indirect yet powerful influence on behavior and results
- Disseminate knowledge and innovation across scales and through boundaries—within and beyond the organization
- Develop more frontline ownership and leadership for change
- Help people see connections and "black holes"
- Help people self-organize and develop groups that are more resilient and able to absorb disruptions
- Tip the balance toward positive change

- Operate without big budgets and extensive planning by tapping the informal social networks and inviting people to contribute.

TIPS AND TRAPS

- Ask the core group to focus on developing a core group that gets things done and a diverse periphery that adds new ideas and growth
- Encourage members to dream BIG when considering whom they want to include in the future
- Do not include more than 10 functions or distinct groups in the legend: it gets too confusing!
- Write down people's names whenever possible instead of positions/titles
- When weaving and connecting people, tell core members to think small (e.g., pairs, small interest groups)
- Learn more from Smart Networks cofounder June Holley at www.networkweaver.com/

RIFFS AND VARIATIONS

- Come back to the maps frequently: update who is involved now and growth patterns
- Use software to make the network maps, providing more detail and metrics
- String webbing sessions together with follow-up action steps via **15% Solutions, Design StoryBoards, 1-2-4-All**

EXAMPLES

- For a hospital core team working to engage everyone in preventing the spread of infections
- For a group of Lean coaches to informally spread skills and methods among frontline staff
- For middle managers in a financial organization to develop prototypes and launch new products in multiple markets
- For provincial government leaders "translating" policy-to-practice initiatives across diverse settings
- For expanding the use of a new technology, the early adopters gathered and mapped out their network to identify potential new users

ATTRIBUTION

Liberating Structure developed by Henri Lipmanowicz and Keith McCandless.
Inspired by June Holley, network weaver.

COLLATERAL MATERIAL

*Below: presentation material we use to introduce **Social Network Webbing**, featuring a map of relationships to improve safety*

 # Network Mapping In Progress
Make a legend, add names of current and desired participants,
step back to consider how to invite others into the work.

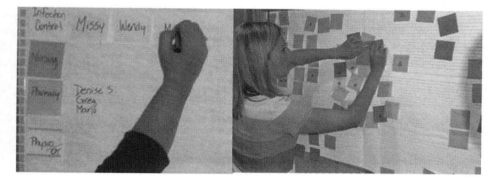

"What I Need From You" (WINFY)

Surfacing Needs and Working across Functions and Disciplines (55 to 70 min.)

What is made possible? People working in different functions and disciplines can quickly improve how they ask each other for what they need to be successful. You can mend misunderstandings or dissolve prejudices developed over time by demystifying what group members need in order to achieve common goals. Since participants articulate core needs to others and each person involved in the exchange is given the chance to respond, you boost clarity, integrity, and transparency while promoting cohesion and coordination across silos: you can put Humpty Dumpty back together again!

FIVE STRUCTURAL ELEMENTS—MIN SPECS

1. Structuring Invitation
- Invite participants to ask for what they need from others (often in different functions or disciplines) to be successful in reaching a specific goal
- Invite them also to respond unambiguously to the requests from others

2. How Space Is Arranged and Materials Needed
- Large room to accommodate 3 to 7 functional clusters of participants in different sections
- Chairs for a group of 3 to 7 people to sit in a circle in the middle of the room
- Paper for participants to record needs and responses

3. How Participation Is Distributed[1]
- Everyone is included in his or her functional cluster
- Everyone has an equal opportunity to contribute

4. How Groups Are Configured
- Three to 7 functional clusters (no limit on number of participants in each cluster)
- One group of 3 to 7 spokespersons to speak on behalf of each functional cluster

5. Sequence of Steps and Time Allocation

- Explain the process by describing the steps below. Reiterate the goal or challenge being addressed to make sure that the context is the same for all. Emphasize that requests must be clear and specific if they are to receive an unambiguous yes or no response. Make it clear that no answers other than *yes, no, I will try*, and *whatever* will be allowed. Position the functional clusters around the room. 3 min.

- Functional clusters use **1-2-4-All** (or 1-2-All) to make a list of their top needs from each of the other functions in the room. Needs are expressed as requests that can be delivered with care and nuance in the following form: "What I need from you is _____." Clusters reduce their lists to two top needs, write these down in their expected form, and select a spokesperson to represent the cluster. 5–15 min.

- All spokespersons gather in a circle in the middle of the room.

- One by one, spokespersons state their two needs to each of the other spokespersons around the circle. At this stage, spokespersons take notes of requests, but no one gives answers or responses. 15 min.

- Working individually (or by conferring with others in their functional cluster), each spokesperson writes down one of four responses to each request: *yes, no, I will try*, or *whatever* (whatever means the request was too vague to provide a specific answer). 5–10 min.

- Addressing one spokesperson in the group at a time, every spokesperson in the circle repeats the requests made by him or her, then shares his or her responses (*yes, no, I will try*, or *whatever*). *No discussion! No elaboration!* 10 min.

- Debrief with **What, So What, Now What?** 15 min.

WHY? PURPOSES

- Learn how to articulate functional and/or personal needs clearly
- Practice asking for what functions and/or individuals need
- Learn how to give clear answers to requests
- Reestablish and/or improve communication inside functional clusters
- Make progress across functional silos
- Mend connections that have been broken
- Get all the issues out on the table at the same time for everyone to see
- Reduce frustration by eliminating preconceptions and rumors

- Build trust so that group members can share accountability with integrity

TIPS AND TRAPS

- Remind participants that a *whatever* response means their request was too vague to provide a specific answer
- Strictly enforce the "no immediate response" rule
- Strictly enforce the rule that the only responses are *yes, no, I will try,* or *whatever* (no further elaboration is allowed)
- Encourage everyone to ask for what they truly need to be successful
- Have fun and encourage a safe amount of drama
- Don't include more than 7 roles/functions (the waters get too muddy)
- In debriefing, try to draw out that people are good at complaining and not so good at asking for what they need. **WINFY** helps you move from complaints to valid requests.
- Use question-and-response cards to help groups sharpen how they express their requests

RIFFS AND VARIATIONS

- Consider a second round if too much appears to be unresolved or unclear: making concrete and clear requests is an essential skill!
- In the debrief, give participants a chance to articulate what was not asked of them: something neglected that would help achieve the groups' purpose but was not requested
- Instead of functional clusters, use the same **WINFY** sequence with a group or a team of individuals who are interdependent
- String together with **Helping Heuristics, Integrated~Autonomy, Appreciative Interviews, Ecocycle**

EXAMPLES

- For a global technical group (with members in multiple countries) facing the need to make decisions in a fast-changing market (see "Getting Commitment, Ownership, and Follow-Through" in Part Three: Stories from the Field).

- For three top executives who are struggling to give consistent direction to the next level of leaders in the organization
- For hospital executives and managers launching a patient-centered care initiative that requires multi-specialty collaboration
- For helping one-on-one relationships become more generative

ATTRIBUTION

Liberating Structure developed by Henri Lipmanowicz and Keith McCandless. Inspired by consultant Kathie Dannemiller and professor Dan Pesut.

COLLATERAL MATERIAL

Below: presentation material we use to introduce **WINFY**

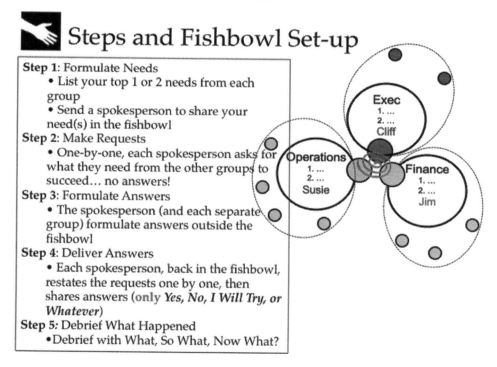

Steps and Fishbowl Set-up

Step 1: Formulate Needs
- List your top 1 or 2 needs from each group
- Send a spokesperson to share your need(s) in the fishbowl

Step 2: Make Requests
- One-by-one, each spokesperson asks for what they need from the other groups to succeed… no answers!

Step 3: Formulate Answers
- The spokesperson (and each separate group) formulate answers outside the fishbowl

Step 4: Deliver Answers
- Each spokesperson, back in the fishbowl, restates the requests one by one, then shares answers (only *Yes, No, I Will Try, or Whatever*)

Step 5: Debrief What Happened
- Debrief with What, So What, Now What?

Exec
1. …
2. …
Cliff

Operations
1. …
2. …
Susie

Finance
1. …
2. …
Jim

Open Space Technology

Liberate Inherent Action and Leadership in Groups of Any Size (90 minutes and up to 3 days)

What is made possible? When people must tackle a common complex challenge, you can release their inherent creativity and leadership as well as their capacity to self-organize. **Open Space** makes it possible to include everybody in constructing agendas and addressing issues that are important to them. Having cocreated the agenda and free to follow their passion, people will take responsibility very quickly for solving problems and moving into action. Letting go of central control (i.e., the agenda and assignments) and putting it in the hands of all the participants generates commitment, action, innovation, and follow-through. You can use **Open Space** with groups as large as a couple of thousand people!

One day a student asked, "What is the most difficult part of painting?" The master answered, "The part of paper where nothing is painted is the most difficult." Painting Zen

FIVE STRUCTURAL ELEMENTS—MIN SPECS

1. Structuring Invitation
- Invite people to come and address a complex problem
- Invite participants to co-construct the agenda by posting sessions that they will convene on topics they are passionate about
- Invite participants to join any session that they care about

2. How Space Is Arranged and Materials Needed
- Chairs in concentric circles for 10–1,000 people in a large room or open space
- Microphones needed for groups larger than 40
- Large blank agenda posted on easels and flip charts, long tapestry paper, or whiteboard
- Agenda to include slots for enough concurrent sessions to accommodate what is likely to emerge given the challenge and the number of participants. (One rule of thumb is that 3 out of 10 participants will post a session, e.g., there will be 15 sessions posted from 50 participants.)

3. How Participation Is Distributed
- Everyone who cares about the challenge at hand and accepts the organizers' invitation is included
- Everyone has an equal opportunity to contribute

- The "Law of Two Feet" governs the participation of all attendees in the various sessions. It says: "Go and attend whichever session you want, but if you find yourself in a session where you are not learning or contributing, use your two feet!"

4. How Groups Are Configured
- Start together in one large circle (or as many concentric circles as needed)
- Continue with groups of various sizes self-organized around agenda topics

5. Sequence of Steps and Time Allocation

	Short Form	Long Form
	90 minutes total time	Up to 3 days
Leader and/or facilitator introduces the concept and mechanics of **Open Space**, including the Law of Two Feet and its Four Principles.	5 min.	20-45 min.
"Marketplace" opens: participants propose topics plus a time and place for groups to meet.	15 min.	20-30 min.
Conveners facilitate sessions; groups develop recommendations and action plans. Notes are taken and published or posted.	2 rounds of 30 min. sessions or 1 round of 60 min.	Several rounds of 60-90 min. sessions
Debrief, proceedings distributed, and closing.	10 min.	60 min. Daily

WHY? PURPOSES
- Generate action and build energy, commitment, and shared leadership
- Address intractable problems or conflicts by unleashing self-organization

- Make sure that ALL of the issues that are most important to the participants are raised, included in the agenda, and addressed
- Make it possible for participants to take responsibility for tackling the issues that they care about and for what does or doesn't happen

TIPS AND TRAPS

- To get started, we recommend reading *Open Space Technology: A User's Guide* by the founder of Open Space, Harrison Owen. All the elements to try **Open Space** for the first time are included and described very clearly.
- A compelling challenge and attractive invitation are key requirements.
- Write up the entire proceedings in a single document, completed and distributed/shared immediately during the meeting.
- The facilitator should introduce the Law of Two Feet, Four Principles, and the mechanics of **Open Space** in a seriously entertaining fashion.
- As the facilitator, notice when you form a judgment (about what is right or wrong) or an idea about how you can help, then "let it go": do one less thing!
- A meeting without the Law of Two Feet—namely, one where the agenda is created by the participants but people are not free to attend the session of their choice—is NOT **Open Space**!

RIFFS AND VARIATIONS

- Reopen the Marketplace a second time each morning (bigger collaborations may emerge)
- String together with **Celebrity Interview**, **Appreciative Interviews**, and/or **TRIZ** before you start **Open Space** and with **25/10 Crowd Sourcing** after closing.
- Other forms of **Open Space** are called unconferences and BarCamps.

EXAMPLES

- For management meetings of all stripes
- Read "Turning a Business Around" in Part Three: Stories from the Field. Alison Joslyn launched a business transformation by inviting all employees to a three-day **Open Space** meeting.

- Read "Inventing Future Health-Care Practice" in Part Three. Chris McCarthy uses Open Space to set direction for collaboration among the creative members of the Innovation Learning Network.
- Immediately after a merger, for bringing together all the employees of both companies to shape next steps and take action together.
- To share IT innovation prototypes and unleash collaborative action among widely distributed grantees.

ATTRIBUTION

Invented by Harrison Owen (see *Open Space Technology: A User's Guide*). Short form developed to fit in Liberating Structures milieu by Henri Lipmanowicz and Keith McCandless.

COLLATERAL MATERIAL

Below: an Open Space circle in Madrid

Generative Relationships S T A R

Reveal Relationship Patterns That Create Surprising Value or Dysfunctions (25 min.)

What is made possible? You can help a group of people understand how they work together and identify changes that they can make to improve group performance. All members of the group diagnose current relationship patterns and decide how to follow up with action steps together, without intermediaries. The STAR compass tool helps group members understand what makes their relationships more or less generative. The compass used in the initial diagnosis can also be used later to evaluate progress in developing relationships that are more generative.

FIVE STRUCTURAL ELEMENTS—MIN SPECS

1. Structuring Invitation
- Invite participants to assess their working group or team in terms of four attributes:

    - **S** Separateness: the amount of diversity in perspective, expertise, and background among group members
    - **T** Tuning: the level of listening deeply, reflecting, and making sense of challenges together
    - **A** Action: the number of opportunities to act on ideas or innovate with group members
    - **R** Reason to work together: the benefits that are gained from working together
    - Invite them to jointly shape action steps to boost generative results

2. How Space Is Arranged and Materials Needed
- Tables for small groups of 4, with a STAR compass graphic and pens for each individual
- A STAR compass graphic on a flip-chart page for each small group
- A STAR compass graphic on a flip-chart page for the whole group

3. How Participation Is Distributed
- Everyone in a working group or team is included

- Everyone has an equal opportunity to contribute

4. How Groups Are Configured
- Individually to make initial assessments
- Small groups
- Whole group

5. Sequence of Steps and Time Allocation
- Participants individually assess *where the team is* in regard to each of the four elements (5 min.):

  - **S** How diverse are we as a group? Do we draw out our diverse perspectives among members?

  - **T** How well are we in tune with one another?

  - **A** How much do we act together?

  - **R** How important is it that we work together? How clear is our purpose?

- In small groups, participants place a dot along each compass point, then talk with their neighbors (1-2-4) about their placements, looking for consensus and differences. 5 min.
- Small groups decide what type of results are generated by the pattern of interaction they have identified (e.g., high **T**uning + no **A**ction = we get along well but accomplish little, high **A**ction + low **T**uning = routine results with no innovation, high **T**uning + high **S**eparateness + high **A**ction + low **R**eason = many false starts, etc.). 5 min.
- In small groups, brainstorm action steps to boost elements that need attention. 5 min.
- Whole group assembles list of action steps and decides "What first steps can we take right now?" 5 min.

WHY? PURPOSES
- Improve the performance of a team
- Help a team become more self-managing and autonomous
- Sharpen the purpose and identity of the group
- Help people step away from blaming individuals and move toward understanding their patterns of interaction

---

- Combine "diagnosis and treatment" without separating the planners from the doers
- Reduce frustration of people not happy with team dynamics and results

TIPS AND TRAPS

- Work up from the individuals to pairs, then table conversations
- Avoid making right or wrong judgments about where people assess the team
- Encourage team members to research, organize, and act on their own remedies
- Finish the activity with at least one specific action for each participant
- Make sure that who is going to do what by when is clear for all

RIFFS AND VARIATIONS

- String together with Liberating Structures that may boost low compass-point assessments:

  - Separateness (Conversation Café; Shift & Share; What, So What, Now What?)
  - Tuning (Wise Crowds; Troika Consulting; Agreement-Certainty Matrix; Heard, Seen, Respected)
  - A Action (25/10 Crowd Sourcing, 15% Solutions, Open Space, Min Specs)
  - Reason (Nine Whys, What I Need From You)

- Use with virtual groups by inviting participants to place their STAR assessments with a dot on the chart on the whiteboard, then chat in pairs and with the whole group about the pattern that emerges. You may want to create a "synthesizer" role to help keep things moving. Generate action steps via a chat version of 1-2-All.

EXAMPLES

- For a strategy retreat, focusing attention on group dynamics and results

- For deciding the composition and purpose of a new team or task force to be formed
- For two people to use in mending their relationship

ATTRIBUTION

Developed by professor Brenda Zimmerman (learn more from Professor Zimmerman at www.change-ability.ca/Change-Ability.html). Adapted by Henri Lipmanowicz and Keith McCandless.

COLLATERAL MATERIAL

Below: presentation material we use to introduce **Generative Relationships STAR**

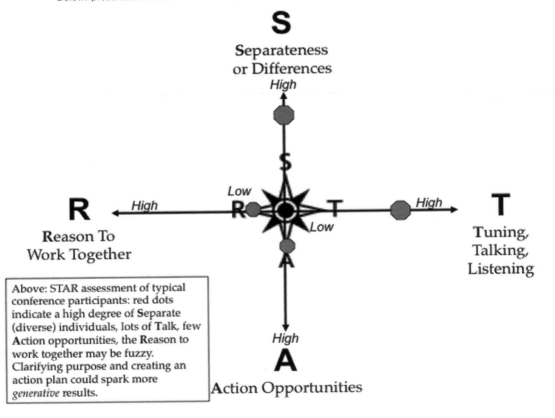

Above: STAR assessment of typical conference participants: red dots indicate a high degree of Separate (diverse) individuals, lots of Talk, few Action opportunities, the Reason to work together may be fuzzy. Clarifying purpose and creating an action plan could spark more *generative* results.

Agreement-and-Certainty Matching Matrix

Sort Challenges into Simple, Complicated, Complex, and Chaotic Domains (45 min.)

What is made possible? You can help individuals or groups avoid the frequent mistake of trying to solve a problem with methods that are not adapted to the nature of their challenge. The combination of two questions makes it possible to easily sort challenges into four categories: *simple, complicated, complex,* and *chaotic.* A problem is simple when it can be solved reliably with practices that are easy to duplicate. It is complicated when experts are required to devise a sophisticated solution that will yield the desired results predictably. A problem is complex when there are several valid ways to proceed but outcomes are not predictable in detail. Chaotic is when the context is too turbulent to identify a path forward. A loose analogy may be used to describe these differences: *simple* is like following a recipe, *complicated* like sending a rocket to the moon, *complex* like raising a child, and *chaotic* is like the game "Pin the Tail on the Donkey." The Liberating Structures Matching Matrix in Chapter 5 can be used as the first step to clarify the nature of a challenge and avoid the mismatches between problems and solutions that are frequently at the root of chronic, recurring problems.

"If I had an hour to solve a problem and my life depended on the solution, I would spend the first 55 minutes determining the proper question to ask...."
Albert Einstein

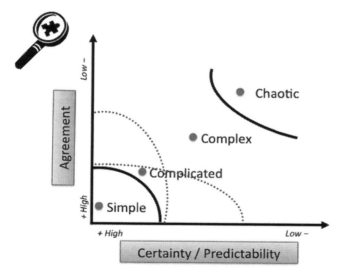

Source: adapted from professors Brenda Zimmerman and Ralph Stacey

FIVE STRUCTURAL ELEMENTS—MIN SPECS

1. Structuring Invitation

- Invite participants to categorize their current challenges as simple, complicated, complex, or chaotic
- Ask them to place every challenge in the matrix based on their answers to two questions: What is the degree of agreement among the participants regarding the challenge and the best way to address it? What is the degree of certainty and predictability about what results will be generated from the solutions proposed for addressing the challenge?
- Ask them to think about the approaches they are using or considering to address each challenge, evaluate how well these fit, and determine where there are mismatches

2. How Space Is Arranged and Materials Needed

- Chairs for people to sit in groups of 4–6, with or without small round tables
- Long open wall with a large tapestry paper illustration of the matrix taped to the wall
- One page with a blank matrix for every participant
- Post-it notes and markers for everybody

3. How Participation Is Distributed

- Everyone involved in the work team or unit under discussion (not only leaders)
- Everyone has an equal opportunity to contribute

4. How Groups Are Configured

- Individually to make initial assessments
- Small groups of 4 to 6
- Whole group

5. Sequence of Steps and Time Allocation

- Ask participants to individually generate the list of challenges that take up their time. 5 min.
- Still working individually, participants place challenges in their individual matrixes. 5 min.
- Ask participants to discuss in pairs. 5 min.
- Invite them to chat with others in a group of 4–6 to find points of agreement, difference, and where there are mismatches. 10 min.

- Invite everyone to post their challenges on the large wall matrix. 5 min.
- Ask participants to form small groups and step back to reflect on, "What pattern do we see? Do any mismatches stand out that we should address?" 5 min.
- Invite whole group to share reflections and decide next steps. 10 min.

WHY? PURPOSES

- Reduce wasted effort by matching challenges with methods
- Identify where local experiments may help solve larger problems
- Make visible to everyone the range and the nature of the challenges facing people in the organization
- Reduce the frustration of people not making progress on key challenges by identifying mismatches
- Share perspectives across functions and levels of the organization

TIPS AND TRAPS

- Clarify what type of challenges and activities are being included
- Work up from the individual, then into pair and table conversations
- Avoid making judgments about where people put their activities
- Explore items that fall into more than one sector by asking, "Does this challenge have multiple dynamics at play? How is it simultaneously simple and complex?"
- Learn more from professor Brenda Zimmerman @ www.change-ability.ca/Change-Ability.html

RIFFS AND VARIATIONS

- Ask, "Where are there mismatches in your approach; what counter-measures make sense?"
- Create a table that captures the mismatches and any action steps that will be taken
- Use the same approach for a single issue people are facing in their work
- Link to or string together with Liberating Structures aimed at developing strategies: **Critical Uncertainties, Purpose-To-Practice, Ecocycle, Panarchy, Integrated~Autonomy, Discovery & Action Dialogue**

EXAMPLES

- For introducing managers trained only in linear cause-and-effect analysis to what is different about complex challenges
- For selecting a mix of change methodologies at the start of a new improvement project
- For helping a planning group move beyond "analysis paralysis" into an action phase
- For organizing the projects of a department

ATTRIBUTION

Liberating Structure developed by Henri Lipmanowicz and Keith McCandless. Adapted from the work of professors Ralph Stacey and Brenda Zimmerman.

COLLATERAL MATERIAL

Below: participant Post-its illustrate Agreement and Certainty Matrix placements for all to see— each Post-it represents an activity or program in the organization

Simple Ethnography

Observe and Record Actual Behaviors of Users in the Field (75 min. to 7 hrs.)

What is made possible? You can enable participants to find novel approaches to challenges by immersing themselves in the activities of the people with local experience—often their colleagues on the front line or anyone who uses their product or service. You open the door to change and innovation by helping participants explore what people actually do and feel in creating, delivering, or using their offering. Their observations and experience can spur rapid performance improvements and expedite prototype development. The combined observations may make it easy to spot important patterns.

"The future is already here. It is just not uniformly distributed."
William Gibson

STRUCTURAL ELEMENTS—MIN SPECS

1. Structuring Invitation
- Invite participants to silently observe people with experience relevant to the challenge at hand and then follow up with interviews for more insight

2. How Space Is Arranged and Materials Needed
- In a local setting (workplace, client organization, neighborhood) with a convenient space for sharing findings, photos, and videos
- Provide notebook, camera, video, permission (if needed)

3. How Participation Is Distributed
- All core-group members working on a challenge are included as ethnographers
- Everyone has an equal opportunity to contribute

4. How Groups Are Configured
- In 1s or 2s distributed among sites being observed
- Whole group for debrief

5. Sequence of Steps and Time Allocation
- Explain the problem to be solved and the current understanding of the situation. 5 min.

- Identify sites to observe and people to shadow that will reveal user experience in depth. 5 min.
- Invite participants to visit sites and observe without speaking interactions and activities, recording details and internal reflections as they go. 10–180 min.
- Ask participants to then select behaviors observed that address the challenge in a novel fashion (in part or in whole) and follow up by asking the individuals they observed what they were feeling and doing as they engaged in the behavior. 20–180 min.
- Reconvene the group of ethnographers and use **1-2-4-All** to compare notes and find patterns across observations or exceptional solutions. 15 min.
- Write up observations or compose stories that highlight needs and opportunities. 10–20 min.
- Feed insights into brainstorming and prototyping efforts. 10 min.
- Repeat steps until the core-group members feel they have a particularly powerful new approach to prototype

WHY? PURPOSES

- Help invisible routines become visible
- Identify fundamental needs and innovative solutions
- Reveal tacit and latent knowledge not accessible by asking users for explicit needs (e.g., with focus groups)
- Show respect and trust by observing and interviewing people on the front line

TIPS AND TRAPS

- Avoid adding meaning and interpretations too quickly to the observations
- Be prepared to repeat steps if the core-group members don't feel they have a particularly powerful new approach to prototype
- Be aware that insight comes from inconspicuous, often overlooked details

- Focus on the intrinsic qualities; ignore material or technological hierarchy
- Look for what is irregular, intimate, unpretentious
- Look for comfort with ambiguity
- Don't ignore what is imperfect, crude, or impermanent—deviance can be positive
- Do one or more rounds of simple ethnography after you implement your new approach

RIFFS AND VARIATIONS

- Use a storytelling template to structure observations (e.g., the Hero's Journey)
- Ask participants to draw or build a model of the challenge (be ready to be surprised by the deeper insights that nonverbal methods produce)
- Include clients in the observations (e.g., invite clients to record their own behaviors and share the images or video with the group)

EXAMPLES

- For sales representatives to discover how some of their colleagues are getting better results without additional resources or privileges
- For understanding how some clinicians are able to attend to the spiritual needs of patients and other are not
- For understanding why patients wander out of hospital isolation-precaution rooms despite repeated warnings
- For understanding how to reduce the patient falls in hospitals
- For understanding the differences between effective and ineffective meetings

ATTRIBUTION

Liberating Structure developed by Henri Lipmanowicz and Keith McCandless. Inspired by Chris McCarthy and ethnographers in the Innovation Learning Network.

COLLATERAL MATERIAL

Below: studying at the feet of people with local expertise via quiet observation and video capture in a Montana hospital

Integrated~Autonomy

Move from Either-or to Robust Both-and Solutions (80 min.)

What is made possible? You can help a group move from *either-or* conflicts to *both-and* strategies and solutions. You can engage everyone in sharper strategic thinking, mutual understanding, and collaborative action by surfacing the advantage of being *both* more integrated *and* more autonomous. Attending to paradox will reveal opportunities for profound leaps in performance by addressing questions such as: What mix of integrative control and autonomous freedom will advance our purpose? Where do our needs for *global* fidelity and consistency meet the needs for *local* customization and creative adaptability? This makes it possible to avoid bipolar swings in strategy that are frequently experienced by many organizations.

"There are two kinds of truth. There are superficial truths, the opposite of which are obviously wrong. But there are also profound truths, whose opposite are equally right." Niels Bohr

FIVE STRUCTURAL ELEMENTS—MIN SPECS

1. Structuring Invitation

- Invite your group to explore the questions, "Will our purpose be best served by increased local autonomy, customization, competition, and freedom among units/sites? Or, will our purpose be best served by increased integration, standardization, and control among units/sites? Or, both?"

2. How Space Is Arranged and Materials Needed

- Chairs for people to sit in groups of 4, with or without small tables
- An "Integrated Autonomy Worksheet" for each participant and a large one on the wall.
- Paper for recording activities and action steps

3. How Participation Is Distributed

- All central unit leaders and local unit leaders involved in the challenge at hand are included
- Everyone has an equal opportunity to contribute

4. How Groups Are Configured

- Individually to generate topics
- Small groups of 4
- Whole group

5. Sequence of Steps and Time Allocation

- Introduce the idea of **Integrated~Autonomy** for the topic at hand by asking, "How is it that we can be more integrated and more autonomous at the same time?" Have examples from past experience ready for sharing. 5 min.

- Use **1-2-4-All** to generate a list of activities that require attention by asking, "Where is there tension between our desire to standardize and the request for more customizing or autonomy?" 10 min.

- Ask participants to work in groups of four, and pick one activity from the list and ask, "What is the rationale for standardizing? What is the rationale for customizing?" 10 min.

- Using **1-2-4** develop action steps that achieve standardization. Using **1-2-4**, develop action steps that achieve customization. 10 min.

- Ask, "Which actions boost *both* standardization (group A) *and* customization (group C)?" See worksheet below. 5 min.

- Ask, "What modifications or creative ideas can be adopted to move some actions from group A to group B or from group C to group B?" See worksheet below. 15 min.

- Using **1-2-4-All**, prioritize the most promising actions that promote *both* integration *and* autonomy. 10 min.

- Refine action steps by developing some effective Liberating Structures strings with the help of **Wise Crowds** or **Troika Consulting** and **15% Solutions**. 15 min.

*Below: presentation materials we use to introduce **Integrated~Autonomy***

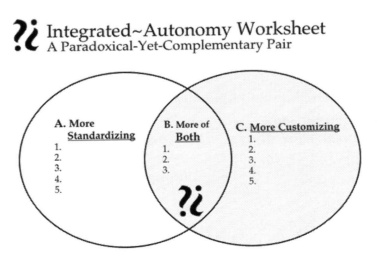

?¿ Integrated~Autonomy Worksheet
A Paradoxical-Yet-Complementary Pair

A. More Standardizing
1.
2.
3.
4.
5.

B. More of Both
1.
2.
3.

C. More Customizing
1.
2.
3.
4.
5.

WHY? PURPOSES

- Develop innovative strategies to move forward.
- Avoid wild or "bipolar" swings in policies, programs, or structures.
- Identify the complementary-yet-paradoxical pairs that are important and manage the paradoxical decisions productively.
- Evaluate decisions by asking, "Are we boosting or attending to both sides?"
- Evaluate and launch new strategies

TIPS AND TRAPS

- A productive starting question has balance and sparks curiosity or a search for what is working. Avoid making one side of the wicked question bad or less valuable to success such as, "How does our effort to be ONE integrated organization squash local autonomy?" Instead make your question equally appreciative of both sides, "How is it that we are both integrated and autonomous in our current operations?"
- Draw on field experience and imagination in asking questions such as, "How can we do more of both?"
- The goal is fidelity in a few core global attributes and differentiation in each local setting
- Laughter and groans (e.g., arrgh) help to identify progress
- You may need to encourage the group to try many experiments simultaneously
- There often are no quick fixes and you may need to return to the challenge periodically with additional rounds of **Integrated~Autonomy**
- When you start, the creative tension between the central and the local sides is relatively invisible. If the group gets stuck or starts to argue, tell each side to put on the hat of the other side and argue the opposite point of view.

RIFFS AND VARIATIONS

- Making progress with **Integrated~Autonomy** can shift *what is possible* for the whole organization as people start to understand that what helps them succeed in addressing a particular challenge applies across the board. Whenever this happens, use **Min Specs** to go deeper into must dos and must not dos.

- Substitute *collaboration* and *competition* for integration and autonomy

EXAMPLES

- For hospital-system leaders to develop the contents of new management contracts for small hospitals in the same region
- For a group of political leaders trying to formulate what should be legislated at the federal level and what should be decided locally
- For infection-control experts trying to create hospital-wide policies that do not inhibit unit-based innovations

ATTRIBUTION

Liberating Structure developed by Henri Lipmanowicz and Keith McCandless.

Critical Uncertainties

Develop Strategies for Operating in a Range of Plausible Yet Unpredictable Futures (100 min.)

What is made possible? You can help a diverse group quickly test the viability of current strategies and build its capacity to respond quickly to future challenges. This Liberating Structure prepares a group for strategy making. It does not produce a plan to be implemented as designed but rather builds resilience: the capacity to actively shape the system and be prepared to respond to surprise. This means being better able to see different futures unfolding, better prepared to act in a distributed fashion, and more ready to absorb disruptions resiliently.

"To be prepared against surprise is to be trained. To be prepared for surprise is to be educated."
James P. Carse

FIVE STRUCTURAL ELEMENTS—MIN SPECS

1. Structuring Invitation
- Invite the group to identify and explore the most critical *and* uncertain "realities" in their operating environment or market
- Then invite them to formulate strategies that would help them operate successfully in those different situations

2. How Space Is Arranged and Materials Needed
- Four groups of chairs around tables
- Paper, Post-it notes, flip charts, or tapestry paper for each group

3. How Participation Is Distributed
- Everyone responsible for planning and executing strategy is included
- Everyone has an equal opportunity to contribute

4. How Groups Are Configured
- Have a group large and diverse enough to break it up into four separate small groups to develop the four scenarios and related strategies
- If not, make two small groups

5. Sequence of Steps and Time Allocation
- Describe the sequence of steps. 2 min.
- Invite participants to make a list of uncertainties they face by asking, "In your/our operating environment, what factors are impossible to predict or control their direction?" 5 min.
- Prioritize the most critical factors by asking, "Which factors threaten your/our ability to operate successfully?" 10 min.

- Based on the group's history and experience, select the two most critical *and* most uncertain (X and Y). 5 min.
- Create a grid with two axes—X & Y—with a "more of ▪⑧less of" continuum for the factor to be represented on each axis. For example, for the X axis, if the number of new products is a critically uncertain factor, one end of the X axis is a large number of new products and the other is no new products. Repeat for the Y factor and axis. For instance, if patent protection is a critical factor, one end of the Y axis is strong patent protection and the other is no patent protection. Four quadrants are created. See example below. 5 min.
- Each of the four groups creatively names and writes a thumbnail scenario for one of the quadrants. 10 min.
- The four groups share their scenarios briefly. 2 min. each
- Each group brainstorms three strategies that would help the group operate successfully in the scenario that it has described. 10 min.
- The four groups share their strategies briefly. 2 min. each
- The whole group sifts results to identify which strategies are robust (strategies that can succeed in multiple quadrants) and which are hedging (strategies that can succeed in only one scenario but protect you from a plausible calamity). The balance of strategies can succeed only in one scenario. 10 min.
- Each small group debriefs with **What, So What, Now What?** 10 min.
- The four groups share their debriefs and the whole group makes first-steps decisions about their Now What. 10 min.

WHY? PURPOSES

- Test the viability of current strategies by exposing assumptions and uncertainties
- Increase capacity of everyone to adapt quickly and absorb disruptions resiliently
- Differentiate priorities in terms of robust and hedging strategies
- Develop more organization-wide confidence in managing the unknowable future
- Widen the range of strategic options

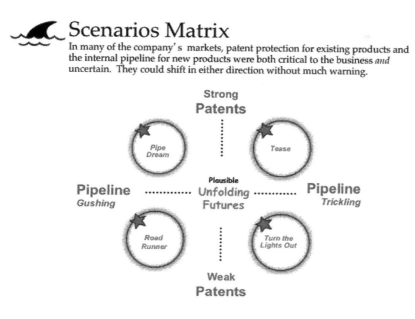

Scenarios Matrix

In many of the company's markets, patent protection for existing products and the internal pipeline for new products were both critical to the business *and* uncertain. They could shift in either direction without much warning.

TIPS AND TRAPS

- When brainstorming uncertainties, recall predictions-gone-wrong and events that caught the group off guard
- Challenge wishful thinking
- Use **1-2-4-All** in very short cycles for each step
- Have fun with naming each quadrant (song and book titles work nicely)
- Have fun developing the scenarios, for instance, by turning them into newspaper reports about a future situation
- Post-it notes help with combining and recombining ideas
- Regardless of role, a few people are naturals: celebrate their skillfulness

RIFFS AND VARIATIONS

- Build from this short session to a full-blown scenario-planning initiative
- For each scenario, invite small groups to dramatize a typical client interaction or product *from the future* that puts your strategies into play

- String together with **Conversation Café, Purpose-To-Practice, WINFY, Open Space, Wicked Questions**, and **Min Specs**

EXAMPLES

- For exploring what features should be included in a product or service that will be launched
- For national policy and operating leaders to shape next steps in a health-care reform initiative
- For IT leaders preparing for implementation challenges across multiple countries in one region
- For executives and operational leaders to create a 10-year strategic vision
- For NGO executive directors responding to unexpected changes in funding and public perception
- For counseling youth in unstable settings, likely to drop out of school or start living on the street

ATTRIBUTION

Liberating Structure developed by Henri Lipmanowicz and Keith McCandless. Inspired by consultant Jay Ogilvy.

Ecocycle Planning

Analyze the Full Portfolio of Activities and Relationships to Identify Obstacles and Opportunities for Progress (95 min.)

What is made possible? You can eliminate or mitigate common bottlenecks that stifle performance by sifting your group's portfolio of activities, identifying which elements are starving for resources and which ones are rigid and hampering progress. The Ecocycle makes it possible to sift, prioritize, and plan actions with everyone involved in the activities at the same time, as opposed to the conventional way of doing it behind closed doors with a small group of people. Additionally, the Ecocycle helps everyone see the forest AND the trees—they see where their activities fit in the larger context with others. **Ecocycle Planning** invites leaders to focus also on creative destruction and renewal in addition to typical themes regarding growth or efficiency. The Ecocycle makes it possible to spur agility, resilience, and sustained performance by including all four phases of development in the planning process.

*Below: presentation material we use to introduce **Ecocycle Planning***

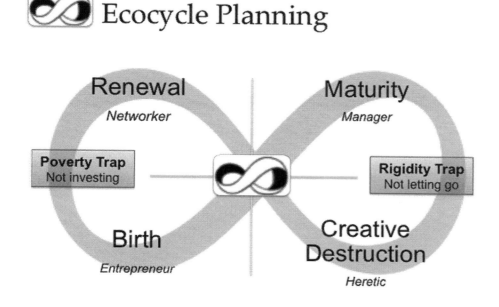

FIVE STRUCTURAL ELEMENTS—MIN SPECS

1. Structuring Invitation

- Invite the group to view, organize, and prioritize current activities using four developmental phases: birth, maturity, creative destruction, and renewal
- Invite the group to formulate action steps linked to each phase: actions that accelerate growth during the birth phase, actions that extend life or increase efficiency during the maturity phase, actions that prune dead wood or compost rigid practices during the creative destruction phase, actions that connect creative people or prepare the ground for birth during the renewal phase. The leadership stance required for each phase can be characterized as entrepreneur, manager, heretic, and networker.

2. How Space Is Arranged and Materials Needed

- A room with an open flat wall and open space for participants to stand comfortably in front of the wall
- Chairs for people to sit in groups of 4, with or without small round tables
- A blank Ecocycle map worksheet for each participant and a large wall-poster version posted on the wall
- Post-it notes for each activity

3. How Participation Is Distributed

- Everybody involved in the work is included, all levels and functions
- Everyone has an equal opportunity to contribute

4. How Groups Are Configured

- **1-2-4-All**
- Small groups for action steps

5. Sequence of Steps and Time Allocation

- Introduce the idea of the Ecocycle and hand out a blank map to each participant. 5 min.
- Ask participants to generate their individual activity lists: "For your working group (e.g., department, function, or whole company), make a list of all the activities (projects, initiatives) that occupy your time." 5 min.
- Ask them to work in pairs to decide the placement of every activity in the Ecocycle. 10 min.

- Invite them to form groups of four and finalize the placement of activities on the Ecocycle map. 15 min.
- Ask each group to put its activities on Post-it notes and create a whole-room map by inviting the groups one by one to place their Post-its on the larger map. 15 min.
- Ask each group to step back and digest the pattern of placements. Ask them to focus on all the activities on which there is consensus about their placement. Ask, "What activities do we need to creatively destroy or stop to move forward? What activities do we need to expand or start to move forward?" 15 min.
- In small groups, for each activity that needs to be stopped (activities that are in the Rigidity Trap), create a first-action step. 10 min. or more depending on the number of activities and groups.
- In small groups, for each activity that needs to start or get more resources (activities in the Poverty trap), create a first-action step. 10 min. or more as above.
- Ask all the groups to focus on all the activities for which there is no consensus. Do a quick round of conversation to make sense of the differences in placement. When possible, create first-action steps to handle each one. 10 min.

WHY? PURPOSES

- Set priorities
- Balance a portfolio of strategies
- Identify waste and opportunities to free up resources
- Bring and hear all perspectives at once
- Create resilience and absorb disruptions by reorganizing programs together
- To reveal the whole picture, the forest AND the trees

TIPS AND TRAPS

- Don't do your first **Ecocycle Planning** session with your group's entire portfolio of market strategies. Start with a simpler program, something tangible with shared experience.
- Remind participants that all phases of the Ecocycle must be parts of a healthy organization

- Be very clear on the domain or type of activities being considered— check activities to be sure they are on a similar scale and domain
- Include views from inside and outside the organization or function (diverse participants and clients can help)
- Preparations and explicit criteria for each quadrant may help or interfere
- Don't hesitate to do a second round
- Identifying the Rigidity and Poverty Traps, plus connecting specific activities with these labels, launches the search for solutions
- Learn more from professor Brenda Zimmerman at http://change-ability.ca and see the excerpt from her book *Edgeware* under the tab Publications

RIFFS AND VARIATIONS

- Ask participants to make a list of all their important *relationships* with internal and external customers/suppliers (in addition to their activities) and to place them on the Ecocycle. Ask them to evaluate the relationships with the same questions used for the activities and to include them in the last four steps of the Ecocycle planning process. Highly recommended!
- String together with **Panarchy, 1-2-4-All, WINFY,** and **Open Space**
- **TRIZ** can help to deepen the Creative Destruction quadrant
- Use with virtual groups by inviting participants to place their Ecocycle assessments with a dot on the whiteboard, then chat in pairs and with the whole group about the pattern that emerges. Before you enter into full-group placements, use silence and paired chat (**1-2-All**) to build understanding. You will need to agree on a short common list of activities or relationships to help simplify mapping. Number or letter each item and invite placements one by one. Sift and sort answers with a whiteboard and a person playing a "synthesizer" role. Don't worry about perfection in the first rounds. Virtual sessions can deepen or complement face-to-face exchanges.
- **What, So What, Now What?** and **25/10 Crowd Sourcing** can help spur action about activities or relationships when the group seems to be stuck.

EXAMPLES

- For service portfolio review with an information technology department
- For nursing executives and academics transforming their approach to education (evaluating the history as well as proposed change initiatives)
- For planning changes in an individual's personal life, sifting through activities and shaping next steps
- For accelerating performance of an executive team in the midst of integrating a newly acquired company (sifting through a mixture of two product lines and research opportunities)

ATTRIBUTION

Adapted by Henri Lipmanowicz and Keith McCandless from professor Brenda Zimmerman (see www.change-ability.ca) and ecologists (see http://www.resalliance.org).

COLLATERAL MATERIAL

*Below: a portfolio of market strategies arrayed around the **Ecocycle** by members of a management team. Each number represents a strategy in play or under consideration.*

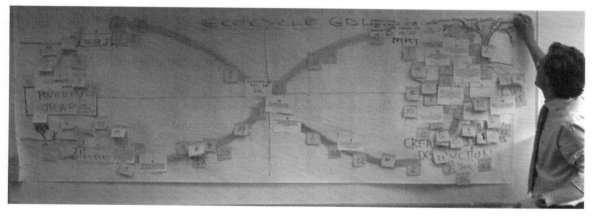

Panarchy

Understand How Embedded Systems Interact, Evolve, Spread Innovation and Transform (2 hrs.)

"If a living system is suffering from ill health, the remedy is to connect it with more of itself." Francisco Varella

What is made possible? You can help a large group of people identify obstacles and opportunities for spreading ideas or innovations at many levels. **Panarchy** enables people to visualize how systems are embedded in systems and helps them understand how these interdependencies influence the spread of change. Participants become more alert to small changes that can help spread ideas up to other system levels; they learn how shifts at larger or lower system levels may release resources to assist them at another level. With better appreciation of the **Ecocycle** dynamics at play, the group creates "opportunity windows" for innovations to spread among levels and across boundaries.

Below: presentation material we use to introduce Panarchy

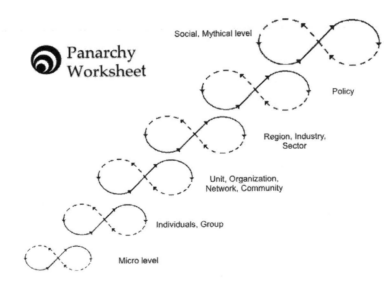

FIVE STRUCTURAL ELEMENTS—MIN SPECS

1. Structuring Invitation

- Invite participants to identify what is contributing to the existence of a challenge at levels above and below them. Ask them also to specify different strategies and opportunities for change within each level and across multiple levels.

2. How Space Is Arranged and Materials Needed
- A room with an unobstructed flat wall and open space for participants to stand comfortably in front of the wall
- A blank Panarchy chart handout
- A large wall-poster or flip-chart version of the Panarchy chart
- Post-it notes for each participant
- Flip-chart pages for the Panarchy graphic

3. How Participation Is Distributed
- Everyone involved in spreading a transformation or innovation effort is included
- Everyone has an equal opportunity to contribute

4. How Groups Are Configured
- Individuals, pairs, groups of 4, whole group: **1-2-4-All**

5. Sequence of Steps and Time Allocation
- Introduce the idea of the **Panarchy** (and the **Ecocycle** if needed). Show an example, such as the MRSA infection Panarchy in Collateral Material below, and hand out a blank Panarchy chart to each participant. 5 min.
- Invite participants to work individually to generate the set of system levels that influence the spread of their ideas/innovation in three steps.
- First step alone to make a list of factors by asking, "What are the smallest-to-the-largest factors influencing your/our chances for success?" Include micro (particles, individual people, teams), meso (organizations, networks), and macro (culture, politics, myths) factors that contribute to the existence of the challenge being addressed. 5 min.
- Second step in pairs to "translate" the factors into levels and create labels for each level (4–7 levels are sufficient). 10 min.
- Third step in groups of four to compare their levels and finalize their chart with Post-its. 10 min.
- If there are multiple groups of four, create a single chart, by inviting each group to place any levels not previously included on the larger chart. 10 min.
- Invite participants to work in groups of four to reflect on the following questions: "On which levels have attention and resources been invested to date? Which levels have been neglected? What do I/we

know about the status and dynamics in play at the different levels?" 10 min.

- In the whole group, share reflections from a few groups. 5 min.
- Ask groups of two or four to explore one level in depth with the **Ecocycle**. Each group should pick one of the 4-7 levels. Distribute people with experience at the different levels to those groups. Ask, "At this level, what is going on right now and what actions are being taken for the challenge that our innovation addresses? Is the response to the challenge in an entrepreneurial, bureaucratic/management, heretical, or renewal phase?" Create a rough draft of Ecocycle assessments for this level. 15 min.
- Collect the Ecocycle assessments from the groups. Each group presents the Ecocycle assessment of their level briefly. 10 min.
- In small groups, brainstorm a list of obstacles and opportunities in regard to efforts to spread ideas/innovations. Ask, "Looking up and down the levels, what opportunities and obstacles do you see for changes *across* the levels? What *windows* for new ideas are opening above? What resources are flowing downward from creative destruction unfolding above? What small-scale developments from below are disrupting the level above?" Encourage the groups to go wild and have fun. 15 min.
- Prioritize the opportunities and obstacles that emerge. 10 min.
- For each opportunity and obstacle on your list, create one first-action step using **1-2-4** by asking, "What action can you take immediately to influence levels above and below you?" And, "Who do you know that has influence in more than one level simultaneously?" 10 min.
- Share action steps with the whole group by placing Post-it notes on each level of the large Panarchy chart. 15 min.
- Invite the group to take a close look at the chart. Use **What, So What, Now What?** to make sense of and prioritize all of the possible next steps. 15 min.
- Revisit and update the Panarchy chart periodically as the group continues work to spread its innovation.

WHY? PURPOSES

- Identify a mix of strategies at multiple levels to move transformation efforts forward

- Create an opportunity for people from many different levels to work together
- Prepare for serendipity as opportunity windows open or close
- Identify people that span levels and can help the group move forward
- Help a whole group see the whole picture (forest AND the trees AND the bioregion)
- Create resilience and absorb disruptions by reorganizing together

TIPS AND TRAPS

- Use **1-2-4-All** for all or most of the steps even if it feels like a chore: the objective is to identify ALL opportunities and obstacles at ALL levels!
- Include people or perspectives from each level (the more participants, the better)
- Look to research when you are unfamiliar with dynamics at smaller and bigger scales
- Do not neglect history and its role in defining what is possible at each level.
- To learn more, see professor Frances Westley's contributions to the SIG Knowledge Hub on scaling (http://sigknowledgehub. com/2012/05/01/introductio-to-scaling/), his work in Panarchy: Understanding Transformations in Human and Natural Systems (Gunderson and Holling, eds.), and other writing.

RIFFS AND VARIATIONS

- String together with **Ecocycle, 1-2-4 Whole, What I Need from You, Social Network Webbing, Celebrity Interview**
- **W³ (What, So What, Now What?)** can help spur focused action steps
- Use **Panarchy** for individuals by asking, "What is contributing to the existence of your challenge at levels above and levels below you? What elements are perpetuating the challenge you are facing? What are the different speeds for effecting changes at each of the levels?"

EXAMPLES

- Native American school administrators advanced education opportunities for their students with innovations ranging from individual student advising to dispelling social myths
- Safety advocates in one hospital planned the spread of their innovations locally, regionally, nationally, and internationally
- Foundation grantees planned dissemination of their disaster-preparedness innovations from prototype to national adoption
- An individual artist sketched out how her work can influence change at different scales

ATTRIBUTION

Adapted by Henri Lipmanowicz and Keith McCandless from the work of professor Frances Westley (see, e.g., Gunderson and Holling, *Panarchy: Understanding Transformations in Human and Natural Systems*)

COLLATERAL MATERIAL

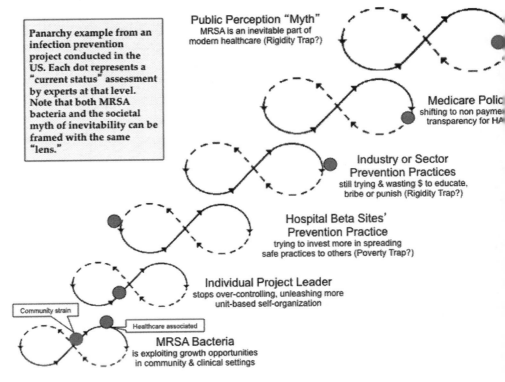

Panarchy example from an infection prevention project conducted in the US. Each dot represents a "current status" assessment by experts at that level. Note that both MRSA bacteria and the societal myth of inevitability can be framed with the same "lens."

Public Perception "Myth"
MRSA is an inevitable part of modern healthcare (Rigidity Trap?)

Medicare Polic
shifting to non paymei
transparency for HA

Industry or Sector Prevention Practices
still trying & wasting $ to educate, bribe or punish (Rigidity Trap?)

Hospital Beta Sites' Prevention Practice
trying to invest more in spreading safe practices to others (Poverty Trap?)

Individual Project Leader
stops over-controlling, unleashing more unit-based self-organization

Community strain

Healthcare associated

MRSA Bacteria
is exploiting growth opportunities in community & clinical settings

Purpose-To-Practice (P2P)

Design the Five Essential Elements for a Resilient and Enduring Initiative (2 hrs.)

What is made possible? By using **P2P** at the start of an initiative, the stakeholders can shape together all the elements that will determine the success of their initiative. The group begins by generating a shared purpose (i.e., why the work is important to each participant and the larger community). All additional elements—principles, participants, structure, and practices—are designed to help achieve the purpose. By shaping these five elements together, participants clarify how they can organize themselves to adapt creatively and scale up for success. For big initiatives, **P2P** makes it possible to include a large number of stakeholders in shaping their future initiative.

"Very real crises mark our time. And as much as we might like it otherwise, it appears that doing what we have always done, only harder, will not solve them."
Charles Johnston

*Below: presentation material we use to introduce **P2P***

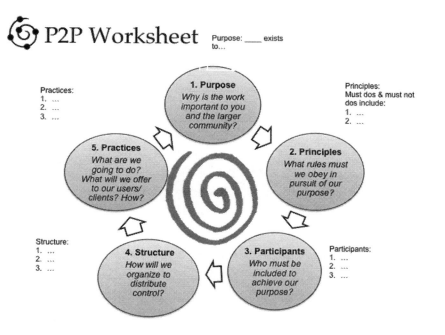

FIVE STRUCTURAL ELEMENTS—MIN SPECS

1. Structuring Invitation
- Invite all or most stakeholders to participate in the design of their new initiative in order to specify its five essential elements: purpose, principles, participants, structure, and practices.

2. How Space Is Arranged and Materials Needed
- Chairs and small tables for people to work in groups of 4
- A large wall with poster paper for recording the P2P result for each element
- For each participant five worksheets, one for each of the five elements

3. How Participation Is Distributed
- All individuals who have a stake in launching the initiative are included
- Everyone has an equal opportunity to contribute

4. How Groups Are Configured
- **1-2-4-All**
- Whole group for finalizing each element

5. Sequence of Steps and Time Allocation
- Introduce the idea of **P2P**, the five elements, and related questions, and hand out blank worksheets. 5 min.
- To clarify the first element, Purpose, ask the question: "Why is the work important to you and the larger community?"
- Use **1-2-4** to generate individual ideas and stories for Purpose. 10 min.
- In groups of four, compare, sift, and amplify the top ideas. 10 min.
- As a whole group, integrate themes and finalize ideas for Purpose. 10 min.
- Move to the remaining **P2P** elements, in turn, repeating the three steps of **1-2-4-All**. Be prepared to go back and revise previous elements as needed (expect some messy nonlinearity). Use the following questions to guide the development of the next four elements:

  - Principles: "What rules must we absolutely obey to succeed in achieving our purpose?"
  - Participants: "Who can contribute to achieving our purpose and must be included?"

- Structure: "How must we organize (both macro- and microstructures) and distribute control to achieve our purpose?"
- Practices: "What are we going to do? What will we offer to our users/clients and how will we do it?"

- After each element, ask, "Has this element shed new light that suggests revisions to previous elements?" 5 min.

- When all elements have been completed, ask participants to step back and take a close look at their draft of the five elements together. Ask them to use **What, So What, Now What?** in small groups to make sense of all of the possible next steps and prioritize them as a whole group. 15 min.
- After the initiative has been launched, invite the participants to revisit their P2P design periodically and adapt elements based on their experience.

WHY? PURPOSES

- Engage and focus everyone's imagination in designing the collective future of participants.
- Avoid "design" by a small group of people behind closed doors
- Pull together all the elements needed to launch and sustain an effort, thereby avoiding a fragmented process
- Develop innovative strategies that can be implemented and spread quickly because there is shared ownership
- Increase resilience and the ability to absorb disruptions by distributing power fairly
- Build the capacity to rapidly adapt any of the elements to changing circumstances

TIPS AND TRAPS

- Crafting a powerful, wildly attractive "purpose" is the most important step: you may want to use **Nine Whys, Appreciative Interviews**, or **TRIZ** to deepen the conversation
- A purpose may be expressed as something positive you are going to start/create or something negative you are going to stop
- Work in quick cycles, failing forward iteratively

- Multiple sessions spread out over weeks or even months may be required
- "Structure" usually is the element that requires the most imagination and leaps away from top-down to more distributed control
- Principles: *Must dos* and *must not dos* often come from hard lessons learned in the field (positive and negative)
- Rely on small groups to do the heavy lifting, and keep it moving
- Keep rounds on schedule and when more time is needed, do two rounds
- Rely on and draw out the inspiring-and-despairing experience of group members
- Invite the participants to use their intuition as the process unfolds
- Invite talented participants to take on roles (e.g., writing, drawing, synthesizing)

RIFFS AND VARIATIONS

- Start with one 30-minute, very rapid cycle covering all five elements to illustrate the need for a strong and clear purpose: without one, it is easy to come up with a half-baked design
- Graphic recording helps to hold attention and focus through the rigorous design process
- You can add questions to enrich the conversation about Practices: What is happening around us that creates an opportunity? What is at stake if we do not take a risk? Where are we starting, honestly?
- When integrating all five elements for a project is too much, just do the one or two design elements that seem most important
- Use the five **P2P** questions routinely as an easy checklist for small projects
- Use with virtual groups by inviting participants to answer the five questions via a chat version of **1-2-All**. Sift and sort answers with a whiteboard and a person playing a "synthesizer" role. Don't worry about perfection in the first rounds. Virtual rounds can deepen or complement face-to-face exchanges.
- Use **P2P** to structure a much longer design session (e.g., a planning or strategy retreat)

EXAMPLES

- By the leaders of the Conversation Café dialogue movement
- The Quality Commons, a group of researchers from eight health systems, used **P2P** to successfully create their consortium

- Going through the first stage of the **P2P**, a management team discovered a much deeper purpose than it expected. The new purpose and shared experience inspired the team to rethink its business model.

ATTRIBUTION

Liberating Structure developed by Henri Lipmanowicz and Keith McCandless. Inspired by Dee Hock (see his book *Birth of the Chaordic Age*).

COLLATERAL MATERIAL

*Below: output for each of the five **P2P** questions*

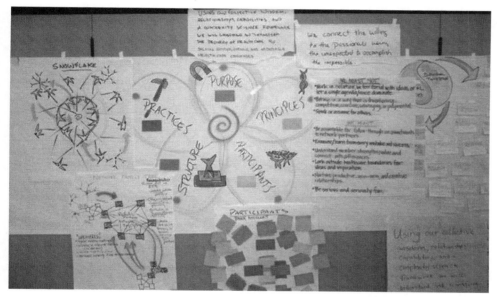

AFTERWORD

Liberating Structures start with something so simple and essential as not to seem worth doing and end with something so powerful and profound that it hardly seems possible.

"Liberating Structures have been life changing for me! I really mean it. And there are ripple effects with other people I'm collaborating with. Loving it."

"Liberating Structures are like magic; every time I use them something that seems impossible just happens as if by magic."

"Using Liberating Structures transformed my way of leading and me as a leader."

"The student feedback I hear has noticeably changed. I increasingly hear: 'This class changed my life;' 'I learned so much about myself in this class;' 'Thank you also for teaching me how to learn.'"

"Liberating Structures have also influenced my interactions with my teenage children. I realized the poor impact I had when I just told them what to do. Now I listen more, let them express their feelings, and let them reach conclusions on what is best for them."

"Employees were once valued for doing what they were told and saying 'yes sir'. Now staff meetings are fun. It feels like magic because people contribute in ways they did not anticipate."

"I have never seen a conversation like this around here. Just about everyone was on the edge of their seat the entire time."

"After experiencing the freedom and the results that you can achieve with them, I cannot imagine going back to the old way."

"We must find a way to get Liberating Structures into the drinking water!"

We continue to be blown away by how positive people are when they tell us what learning to use Liberating Structures has meant to them. Their gratitude

"We must find a way to get Liberating Structures into the drinking water!"

has been our greatest reward both emotionally and professionally. We love the stories of all the small and big successes that Liberating Structures have made possible for them. We glow in the pleasure they get from their transformed relationships and working conditions.

Feedback of this sort has convinced us that Liberating Structures have universal and enduring value. This is what motivated us to dig deeply to uncover the fundamental principles behind Liberating Structures and document our fieldwork. It was the people who learned and used Liberating Structures who convinced us to create a website and pushed us to write a book. *It took a good hard push.*

In our work with all kinds of organizations around the world, we have yet to meet anyone who could not address one or more challenges he or she is facing more effectively with Liberating Structures. This tells us that everybody would benefit from learning at least a few of them. Every teacher and professor should use some routinely. Exposure to Liberating Structures in the classroom would prepare students to be more effective contributors in the workplace. Managers should know at least all the basic Liberating Structures. Frontline workers would improve their everyday outcomes by simply mastering a few on their own. Internal and external consultants would enlarge the scope and impact of their work by becoming skilled at using Liberating Structures and would expand their offerings to their clients. Yet only a tiny fraction of the seven billion-plus people in the world have even heard of Liberating Structures!

We want to make it as easy as possible for everyone to feel free to use, copy, and disseminate this material and make his or her corner of the world a better place.

This is why we have chosen not to copyright any of our work and instead publish it under a Creative Commons License. We want to make it as easy as possible for everyone to feel free to use, copy, and disseminate this material and make his or her corner of the world a better place.

Join us in getting Liberating Structures into the drinking water!

NOTES

PART ONE: THE HIDDEN STRUCTURES OF ENGAGEMENT

Chapter 1. Introduction: Small Changes, Big Differences

Unless otherwise noted, all examples and stories in this book are actual cases or composites of experiences from our consulting practice or related in our workshops; they are used with the permission of the individuals involved. The titles and affiliations of the subjects or contributors of this material may have changed after the book's publication date; whenever possible, we have updated this information on our website.

Chapter 3. Liberating Structures for Everyone

[1] The term *Liberating Structures* was first introduced by William Torbert, a professor at Boston College. He explored the notion of forms of organization structure that gave guidance to people in a way that they developed skills to guide themselves. He advanced a theory of power that generates productivity, justice, and inquiry; and a theory of "liberating structure" through which organizations can generate continual quality improvement (contributed by Lisa Kimball).

[2] Gallup Inc. "State of the American Workplace: Employee Engagement Insights for U.S. Business Leaders," 2013. http://www.gallup.com/strategicconsulting/163007/state-american-workplace.aspx accessed July 14, 2013. Gallup defines engaged employees as "those who are involved in, enthusiastic about, and committed to their work and contribute to their organization in a positive manner" (p. 12).

[3] Adapted from Edgar Schein, *Organizational Culture and Leadership*, 4th ed. (San Francisco: Jossey-Bass, 2010).

PART THREE: STORIES FROM THE FIELD

[1] Except as noted, the stories here were developed from interviews we conducted with twenty-five leaders using Liberating Structures all over the world. We selected these twelve examples for their ability to show the power of Liberating

Structures to address many different types of issues and opportunities in a broad range of organizations.

² Ori Brafman and Rod A. Beckstrom. *The Starfish and The Spider: The Unstoppable Power Of Leaderless Organizations* (New York: Portfolio, 2007).

³ Professor Singhal recommends the following videos for additional examples: *UnScripted: Liberating Structures* by Arvind Singhal https://vimeo. com/51546509 10'20"; *Liberating Structures: Inviting and Unleashing All: Lipmanowicz in Convo with Singhal* https://vimeo.com/50352840 8' 30"; *Liberating Classroom: Lipmanowicz in Convo with Singhal* https://vimeo. com/50347352 8' 20"

⁴ Positive Deviance is based on the observation that in every community there are certain individuals or groups whose uncommon behaviors and strategies enable them to find better solutions to problems than their peers, while having access to the same resources and facing similar or worse challenges. The Positive Deviance approach is an asset-based, problem-solving, and community-driven approach that enables the community to discover these successful behaviors and strategies and develop a plan of action to promote their adoption by all concerned. See, e.g., Pascale, Richard, Jerry Sternin, and Monique Sternin, T*he Power of Positive Deviance* (Boston: Harvard Business Press, 2010) and http://www.positivedeviance.org/index.html

⁵ The CBC news show *The National* featured Michael and the hospitals in this project in a segment aired on March 19, 2012 called "Germ War: One of Canada's Leading Infection Control Experts Has Started a Simple But Unorthodox Project That's Getting Incredible Results in the Battle against Hospital Infections."http://www.cbc.ca/player/Shows/Shows/The+National/ Health/ID/2213462958/?page=6

⁶ KGH was part of a demonstration project to prevent infections in five hospital sites across Canada that concluded in 2011 *[see Inspiring Enduring Culture Change While Preventing Hospital Infections in Part Three: Stories from the Field]*. Sherry served as leader of a core group that managed the prevention effort within her unit and across hospital departments. To coordinate action and attract cross-functional participation, the group employed **Social Network Webbing**.

ACKNOWLEDGMENTS AND LEARNING RESOURCES

Acknowledgments

Through thick and thin, hundreds of people kindly supported us in the developmental years (2003–2013). Here we name a handful.

Curt Lindberg brought together a fabulous network of complexity-crazed scholars and leaders. This community intellectually *clothed and fed us* in the beginning. Inklings of a Liberating Structures strategy were launched in Ohio with the front line of the Veterans Administration health system. Among complexity scholars, Brenda Zimmerman shines like the North Star. Her theoretical brilliance and practical bent illuminated a path forward. Liz Rykert was the first dedicated reader/editor, working through the details of each Liberating Structure's description.

Grey Warner opened the door wide for getting started in Latin America. Alison Joslyn was the first executive to boldly try everything we had to offer. We inspired her and she inspired us in equal measure. Tadeu Alves went out on a limb to sponsor our first workshop in Brazil. Its success sowed the seeds for leaders to follow suit in Mexico, Central America, Colombia, Peru, Chile, and Puerto Rico. We owe special gratitude to all the frontline people in Latin America who had the courage to break new ground and innovate. Their accomplishments taught us a lot about what Liberating Structures made possible. Big hugs to David Gasser, Nicole Schmidlin, Nilton Tojar, Gracio Reis, Marcio Martins, Pablo Quintana, Ricardo Schrader, Nilda Bigott, Sidnei Castro, Vanessa Vertiz, Eduardo Guerra, Andres Bruzual Cristobal Bravo, Sean Hughes, Rafael Suarez, and Tim Daveler. Special kudos to the indefatigable Dave Raimondo!

As Liberating Structures were developing momentum in Latin America, a US-based group was working with Positive Deviance to prevent the spread of superbugs. Sharon Benjamin, Kevin Buck, Joelle Everett, Lisa Kimball, Mark Munger, Jerry Sternin, Monique Sternin, and Margaret Toth shared their talents as we practiced side by side. Diane Magrane believed in us and challenged us to try Liberating Structures in medical-school settings. In our work with community leaders in Montana, Harvey Stewart insisted we develop principles. Linda DeWolf and Chris McCarthy helped launch the Innovation Learning Network with a Liberating Structures twist. Michael Gardam invited us to help guide a Canada-wide superbug-prevention effort.

In Europe, Antonio Mosquera, Jan Van Acker, Kari Jarvinen, and Guy Eiferman opened the doors to their organizations and gave us the opportunity to demonstrate the adaptability of Liberating Structures to many different cultural environments. There, too, progress and learning rested on the shoulders of courageous frontline early adopters. Big hugs to Cristina Lopez Vilchez, Miguel Angel Soria, Erik Plas, Istvan Grof, Philippe Decerf, Ans Heirman, Reginald Decraene, Bruno Klucasr, Donia Cherifi, Veronique Rosset, and Clarisse Lhoste.

The application of Liberating Structures in education and social change is expanding and spreading in large part thanks to professor Arvind Singhal. He created and nurtures a growing community of Liberating Structures Changemakers. Big hugs to professor Lucia Dura, professor Helen Hua Wang, professor Harry Meeuwsen, professor Robert Ulmer, Dr. Virginia Lacayo, professor Marie Lindquist, Dr. Karen Greiner, Erin Stock, Marc Peters, Rafael Obregon, Acadia Roher, and Carliene Quist.

Fabulous designer Lesley Jacobs gave playful form to each Liberating Structure. Our developmental editor, Leslie Stephen, made this book possible by pulling out of us the best each had to offer and filling the gaps. A deep bow to Annie Jacobs for style editing, head shrinking, and loving care after far too many days away from home. Endless gratitude goes to Riitta Lipmanowicz for her selfless nurturing, infinite patience, and endless reservoir of TLC. It could have never happened without you.

Attributions and Learning Resources

More than any single book, *Edgeware* launched our quest for practical applications of complexity science. We stand on the shoulders of Curt Lindberg, Paul Plsek, and Brenda Zimmerman. The view was fabulous! Earlier, in the 1980s, consultants Lisa Kimball and Frank Burns started work with groups to "focus beyond meeting content-only to designing engaging experiences." They borrowed a concept with a catchy name from a Boston University professor named William Torbert—Liberating Structures.

In the Field Guide, we give attribution and credit to authors and developers who have inspired us. With a deep bow to these pioneers, thank you. Earlier influences are hard to trace but no less important. There are other mothers, fathers, and gurus behind most of the methods. Let us know whom we missed.

In addition, to build an understanding of the theories behind Liberating Structures, we recommend the following books and articles:

Alexander, Christopher, Sara Ishikawa, and Murray Silverstein. *A Pattern Language: Towns, Buildings, Construction.* Oxford: Oxford University Press, 1977.

Anderson, Ruth A., and Reuben R. McDaniel Jr. "Taking Complexity Science Seriously: New Research, New Methods." In *On the Edge: Nursing in the Age of Complexity,* edited by Clair Lindberg, Sue Nash, and Curt Lindberg, 73–95. Bordertown, N.J.: Plexus Press, 2008.

Arrien, Angeles. *Signs of Life: The Five Universal Shapes and How to Use Them.* New York: Tarcher/Penguin, 1998.

Axelrod, Richard H. *Terms of Engagement: Changing the Way We Change Organizations.* San Francisco: Berrett-Koehler, 2000.

Beinhocker, Eric D. "Strategy at the Edge of Chaos." McKinsey Quarterly, no. 1 (1997): 24–39.

Bellman, Geoffrey M. *The Consultant's Calling: Bringing Who You Are to What You Do.* San Francisco: Jossey-Bass, 1992.

Block, Peter. *Community: The Structure of Belonging.* San Francisco: Berrett-Koehler, 2008.

Boal, Augusto. *Theatre of the Oppressed.* New York: Theatre Communications Group, 1985.

Brafman, Ori, and Rod A. Beckstrom. *The Starfish and the Spider: The Unstoppable Power of Leaderless Organizations.* New York: Portfolio, 2010.

Caballero, María Cristina. "Academic Turns City into a Social Experiment: Mayor Mockus of Bogotá and His Spectacularly Applied Theory." Harvard Gazette, March 11, 2004.

Cooperrider, David L. "Positive Image, Positive Action: The Affirmative Basis of Organizing." In *Appreciative Management and Leadership: The Power of Positive Thought and Action in*

Organizations, edited by Suresh Srivasta and David L. Cooperrider, 91–125. San Francisco: Jossey-Bass, 1990.

Giddens, Anthony. *Central Problems in Social Theory: Action, Structure, and Contradiction in Social Analysis.* London: Macmillan, 1979

Greenhalgh, Trisha, Glenn Robert, Fraser Macfarlane, Paul Bate, and Olivia Kyriakidou. "Diffusion of Innovations in Service Organizations: Systematic Review and Recommendations," Milbank Quarterly 82, no. 4 (2004): 581–629.

Gunderson, Lance, and C. S. Holling, eds. *Panarchy: Understanding Transformations in Human and Natural Systems.* Washington, DC: Island Press, 2002.

Hand, Eric. "Citizen Science: People Power." Nature 466 (2010): 685–87.

Heifetz, Ronald A. *Leadership without Easy Answers.* Cambridge, MA: Belknap Press, 1994.

Hock, Dee, and VISA International. *Birth of the Chaordic Age.* San Francisco: Berrett-Koehler, 2000.

Holman, Peggy, Tom Devane, and Steven Cady. *The Change Handbook: The Definitive Resource on Today's Best Methods for Engaging Whole Systems.* San Francisco: Berrett-Koehler, 2007.

Lanham, Holly Jordan et al. "How Improving Practice Relationships among Clinicians and Nonclinicians Can Improve Quality in Primary Care." Joint Commission Journal on Quality and Patient Safety 35 (September 2009): 457–66.

Kelso, J. A. Scott, and David A. Engstrom. *The Complementary Nature.* Cambridge, MA: MIT Press, 2010.

Kimball, Lisa. "Liberating Structures: A New Pattern Language for Engagement." OD Practitioner 43, no. 3 (2011): 8–11.

Lipmanowicz, Henri, and Keith McCandless. "Liberating Structures: Innovating by Including and Unleashing Everyone." *Performance* 2, no. 4 (2009): 6–19.

Macy, Joanna, and Molly Young Brown. *Coming Back to Life: Practices to Reconnect Our Lives, Our World.* Gabriola Island, BC: New Society, 1998.

Malone, Thomas W., Robert Laubacher, and Chrysanthos Dellarocas. "Harnessing Crowds: Mapping the Genome of Collective Intelligence." Working paper 2009-001, MIT Center for Collective Intelligence, 2009.

McKnight, John. *The Careless Society: Community and Its Counterfeits*. New York: Basic Books, 1996.

Morgan, Gareth. *Images of Organization*. Thousand Oaks, CA: Sage, 1997.

Oshry, Barry. *Seeing Systems: Unlocking the Mysteries of Organizational Life*. San Francisco: Berrett-Koehler, 1995.

Owen, Harrison. *Open Space Technology: A User's Guide*, 3rd ed. (San Francisco: Berrett-Koehler, 2008).

Palmer, Parker J. *The Courage to Teach: Exploring the Inner Landscape of a Teacher's Life*. San Francisco: Jossey-Bass, 1998.

Pascale, Richard, and Jerry Sternin. "Your Company's Secret Change Agents." *Harvard Business Review*, May 2005. http://hbr.org/2005/05, your-companys-secret-change-agents.

Patton, Michael Quinn. *Developmental Evaluation: Applying Complexity Concepts to Enhance Innovation and Use*. New York: Guilford Press, 2010

Schein, Edgar H. *Helping: How to Offer, Give, and Receive Help*. San Francisco: Berrett-Koehler, 2009.

———. *Organizational Culture and Leadership*. San Francisco: Jossey-Bass, 2004.

Singhal, Arvind, Prucia Buscell, and Keith McCandless. Saving Lives by Changing Relationships: Positive Deviance for MRSA Control and Prevention in a U.S. Hospital. Positive Deviance Wisdom Series, no. 3. Boston: Tufts University, Positive Deviance Initiative, 2009.

Stacey, Ralph D. *Complex Responsive Processes in Organizations: Learning and Knowledge Creation*. London: Routledge, 2001.

Suchman, Anthony L. "A New Theoretical Foundation for Relationship-Centered Care." In supplement 1, *Journal of General Internal Medicine* 21 (January 2006): S40–S44.

Surowiecki, James. *The Wisdom of Crowds*. New York: Anchor, 2005.

Torbert, William R. *The Power of Balance: Transforming Self, Society, and Scientific Inquiry*. Thousand Oaks, CA: Sage, 1991.

Weick, Karl E., and Kathleen M. Sutcliffe. *Managing the Unexpected: Resilient Performance in an Age of Uncertainty*. San Francisco: Jossey-Bass, 2007.

Weick, Karl E., Kathleen M. Sutcliffe, and David Obstfeld. "Organizing for High Reliability: Processes of Collective Mindfulness." *Research in Organizational Behavior* 21, no. s 81 (1999): 81–123.

Westley, Frances, Brenda Zimmerman, and Michael Q. Patton. *Getting to Maybe: How the World Is Changed*. Toronto: Random House of Canada, 2006.

Wheatley, Margaret J., and Myron Kellner-Rogers. *A Simpler Way*. San Francisco: Berrett-Koehler, 1996.

Zimmerman, Brenda. "HIV/AIDS in the Developing World: The Brazil Story." In "Complicated and Complex Systems: What Would Successful Reform of Medicare Look Like?," by Shalom Glouberman and Brenda Zimmerman, discussion paper no. 8, York University,Toronto, July 2002, 16–20

Zimmerman, Brenda, Curt Lindberg, and Paul Plsek. *Edgeware: Insights from Complexity Science for Health Care Leaders*. Irving, TX: VHA, 1998.

ABOUT THE AUTHORS

Henri Lipmanowicz and Keith McCandless have partnered since 2002 to develop Liberating Structures. They have worked with organizations ranging from neighborhood groups to global business enterprises in more than thirty countries. Updates on their ongoing work are reported on their website www.liberatingstructures.com.

Henri Lipmanowicz is the former president of Merck's Intercontinental Region and Japan and a cofounder of the Plexus Institute.

My previous passion was building organizations all over the world where people thrived and were successful beyond their wildest expectations. My current passion is the development of Liberating Structures and their dissemination across all five continents. One passion follows naturally the other since Liberating Structures make it possible for people to build organizations where they flourish and succeed beyond their expectations.

I enjoy mentoring people and seeing them grow. I love asking questions and looking at issues from unexpected angles. I thrive on complexity and take pleasure in challenging senior leaders.

Liberating Structures is a labor of love and I am excited about their present and future contributions. Coaching people about their use has been invariably rewarding and has convinced me that everybody can benefit from learning how to use them. That is why I hope that more and more students will start learning about Liberating Structures in educational settings so that they can be better prepared to use them at work.

Henri retired from Merck in 1998 after a thirty-year career during which he progressed from managing director in Finland to president of the

Intercontinental Region and Japan (the world minus the United States and Western Europe) and a member of Merck Management Committee. In 2000, Henri cofounded the Plexus Institute and served as chairman of the board until 2010.

Born in Carcassonne, France, Henri holds a MS degree in industrial engineering and management from Columbia University and a MS degree in chemical engineering from France. His career gave him the opportunity to live in seven countries and made him a perpetual world traveler. He resides in the United States with his Finnish wife; their joy in their two daughters and seven grandchildren is beyond their wildest expectations. While in France, he drives around in a 1961 Citroen 2CV.

Keith McCandless is cofounder of the Social Invention Group.

I help people in organizations innovate and manage complexity by working with groups to unleash creativity, discover opportunities, and build on momentum.

I am a founding partner of the Social Invention Group since 2000, and my eclectic skills are grounded in organization development, complexity science, business strategy, and graphic facilitation—all with an improvisational twist.

It was kismet that I met Henri while serving on the Scientific Advisory Board of the Plexus Institute. We shared a hunch that complexity science had practical applications and could be accessible to everyone. My keen interest in transformational learning and planning methods clicked with Henri's business acumen as we fielded early prototypes. Over twelve years, our hunch metamorphosed into a powerful repertoire for changemakers. Gleefully, we cut across academic disciplines, tapped spiritual practices, roamed the planet, and deepened scientific insights along the way.

What delights me most is the range of challenges, big and small, where this work can have a positive influence. Professional, functional, and interpersonal boundaries seem to dissolve when using Liberating Structures. I love creating the conditions for social inventiveness to flourish and to help people to take on their most entangled challenges with newfound confidence.

From 1992–2000, Keith led executive learning initiatives for the Health Forum (HF) in San Francisco. He was responsible for working with field-based learning collaboratives and managing education and research efforts. Prior to the Health Forum, Keith founded and served as the executive director of the Foundation for Health Care Quality in Seattle. The foundation brought together business and health leaders in a unique partnership to improve value in health care.

Born in Cincinnati, Ohio, he holds a master's in management of human services from Brandeis University in Boston and a BA from Evergreen State College in Olympia, Washington. Keith lives in Seattle with his wife, Anne, and Deacon, a whippet with talent to amuse.

Index

Page references followed by *fig* indicate an illustrated diagram; followed by *t* indicate a table.

what leaders should expect
from, 80
whom to include in, 79*fig*–80
Impromptu Networking
description of, 68*fig*
Field Guide on, 166, 171–173
"Fixing a Broken Child Welfare
System" (Jaasko-Fisher) use
of, 120–121, 173
used with Flemish cardiologists,
71
Immersion Workshop inclusion
of, 82*fig*
"Inclusive High-Stakes Decision
Making Made Easy"
(Yeatman) use of, 123, 127
for launching a multi-stakeholder collaborative project,
96–97
leadership team retreat: storyboard: part 1 use of, 99*fig*
Matching Matrix goals to, 69*fig*
National Summit storyboard:
part 1 use of, 105*fig*, 106
noticing patterns together
string inclusion of, 89
suggested as safe to use first, 76
vignette on classroom approach
using, 1, 2
Improv Prototyping
description of, 68*fig*
Discovery & Action Dialogues
(DAD) used with, 205
"Dramatizing Behavior Change
to Stop Infections"
(Belanger) use of, 151–152

Field Guide on, 166, 232–235
Helping Heuristics used with,
238
hospital infection rate reduced
using, 2, 3
Immersion Workshop inclusion
of, 82*fig*
"Inspiring Enduring Culture
Change While Preventing
Hospital Infections"
(Gardam) use of, 149
Matching Matrix goals to, 69*fig*
1-2-4-All used with, 233
riffs and variations for using,
234
Shift & Share used with, 215
User Experience Fishbowl used
with, 242
Wicked Questions used with,
180
Include everyone principle
advocating including people before the fact, 55
description of, 27, 28, 30, 54*t*
examining the possibilities of,
54–56
how trust grows through the experience of, 55
Immersion Workshop application of, 79*fig*–80
Matching Matrix for unleashing
local action goal in keeping
with, 69*fig*, 70
"Inclusive High-Stakes Decision
Making Made Easy" (Yeatman),
116, 123–127

43983516R00203

Made in the USA
Middletown, DE
01 May 2019